A Collection of

CLASSIC
SOUTHERN
HUMOR II

A Collection of
CLASSIC SOUTHERN HUMOR II

More Fiction and Occasional Fact by Some of the South's Best Storytellers.

Edited by George William Koon

PEACHTREE PUBLISHERS, LTD.

Published by
PEACHTREE PUBLISHERS, LTD.
494 Armour Circle, N.E.
Atlanta, Georgia 30324

Manufactured in the United States of America

1st printing

Library of Congress Catalog Number 84-60018

ISBN 0-931948-88-6 Hardcover
ISBN 0-931948-95-9 Trade Paper

Cover design by Cynthia McDaniel Davis

For Holly and Mary.

Also edited by George William Koon:

A Collection of Classic Southern Humor

Contents

Preface

The South's Fine Frenzy

The poet's eye, in a fine frenzy rolling,
Doth glance from heaven to earth, from earth to heaven,
And as imagination bodies forth
The forms of things unknown, the poet's pen
Turns them to shapes, and gives to airy nothing
A local habitation and a name.

A Midsummer Night's Dream

SHAKESPEARE KNEW, of course, that *frenzy* meant madness, and when he said that creativity is a "fine frenzy" he implied that genius is a step either just beyond or just before insanity. No genius conforms better to that definition than that which produces humor. For like madness, humor dwells in inconsistency. It requires that we wear a suit when we get hit with a pie, that only those most smug and secure slip on banana peels.

The South supplies appropriate inconsistency in great quantity. It thrives on the contradictions that identify our deep madness as they generate our best comedy. If the region clings to tradition, it crawls with rednecks anxious to be at least middle class. Such explains why Faulkner put Compson and Snopes into the same fictional world. If it promotes high morality, it allows secret passions that confirm all that Tennessee Williams wrote. If it is the Bible Belt, it is, as Flannery O'Connor knew so well, the scene of a fair share of the nation's violent crime. If the New South has glossy restaurants in glossy Atlanta hotels, it still has plenty of South Georgia waitresses who want to know not if you want grits but where you want them.

Much of this inconsistency is supplied by the South's usually stubborn resistance to change. The region has maintained many of its basic characteristics and thus has come to be a highly identifiable American institution, an institution that seems to become more entrenched as American attitudes and ways change more rapidly. Its consistency, sometimes apparently mad, makes the perfect background for comedy. All we have to do is drop in some item or character which contradicts its directions, just as we drop Hawkeye Pierce and Judy Benjamin into one of the most clearly defined institutions, the U.S. Army.

The best string of stories in my own family involves the struggles of my grandfathers to come to terms with the auto-mobile, an item which certainly contradicted their way of life. My father's father did not learn to drive until he was fifty; even then he refused to try to back up, as if reverse were just too modern for him. And the family spent much time plucking him out of tight spots. My mother's father, a railroad engineer, drove only once. He missed his first curve and cursed his Model T for not following the road the way his Southern Railway engine followed the tracks. Faulkner seized on this kind of story, this mythology, when in *The Reivers,* he made fine comedy out of the advent of the Ford in Yoknapatawpha County. And Flannery O'Connor turned some of these tales to religious purposes in the great comic novel, *Wise Blood,* where Hazel Motes, who believes that "Nobody with a good car needs to be justified," forms the Church without Christ in an old Essex that stalls in front of every Jesus Saves sign in Georgia.

Walker Percy turns the process around in *Lost in the Cosmos* where he has a stubborn past invade an upbeat present. He arranges for John Calvin and John Pelham to wander into "The Phil Donahue Show" where the host is directing a discussion of

viii

promiscuity. The juxtaposition of the severe Calvin and the gallant and committed Pelham with Donahue's guests — a homosexual, a philandering businessman, a pregnant fourteen-year-old, a very rational sex therapist (Dr. Joyce Friday), and a few dozen sincerely philosophical housewives — makes for grand comedy and important social commentary.

Our rather clear delineations of social and religious strata also make way for some frenzy. For example, Faulkner has Will Varner and Flem Snopes, employer and employee, struggle to see just who is in charge as lower class scratches its way up in the opening of *The Hamlet.* We get wonderful conflicts when Raney Bell, a serious Baptist from Bethel, Georgia, marries Charles Shepherd, one of Atlanta's highest Episcopalians. The wedding, and much more hilarity having to do with a Baptist/Anglo-Catholic honeymoon, take place in Clyde Edgerton's fine novel, *Raney.* No one knows just why the South produces such an abundance of Baptists hand-in-hand with such a large flock of genuflecting Episcopalians. But it does. And Edgerton has been shrewd and skillful in defining the wonderful incongruity.

If we want madness specifically and well laid out, we can turn to Eudora Welty's great comic novel *The Ponder Heart,* which deals mainly with the adventures of the daffy Uncle Daniel, a child/adult who is lovable and just a little off. One of the best scenes has Daniel home on leave from the state "institution." When Grandpa returns him to incarceration on Sunday, Daniel convinces the folks at the institution that it is Grandpa who is being returned. After all, they are used to seeing the young bring in the old. To the surprise of the family, it is Uncle Daniel who drives home to Clay while Grandpa frets among the straitjackets. As Shakespeare had it, distinguishing madness from genius is not easy.

I do not mean that the South has any corner on madness. The rest of the world shares our insanity, if not so dramatically. But there are at least two tactics for dealing with a world seemingly mad. One involves conceding the madness; more than a few contemporary writers have followed that course. Annie Dillard, in an interesting little book called *Living By Fiction,* suggests that much recent fiction marks the world as senseless. She adds that many of the writers employ what she calls "narrative collage," a broken narrative device appropriate for dealing with "the fragmentation of the great world." She comments on writers such as Beckett, Barthelme, Borges, Fuentes, and Pynchon. And she mentions Julio Cortazar, whose novel *Hopscotch* appeared originally in a loose-leaf notebook so that the pages could be put into any order the reader chose. Art is to be as mad and confused as life.

For the most part, Southern writers seem to have resisted this movement which some call Post-Modernism. The New Orleans writer John Kennedy Toole, represented in the first volume of this collection, may have been tempted by it, but even his brilliantly comic *A Confederacy of Dunces* has far more coherence than this literary movement would allow. One may want to conclude, then, that the South is behind the times — even when it comes to literary trends.

A happier conclusion, though, involves a second approach to madness, an approach which has us expanding our point of view to make room for the confusion and contrariness of human nature. I want to argue that most Southern writers have taken this second course, that the region's perspective is too broad and too strong to give in to meaninglessness. Humor, I claim, is one of the major attempts to accommodate madness. Thus it becomes a form of optimism, a form that is happy without being naive. And as humor gestures toward an acceptance of human nature, it makes our frenzy fine.

I trust that the following collection illustrates my case. Like the first volume, it mixes old and new, the famous and the lesser known. Volume two has another thing in common with its predecessor: It opens with a piece by Eudora Welty, the country's finest humorist and probably its best living author. After that, it offers work by thirteen writers who take humor from Martha Hall's near-slapstick to its very serious use by Jefferson Humphries. It ranges from the past of Mark Twain to the present of Tom Wolfe, from the happy spoof of materialism in *The Ponder Heart* to the sharp-edged satire of *Lost in the Cosmos*.

The volume, of course, is not comprehensive; the South produces too much good humor for one project. But, taken with its companion volume, published in 1984, this collection should be representative of the South's best comedy in its many forms and applications. Our purpose here, however, is not to teach lessons or establish frail literary theory. Rather, it is to make available good work that readers, Southern and frenzied or otherwise, will enjoy.

George William Koon
Clemson University

A Collection of

CLASSIC SOUTHERN HUMOR II

Eudora Welty

from The Ponder Heart

MY UNCLE DANIEL'S just like your uncle, if you've got one — only he has one weakness. He loves society and he gets carried away. If he hears our voices, he'll come right down those stairs, supper ready or no. When he sees you sitting in the lobby of the Beulah, he'll take the other end of the sofa and then move closer up to see what you've got to say for yourself; and then he's liable to give you a little hug and start trying to give you something. Don't do you any good to be bashful. He won't let you refuse. All he might do is forget tomorrow what he gave you today, and give it to you all over again. Sweetest disposition in the world. That's his big gray Stetson hanging on the rack right over your head — see what a large head size he wears?

Things I could think of without being asked that he's given away would be — a string of hams, a fine suit of clothes, a white-face heifer calf, two trips to Memphis, pair of fantail pigeons, fine Shetland pony (loves children), brooder and incubator, good nanny goat, bad billy, cypress cistern, field of white Dutch clover, two wheels and some laying pullets (they were together), cow pasture during drouth (he has everlasting springs), innumerable fresh eggs, a pick-up truck — even his own cemetery lot, but they wouldn't accept it. And I'm not counting this week. He's been a general favorite all these years.

Grandpa Ponder (in his grave now) might have any fine day waked up to find himself in too pretty a fix to get out of, but he had too much character. And besides, Edna Earle, I used to say to myself, if the worst does come to the worst, Grandpa *is* rich.

When I used to spot Grandpa's Studebaker out front, lighting from the country, and Grandpa heading up the walk, with no Uncle Daniel by his side, and his beard beginning to shake under his chin, and he had a beautiful beard, I'd yell back to the kitchen, "Ada! Be making Mr. Sam some good strong iced tea!" Grandpa was of the old school, and wanted people to measure up — everybody in general, and Uncle Daniel and me in particular. He and Grandma raised me, too. "Clear out, you all," I'd say to who all was in here. "Here comes Grandpa Ponder, and no telling what he has to tell me." I was his favorite grandchild, besides being the only one left alive or in calling distance.

"Now what, sir?" I'd say to Grandpa. "Sit down first, on that good old sofa — give me your stick, and here comes you some strong tea. What's the latest?"

He'd come to tell me the latest Uncle Daniel had given away. The incubator to the letter carrier — that would be a likely thing, and just as easy for Uncle Daniel as parting with the rosebud out of his coat. Not that Uncle Daniel ever got a *letter* in his life, out of that old slow poke postman.

"I only wish for your sake, Grandpa," I'd say sometimes, "you'd never told Uncle Daniel all you had."

He'd say, "Miss, I didn't. And further than that, one thing I'm never going to tell him about is money. And don't let me hear you tell him, Edna Earle."

"Who's the smart one of the family?" I'd say, and give him a little peck.

My papa was Grandpa's oldest child and Uncle Daniel was Grandpa's baby. They had him late — mighty late. They used to let him skate on the dining room table. So that put Uncle Daniel and me pretty close together — we liked-to caught up with each other. I did pass him in the seventh grade, and hated to do it, but I was liable to have passed anybody. People told me I ought to have been the *teacher*.

It's always taken a lot out of me, being smart. I say to people who only pass through here, "Now just a minute. Not so fast. Could *you* hope to account for twelve bedrooms, two bathrooms, two staircases, five porches, lobby, dining room, pantry and kitchen, every day of your life, and still be out here looking pretty when they come in? And two Negroes? And that plant?" Most people ask the name of that plant

2

before they leave. All I can tell them is, Grandma called it Miss Ouida Sampson after the lady that wished it on her. When I was younger, I used to take a blue ribbon on it at the County Fair. Now I just leave it alone. It blooms now and then.

But oh, when the place used to be busy! And when Uncle Daniel would start on a spree of giving away — it comes in sprees — and I would be trying to hold Grandpa down and account for this whole hotel at the same time — and Court would fling open in session across the street and the town fill up, up, up — and Mr. Springer would sure as Fate throttle into town and want that first-floor room, there where the door's open, and count on me to go to the movie with him, tired traveling man — oh, it was Edna Earle this, and Edna Earle that, every minute of my day and time. This is like the grave compared. *You're* only here because your car broke down, and I'm afraid you're allowing a Bodkin to fix it.

And listen: if you read, you'll put your eyes out. Let's just talk.

You'd know it was Uncle Daniel the minute you saw him. He's unmistakable. He's big and well known. He has the Ponder head — large, of course, and well set, with short white hair over it thick and curly, growing down his forehead round like a little bib. He has Grandma's complexion. And big, forget-me-not blue eyes like mine, and puts on a sweet red bow tie every morning, and carries a large-size Stetson in his hand — always just swept it off to somebody. He dresses fit to kill, you know, in a snow-white suit. But do you know he's up in his fifties now? Don't believe it if you don't want to. And still the sweetest, most unspoiled thing in the world. He has the nicest, politest manners — he's good as gold. And it's not just because he's kin to me I say it. I don't run the Beulah Hotel for nothing: I size people up: I'm sizing you up right now. People come here, pass through this book, in and out, over the years — and in the whole shooting-match, I don't care from where or how far they've come, not one can hold a candle to Uncle Daniel for looks or manners. If he ever did a thing to be sorry for, it's more than he ever intended.

Oh, even the children have always reckoned he was theirs to play with. When they'd see him coming they'd start jumping up and down

3

till he'd catch them and tickle their ribs and give them the change he carried. Grandpa used to make short work of them.

Grandpa worshiped Uncle Daniel. Oh, Grandpa in his panama and his seersucker suit, and Uncle Daniel in his red tie and Stetson and little Sweetheart rose in his lapel! They did set up a pair. Grandpa despised to come to town, but Uncle Daniel loved it, so Grandpa came in with him every Saturday. That was the way you knew where you were and the day of the week it was — those two hats announcing themselves, rounding the square and making it through the crowd. Uncle Daniel would always go a step or two behind, to exchange a few words, and Grandpa would go fording a way in front with his walking cane, through farmers and children and Negroes and dogs and the countryside in general. His nature was impatient, as time went by.

Nothing on earth, though, would have made Grandpa even consider getting strict with Uncle Daniel but Uncle Daniel giving away this hotel, of all things. He gave it to me, fifteen long years ago, and I don't know what it would have done without me. But "Edna Earle," says Grandpa, "this puts me in a quandary."

Not that Grandpa minded me having the hotel. It was Grandma's by inheritance, and used to be perfectly beautiful before it lost its paint, and the sign and the trees blew down in front, but he didn't care for where it stood, right in the heart of Clay. And with the town gone down so — with nearly all of *us* gone (Papa for one left home at an early age, nobody ever makes the mistake of asking about *him*, and Mama never did hold up — she just had me and quit; she was the last of the Bells) — and with the wrong element going spang through the middle of it at ninety miles an hour on that new highway, he'd a heap rather *not* have a hotel than have it. And it's true that often the people that come in off the road and demand a room right this minute, or ask you ahead what you have for dinner, are not the people you'd care to spend the rest of your life with at all. For Grandpa that settled it. He let Miss Cora Ewbanks run it as she pleased, and she was the one let the sign blow down, and all the rest. She died very shortly after she left it — an old maid.

The majority of what Uncle Daniel had given away up to then was stuff you could pick up and cart away — miscellaneous is a good word for it. But the Beulah was solid. It looked like it had dawned on Uncle Daniel about *property*. (Pastures don't count — you can take them back by just setting their cows back on the road.) Grandpa was getting plenty old, and he had a funny feeling that once *property* started going, next might go the Ponder place itself, and the land and the crop around it, and everything right out from under Uncle Daniel's feet, for all *you* could predict, once Grandpa wasn't there to stop him. Once Grandpa was in his grave, and Uncle Daniel shook free, he might succeed in giving those away to somebody not kin or responsible at all, or not even local, who might not understand what they had to do. Grandpa said that people exist in the realm of reason that are ready to take advantage of an open disposition, and the bank might be compelled to honor that — because of signatures or witnesses or whatever monkey-foolishness people go through with if they're strangers or up to something.

Grandpa just wanted to teach Uncle Daniel a lesson. But what he did was threaten him with the asylum. That wasn't the way to do it.

I said, "Grandpa, you're burning your bridges before you get to them, I think."

But Grandpa said, "Miss, I don't want to hear any more about it. I've warned him, now." So he warned him for nine years.

And as for Uncle Daniel, he went right ahead, attracting love and friendship with the best will and the lightest heart in the world. He loved being happy! He loved happiness like I love tea.

And then in April, just at Easter time, Grandpa spent some money himself, got that new Studebaker, and without saying kiss-my-foot to me, Grandpa and old Judge Tip Clanahan up and took Uncle Daniel through the country to Jackson in that brand-new automobile, and consigned him.

"That'll correct him, I expect," said Grandpa.

Child-foolishness! Oh, Grandpa lived to be sorry. Imagine that house without Uncle Daniel in it. I grew up there, but all you really need to know about is it's a good three miles out in the country from where you are now, in woods full of hoot-owls.

To be fair, that wasn't till after Grandpa'd tried praying over Uncle Daniel for years and years, and worn out two preachers praying over them both. Only I was praying against Grandpa and preachers and Judge Tip Clanahan to boot, because whatever *you* say about it, I abhor the asylum.

Oh, of course, from the word Go, Uncle Daniel got more vacations than anybody else down there. In the first place, they couldn't find anything the matter with him, and in the second place, he was so precious that he only had to ask for something. It seemed to me he was back home visiting more than he ever was gone between times, and pop full of stories. He had a pass from the asylum, and my great-grand-father Bell had been a big railroad man, so he had a pass on the branch-line train, and it was the last year we had a passenger train at all, so it worked out grand. Little train just hauls cross-ties now. Everybody missed Uncle Daniel so bad while he was gone, they spent all their time at the post office sending him things to eat. Divinity travels perfectly, if you ever need to know.

Of course, let him come home and he'd give away something. You can't stop that all at once. He came home and gave the girl at the bank a trip to Lookout Mountain and Rock City Cave, and then was going along with her to watch her enjoy both, and who prevailed on him then? Edna Earle. I said, "Dear heart, *I* know the asylum's no place for you, but neither is the top of a real high mountain or a cave in the cold dark ground. Here's the place." And he said, "All right, Edna Earle, but make me some candy." He's good as gold, but you have to know the way to treat him; he's a man, the same as they all are.

But he had a heap to tell. You ought to have heard some of the tales! It didn't matter if you didn't know the people: something goes on there all the time! I hope I'm not speaking of kin of present company. We'd start laughing clear around town, the minute Uncle Daniel hopped off the train, and never let up till Grandpa came chugging in to get him, to set him on the down-train. Grandpa did keep at it. And I don't know how it worked, but Uncle Daniel *was* beginning to be less open-handed. He commenced slacking up on giving away with having so much to tell.

The sight of a stranger was always meat and drink to him. The stranger don't have to open his mouth. Uncle Daniel is ready to do all the talking. That's understood. I used to dread he might get hold of one of these occasional travelers that wouldn't come in unless they had to — the kind that would break in on a story with a set of questions, and wind it up with a list of what Uncle Daniel's faults were: some Yankee. But Uncle Daniel seemed to have a sixth sense and avoid those, and light on somebody from nearer home always. He'd be crazy about you.

Grandpa was a little inclined to slow him down, of course. He'd say, "Who? — What, Daniel? — When? — Start over!" He was the poorest listener in the world, though I ought not to say that now when he's in his grave. But all the time, whatever Uncle Daniel might take into his head to tell you, rest assured it was the Lord's truth to start with, and exactly the way he'd see it. He never told a lie in his life. Grandpa couldn't get past that, poor Grandpa. That's why he never could punish him.

I used to say Mr. Springer was the perfect listener. A drug salesman with a wide, wide territory, in seldom enough to forget between times, and knowing us well enough not to try to interrupt. And too tired to object to hearing something over. If anything, he laughed too soon. He used to sit and beg for Uncle Daniel's favorite tale, the one about the time he turned the tables on Grandpa.

Turned the tables not on purpose! Uncle Daniel is a perfect gentleman, and something like that has to *happen*; he wouldn't contrive it.

Grandpa one time, for a treat, brought Uncle Daniel home to vote, and took him back to the asylum through the country, in the new Studebaker. They started too early and got there too early — I told them! And there was a new lady busying herself out at the front, instead of the good old one. "Low-in-the-hole!" as Uncle Daniel says, the lady asked *him* who the old *man* was. Uncle Daniel was far and away the best dressed and most cheerful of the two, of course. Uncle Daniel says, "Man alive! Don't you know that's *Mr. Ponder*?" And the lady was loading the Coca-Cola machine and says, "Oh, foot, I can't remember everybody," and called somebody and they took Grandpa. Hat, stick, and everything, they backed him right down the hall and

7

shut the door on him boom. And Uncle Daniel waited and dallied and had a Coca-Cola with his nickel when they got cold, and then lifted his hat and politely backed out the front door and found Grandpa's car with the engine running still under the crape myrtle tree, and drove it on home and got here with it — though by the time he did, he was as surprised as Grandpa. And that's where he ends his story. Bless his heart. And that's where Mr. Springer would turn loose and laugh till Uncle Daniel had to beat him on the back to save him.

The rest of it is, that down in Jackson, the madder Grandpa got, the less stock they took in him, of course. That's what crazy *is*. They took Grandpa's walking stick away from him like he was anybody else. Judge Tip Clanahan had to learn about it from Uncle Daniel and then send down to get Grandpa out, and when Grandpa did get loose, they nearly gave him back the wrong stick. They would have heard from him about *that*.

When Uncle Daniel got here with that tale, everybody in town had a conniption fit trying to believe it, except Judge Tip. Uncle Daniel thought it was a joke on the *lady*. It took Grandpa all day long from the time he left here to make it on back, with the help of Judge Clanahan's long-legged grandson and no telling what papers. *He* might as well not have left home, he wouldn't stop to tell us a word.

There's more than one moral to be drawn there, as I told Mr. Springer at the time, about straying too far from where you're known and all — having too wide a territory. Especially if you light out wearing a seersucker suit you wouldn't let the rummage sale have, though it's old as the hills. By the time you have to *prove* who you are when you get there, it may be too late when you get back. *Think* about Grandpa Ponder having to call for witnesses the minute he gets fifty miles off in one direction. I think that helped put him in his grave. It went a long way toward making him touchy about what Uncle Daniel had gone and done in the meanwhile. You see, by the time Grandpa made it back, something had happened at home. Something will every time, if you're not there to see it.

Uncle Daniel had got clear up to his forties before we ever dreamed that such a thing as love flittered through his mind. He's so *sweet*. Sometimes I think if we hadn't showed him that widow! But he was bound to see her: he has eyes: Miss Teacake Magee, lived here all her life. She sings in the choir of the Baptist Church every blessed Sunday: couldn't get *her* out. And sings louder than all the rest put together, so loud it would make you lose your place.

I'll go back a little for a minute. Of course we're all good Presbyterians. Grandpa was an elder. The Beulah Bible Class and the Beulah Hotel are both named after Grandma. And my other grandma was the second-to-longest-living Sunday School teacher they've ever had, very highly regarded. My poor little mama got a pageant written before she died, and I still conduct the rummage sales for the Negroes every Saturday afternoon in the corner of the yard and bring in a sum for the missionaries in Africa that I think would surprise you.

Miss Teacake Magee is of course a Sistrunk (the Sistrunks are *all* Baptists — big Baptists) and Professor Magee's widow. He wasn't professor *of* anything, just real smart — smarter than the Sistrunks, anyway. He'd never worked either — he was like Uncle Daniel in that respect. With Miss Teacake, everything dates from "Since I lost Professor Magee." A passenger train hit him. That shows you how long ago *his* time was.

Uncle Daniel *thought* what he was wild about at that time was the Fair. And I kept saying to myself, maybe that *was* it. He carried my plant over Monday, in the tub, and entered it for me as usual, under "Best Other Than Named" — it took the blue ribbon — and went on through the flowers and quilts and the art, passing out compliments on both sides of him, and out the other door of the Fine Arts Tent and was loose on the midway. From then on, the whole week long, he'd go back to the Fair every whipstitch — morning, noon, or night, hand in hand with any soul, man, woman, or child, that chose to let him — and spend his change on them and stay till the cows come home. He'd even go by himself. I went with him till I dropped. And we'd no more leave than he'd clamp my arm. "Edna Earle, look back yonder down the hill at all those lights still a-burning!" Like he'd never seen lights before. He'd say, "Sh! Listen at Intrepid Elsie Fleming!"

Eudora Welty

Intrepid Elsie Fleming rode a motorcycle around the Wall of Death
— which let her do, if she wants to ride a motorcycle that bad. It was
the time she wasn't riding I objected to — when she was out front on
the platform warming up her motor. That was nearly the whole time.
You could hear her day and night in the remotest parts of this hotel and
with the sheet over your head, clear over the sound of the Merry-Go-
Round and all. She dressed up in pants.

Uncle Daniel said he had to admire that. He admired everything he
saw at the Fair that year, to tell the truth, and everything he heard, and
always expected to win the Indian blanket; never did — *they* never let
him. I'll never forget when I first realized what flittered through his
mind.

He'd belted me into the Ferris Wheel, then vanished, instead of
climbing into the next car. And the first thing I made out from the
middle of the air was Uncle Daniel's big round hat up on the platform
of the Escapades side-show, right in the middle of those ostrich plumes.
There he was — passing down the line of those girls doing their come-
on dance out front, and handing them ice cream cones, right while they
were shaking their heels to the music, not in very good time. He'd got
the cream from the Baptist ladies' tent — banana, and melting fast.
And I couldn't get off the Ferris Wheel till I'd been around my nine
times, no matter how often I told them who I was. When I finally got
loose, I flew up to Uncle Daniel and he stood there and hardly knew
me, licking away and beside himself with pride and joy. And his sixty
cents was gone, too. Well, he would have followed the Fair to Silver
City when it left, if I'd turned around good.

He kept telling me for a week after, that those dancing girls wore
beyond compare the prettiest dresses and feather-pieces he ever saw on
ladies' backs in his life, and could dance like the fairies. "They every
one smiled at me," he said. "And yet I liked Miss Elsie Fleming very
well, too." So the only thing to be thankful for is he didn't try to treat
Intrepid Elsie Fleming — she might have bitten him.

As for Grandpa, I didn't tell him about the twelve banana ice cream
cones and where they went, but he heard — he played dominoes with
Judge Tip — and as soon as he got home from the Clanahans' he took a

spell with his heart. The Ponder heart! So of course we were all running and flying to do his bidding, everything under the sun he said. I never saw such lovely things as people sent — I gained ten pounds, and begged people to spare us more. Of course I was running out there day and night and tending to the Beulah between times. One morning when I carried Grandpa his early coffee, he said to me, "Edna Earle, I've been debating, and I've just come to a conclusion."

"What now, Grandpa?" I said. "Tell me real slow."

Well, he did, and to make a long story short, he had his way; and after that he never had another spell in his life till the one that killed him — when Uncle Daniel had *his* way. The heart's a remarkable thing, if you ask me. "I'm fixing to be strict for the first time with the boy," was Grandpa's conclusion. "I'm going to fork up a good wife for him. And you put your mind on who."

"I'll do my best, Grandpa," I said. "But remember we haven't got the whole wide world to choose from any more. Mamie Clanahan's already engaged to the man that came to put the dial telephones in Clay. Suppose we cross the street to the Baptist Church the first Sunday you're out of danger."

So up rose Miss Teacake Magee from the choir — her solo always came during collection, to cover up people rattling change and dropping money on the floor — and when I told Uncle Daniel to just listen to that, it didn't throw such a shadow over his countenance as you might have thought.

"Miss Teacake's got more breath in her than those at the Fair, that's what she's got," he whispers back to me. And before I could stop his hand, he'd dropped three silver dollars, his whole month's allowance, in the collection plate, with a clatter that echoed all over that church. Grandpa fished the dollars out when the plate came by him, and sent me a frown, but he didn't catch on. Uncle Daniel sat there with his mouth in an O clear through the rest of the solo. It seems to me it was "Work, for the Night Is Coming." But I was saying to myself, Well, Edna Earle, she's a Sistrunk. And a widow well taken care of. And she makes and sells those gorgeous cakes that melt in your mouth — she's an artist. Forget about her singing. So going out of church, I says,

11

"Eureka, Grandpa. I've found her." And whispers in his ear.

"Go ahead, then, girl," says he.

If you'd ever known Grandpa, you'd have been as surprised as I was when Grandpa didn't object right away, and conclude we'd better find somebody smarter than that or drop the whole idea. Grandpa would be a lot more willing to stalk up on a wedding and stop it, than to encourage one to go on. Anybody's — yours, mine, or the Queen of Sheba's. He regarded getting married as a show of weakness of character in nearly every case but his own, because he was smart enough to pick a wife very nearly as smart as he was. But he was ready to try anything once for Uncle Daniel, and Miss Teacake got by simply because Grandpa knew who she was — and a little bit because of her hair as black as tar — something she gets from Silver City and puts on herself in front of the mirror.

Poor Grandpa! Suppose I'd even *attempted*, over the years, to step off — I dread to think of the lengths Grandpa would have gone to to stop it. Of course, I'm intended to look after Uncle Daniel and everybody knows it, but in plenty of marriages there's three — three all your life. Because nearly everybody's got somebody. I used to think if I ever did step off with, say, Mr. Springer, Uncle Daniel wouldn't mind; he always could make Mr. Springer laugh. And I could name the oldest child after Grandpa and win him over quick before he knew it. Grandpa adored compliments, though he tried to hide it. Ponder Springer — that sounds perfectly plausible to me, or did at one time.

At any rate, Uncle Daniel and Miss Teacake got married. I just asked her for recipes enough times, and told her the real secret of cheese straws — beat it three hundred strokes — and took back a few unimportant things I've said about the Baptists. The wedding was at the Sistrunks', in the music room, and Miss Teacake insisted on singing at her own wedding — sang "The Sweetest Story Ever Told."

It was bad luck. The marriage didn't hold out. We were awfully disappointed in Miss Teacake, but glad to have Uncle Daniel back. What Uncle Daniel told me he didn't take to — I asked him because I was curious — was hearing spool-heels coming and going on Professor Magee's floor. But he never had a word to say against Miss Teacake: I think he liked her. Uncle Daniel has a remarkable affection for every-body and everything in creation. I asked him one question about her and got this hotel. Miss Teacake's settled down again now, and don't seem to be considering catching anybody else in particular. Still singing.

So Grandpa carried Uncle Daniel to the asylum, and before too long, Uncle Daniel turned the tables on Grandpa, and never had to go back *there*.

Tennessee Williams

The Yellow Bird

ALMA WAS THE daughter of a Protestant minister named Increase Tutwiler, the last of a string of Increase Tutwilers who had occupied pulpits since the Reformation came to England. The first American progenitor had settled in Salem, and around him and his wife, Goody Tutwiler, née Woodson, had revolved one of the most sensational of the Salem witch-trials. Goody Tutwiler was cried out against by the Circle Girls, a group of hysterical young ladies of Salem who were thrown into fits whenever a witch came near them. They claimed that Goody Tutwiler afflicted them with pins and needles and made them sign their names in the devil's book quite against their wishes. Also one of them declared that Goody Tutwiler had appeared to them with a yellow bird which she called by the name of Bobo and which served as interlocutor between herself and the devil to whom she was sworn. The Reverend Tutwiler was so impressed by these accusations, as well as by the fits of the Circle Girls when his wife entered their presence in court, that he himself finally cried out against her and testified that the yellow bird named Bobo had flown into his church one Sabbath and, visible only to himself, had perched on his pulpit and whispered indecent things to him about several younger women in the congregation. Goody Tutwiler was accordingly condemned and hanged, but this was by no means the last of the yellow bird named Bobo. It had manifested itself in one form or another, and its continual nagging had left the Puritan spirit fiercely aglow, from Salem to Hobbs, Arkansas, where the Increase Tutwiler of this story was preaching.

Increase Tutwiler was a long-winded preacher. His wife sat in the front pew of the church with a palm-leaf fan which she would agitate violently when her husband had preached too long for anybody's endurance. But it was not always easy to catch his attention, and Alma, the daughter, would finally have to break into the offertory hymn in order to turn him off. Alma played the organ, the primitive kind of organ that had to be supplied with air by an old Negro operating a pump in a stifling cubicle behind the wall. On one occasion the old Negro had fallen asleep, and no amount of discreet rapping availed to wake him up. The minister's wife had plucked nervously at the strings of her palm-leaf fan till it began to fall to pieces, but without the organ to stop him, Increase Tutwiler ranted on and on, exceeding the two-hour mark. It was by no means a cool summer day, and the interior of the church was yellow oak, a material that made you feel as if you were sitting in the middle of a fried egg.

At last Alma despaired of reviving the Negro and got to her feet. "Papa," she said. But the old man didn't look at her. "Papa," she repeated, but he went right on. The whole congregation was whispering and murmuring. One stout old lady seemed to have collapsed, because two people were fanning her from either side and holding a small bottle to her nostrils. Alma and her mother exchanged desperate glances. The mother half got out of her seat. Alma gave her a signal to remain seated. She picked up the hymnbook and brought it down with such terrific force on the bench that dust and fiber spurted in all directions. The minister stopped short. He turned a dazed look in Alma's direction. "Papa," she said, "it's fifteen minutes after twelve and Henry's asleep and these folks have got to get to dinner, so for the love of God, quit preaching."

Now Alma had the reputation of being a very quiet and shy girl, so this speech was nothing short of sensational. The news of it spread throughout the Delta, for Mr. Tutwiler's sermons had achieved a sort of unhappy fame for many miles about. Perhaps Alma was somewhat pleased and impressed by this little celebration that she was accordingly given on people's tongues the next few months, for she was never quite the same shy girl afterwards. She had not had very much fun out of being a minister's daughter. The boys had steered clear of the rectory, because when they got around there they were exposed to Mr. Tutwiler's inquisitions. A boy and Alma would have no chance to talk in the Tutwiler porch or parlor while the old man was around. He was obsessed with the idea that Alma might get to smoking, which he thought was the initial and, once taken, irretrievable step toward perdition. "If Alma gets to smoking," he told his wife, "I'm going to denounce her from the pulpit and put her out of the house." Every time he said this Alma's mother would scream and go into a faint, as she knew that every girl who is driven out of her father's house goes right into a good-time house. She was unable to conceive of anything in between.

Now Alma was pushing thirty and still unmarried, but about six months after the episode in the church, things really started popping around the minister's house. Alma had gotten to smoking in the attic, and her mother knew about it. Mrs. Tutwiler's hair had been turning slowly gray for a number of years, but after Alma took to smoking in the attic, it turned snow-white almost overnight. Mrs. Tutwiler concealed the terrible knowledge that Alma was smoking in the attic from her husband, and she didn't even dare raise her voice to Alma about it because the old man might hear. All she could do was stuff the attic door around with newspapers. Alma *would* smoke; she claimed it had gotten a hold on her and she couldn't stop it now. At first she only smoked twice a day, but she began to smoke more as the habit grew on her. Several times the old man had said he smelled smoke in the house, but so far he hadn't dreamed that his daughter would dare take up smoking. But his wife knew he would soon find out about it, and Alma knew he would too. The question was whether Alma cared. Once she came downstairs with a cigarette in her mouth, smoking it, and her mother barely snatched it out of her mouth before the old man saw her. Mrs. Tutwiler went into a faint, but Alma paid no attention to her, just went on out of the house, lit another cigarette, and walked down the street to the drugstore.

It was unavoidable that sooner or later people who had seen Alma

smoking outside the house, which she now began to do pretty regu-
larly, would carry the news back to the preacher. There were plenty of
old women who were ready and able to do it. They had seen her
smoking in the White Star drugstore while she was having her afternoon Coke, puffing on the cigarette between sips of the Coke and
carrying on a conversation with the soda-jerk, just like anyone from
that set of notorious high school girls that the whole town had been
talking about for several generations. So one day the minister came
into his wife's bedroom and said to her, "I have been told that Alma has
taken to smoking."

His manner was deceptively calm. The wife sensed that this was not
an occasion for her to go into a faint, so she didn't. She had to keep her
wits about her this time — that is, if she had any left after all she had
been through with Alma's smoking.

"Well," she said, "I don't know what to do about it. It's true."

"You know what I've always said," her husband replied. "If Alma
gets to smoking, out she goes."

"Do you want her to go into a good-time house?" inquired Mrs.
Tutwiler.

"If that's where she's going, she can go," said the preacher, "but not
until I've given her something that she'll always remember."

He was waiting for Alma when she came in from her afternoon smoke
and Coke at the White Star drugstore. Soon as she walked into the door
he gave her a good, hard slap, with the palm of his hand on her mouth,
so that her front teeth bit into her lip and it started bleeding. Alma
didn't blink an eye, she just drew back her right arm and returned the
slap with good measure. She had bought a bottle of something at the
drugstore, and while her father stood there, stupefied, watching her,
she went upstairs with the mysterious bottle in brown wrapping paper.
And when she came back down they saw that she had peroxided her
hair and put on lipstick. Alma's mother screamed and went into one of
her faints, because it was evident to her that Alma was going right over
to one of the good-time houses on Front Street. But all the iron had

gone out of the minister's character then. He clung to Alma's arm. He begged and pleaded with her not to go there. Alma lit up a cigarette right there in front of him and said, "Listen here, I'm going to do as I please around here from now on, and I don't want any more interference from you!"

Before this conversation was finished the mother came out of her faint. It was the worst faint she had ever gone into, particularly since nobody had bothered to pick her up off the floor. "Alma," she said weakly, "Alma!" Then she said her husband's name several times, but neither of them paid any attention to her, so she got up without any assistance and began to take a part in the conversation. "Alma," she said, "you can't go out of this house until that hair of yours grows in dark again."

"That's what you think," said Alma.

She put the cigarette back in her mouth and went out the screen door, puffing and drawing on it and breathing smoke out of her nostrils all the way down the front walk and down to the White Star drugstore, where she had another Coke and resumed her conversation with the boy at the soda-counter. His name was Stuff — that was what people called him — and it was he who had suggested to Alma that she would look good as a blonde. He was ten years younger than Alma but he had more girls than pimples.

It was astonishing the way Alma came up fast on the outside in Stuff's affections. With the new blond hair you could hardly call her a dark horse, but she was certainly running away with the field. In two weeks' time after the peroxide she was going steady with Stuff; for Alma was smart enough to know there were plenty of good times to be had outside the good-time houses on Front Street, and Stuff knew that, too. Stuff was not to be in sole possession of her heart. There were other contenders, and Alma could choose among them. She started going out nights as rapidly as she had taken up smoking. She stole the keys to her father's Ford sedan and drove to such near-by towns as Lakewater, Sunset, and Lyons. She picked up men on the highway and went out "juking" with them, making the rounds of the highway drinking places; never got home till three or four in the morning. It was impossible to see how one human constitution could stand up under the strain of so much running around to night places, but Alma had all the vigor that comes from generations of firm believers. It could have gone into anything and made a sensation. Well, that's how it was. There was no stopping her once she got started.

The home situation was indescribably bad. It was generally stated that Alma's mother had suffered a collapse and that her father was spending all his time praying, and there was some degree of truth in both reports. Very little sympathy for Alma came from the older residents of the community. Certain little perfunctory steps were taken to curb the girl's behavior. The father got the car-key out of her pocket one night when she came in drunk and fell asleep on the sofa, but Alma had already had some duplicates of it made. He locked the garage one night. Alma climbed through the window and drove the car straight through the closed door.

"She's lost her mind," said the mother. "It's that hair-bleaching that's done it. It went right through her scalp and now it's affecting her brain."

They sat up all that night waiting for her, but she didn't come home. She had run her course in that town, and the next thing they heard from Alma was a card from New Orleans. She had got all the way down there. "Don't sit up," she wrote. "I'm gone for good. I'm never coming back."

Six years later Alma was a character in the old French Quarter of New Orleans. She hung out mostly on "Monkey-Wrench Corner" and picked up men around there. It was certainly not necessary to go into a good-time house to have a good time in the Quarter, and it hadn't taken her long to find that out. It might have seemed to some people that Alma was living a wasteful and profligate existence, but if the penalty for it was death, well, she was a long time dying. In fact she seemed to prosper on her new life. It apparently did not have a dissipating effect on her. She took pretty good care of herself so that it wouldn't, eating well and drinking just enough to be happy. Her face had a bright and innocent look in the mornings, and even when she was alone in her room it sometimes seemed as if she weren't alone — as if someone were with her, a disembodied someone, perhaps a remote ancestor of liberal tendencies who had been displeased by the channel his blood had taken till Alma kicked over the traces and jumped right back to the plumed-hat cavaliers.

Of course, her parents never came near her again, but once they dispatched as emissary a young married woman they trusted.

The woman called on Alma in her miserable little furnished room — or crib, as it actually was — on the shabbiest block of Bourbon Street in the Quarter.

"How do you live?" asked the woman.

"What?" said Alma, innocently.

"I mean how do you get along?"

"Oh," said Alma, "people give me things."

"You mean you accept gifts from them?"

"Yes, on a give-and-take basis," Alma told her.

The woman looked around her. The bed was unmade and looked as if it had been that way for weeks. The two-burner stove was loaded with unwashed pots in some of which grew a pale fungus. Tickets from pawnshops were stuck round the edge of the mirror along with many, many photographs of young men, some splitting their faces with enormous grins while others stared softly at space.

"These photographs," said the woman, "are these — are these your friends?"

"Yes," said Alma, with a happy smile. "Friends and acquaintances, strangers that pass in the night!"

"Well, I'm not going to mention this to your father!"

"Oh, go on and tell the old stick-in-the-mud," said Alma. She lit a cigarette and blew the smoke at her caller.

The woman looked around once more and noticed that the doors of the big armoire hung open on white summer dresses that were covered with grass stains.

"You go on picnics?" she asked.

"Yes, but not church ones," said Alma.

21

The woman tried to think of something more to ask but she was not gifted with an agile mind, and Alma's attitude was not encouraging.

"Well," she said finally, "I had better be going."

"Hurry back," said Alma, without getting up or looking in the woman's direction.

Shortly thereafter Alma discovered that she was becoming a mother.

She bore a child, a male one, and not knowing who was the father, she named it John after the lover that she had liked best, a man now dead. The son was perfect, very blond and glowing, a lusty infant.

Now from this point on the story takes a strange turn that may be highly disagreeable to some readers, if any still hoped it was going to avoid the fantastic.

This child of Alma's would have been hanged in Salem. If the Circle Girls had not cried out against Alma (which they certainly would have done), they would have gone into fifty screaming fits over Alma's boy.

He was thoroughly bewitched. At half-past six every morning he crawled out of the house and late in the evening he returned with fists full of gold and jewels that smelled of the sea.

Alma grew very rich indeed. She and the child went North. The child grew up in a perfectly normal way to youth and to young manhood, and then he no longer crawled out and brought back riches. In fact that old habit seemed to have slipped his mind somehow, and no mention was ever made of it. Though he and his mother did not pay much attention to each other, there was a great and silent respect between them while each went about his business.

When Alma's time came to die, she lay on the bed and wished her son would come home, for lately the son had gone on a long sea-voyage for unexplained reasons. And while she was waiting, while she lay there dying, the bed began to rock like a ship on the ocean, and all at once not John the Second, but John the First appeared, like Neptune out of the ocean. He bore a cornucopia that was dripping with seaweed and his bare chest and legs had acquired a greenish patina such as a bronze statue comes to be covered with. Over the bed he emptied his horn of plenty which had been stuffed with treasure from wrecked Spanish galleons: rubies, emeralds, diamonds, rings, and necklaces of rare gold, and great loops of pearls with the slime of the sea clinging to them.

"Some people," he said, "don't even die empty-handed."

And off he went, and Alma went off with him.

The fortune was left to The Home For Reckless Spenders. And in due time the son, the sailor, came home, and a monument was put up. It was a curious thing, this monument. It showed three figures of indeterminate gender astride a leaping dolphin. One bore a crucifix, one a cornucopia, and one a Grecian lyre. On the side of the plunging fish, the arrogant dolphin, was a name inscribed, the odd name of Bobo, which was the name of the small yellow bird that the devil and Goody Tutwiler had used as a go-between in their machinations.

Jesse Hill Ford

The Surest Thing in Show Business

T HINGS DIDN'T PAN out in Texas, so my wife, Jerry, and me, we come East in our old car, hauling a trailer loaded with three hundred pounds of snakes, an old cheetah, and a bear cub. We found this place we could rent on the highway, just outside the Great Smoky Mountains National Park, on the Tennessee side, so we decided to give her a try. It had a large clear space for parking and was on a long mountain grade going into the Smokies. A long grade that way will get you traffic that stops because the motor gets overheated, and then too, the kids will be yelling they want to see the snakes. So between the radiator and the kids, Daddy, he can't do nothing but stop.

Jerry, my wife, she helped me paint the signs, thirty-nine of them, all bright yellow and red enough to dazzle your eyes, and we tacked them up for two miles along the road on either side of the place, but mostly on the downgrade side. I was able to pick up three fair-size iguana lizards and a couple of pretty good Gila monsters from other reptile folks passing through on the way to Florida, and by the time traffic started really coming through in June, Jerry and me had a nice palisade wall, an admission booth, a free ice-water fountain, a free radiator water tank, and a Cherokee squaw named Lizzie who held down the candy, cigarettes, and souvenir stand.

Lizzie was okay, only she cussed and swore when she got excited, which had got her fired from her job at a souvenir joint inside the park. And, too, she was somewhat of a problem at first because she wanted to call me a swear word, and I don't like to have nobody but myself to swear around Jerry. What Lizzie called me sounded like *sumitch*, all one word: "Gimme some change for this goddam drawer, sumitch."

25

She wouldn't call me by my own name, Jake, so finally we hit on a sort of middle bargain. "How about just calling me Mitch?" I says. And after some practice it worked out okay, and that's how come we changed the name to Mitch and Jerry's Reptile Show in place of Jake and Jerry's. For in show business you got to be ready to wheel and deal and bargain a little if you make it. And any show around the Smokies that don't have at least one real Indian is like a kite without no tail.

By July we was going full blast, and I had took on an old man and a boy to milk a couple of afternoons a week so I could tend to building more animal cages and ordering hot snakes in place of the old ones we brought with us. The old man couldn't do no more than hang a snake's mouth over a milk jar and grin — I mean he didn't actually milk out no venom and never learned — but he had a good line of gab and always drank a little dab of colored water he hid in the jar ahead of time, and the crowd liked him. Another thing, the old man put on he was more feeble than he really was and made his hands look real shaky so they figured he was going to get bit any second. And that's the whole secret. You go in there to make them believe you might get bit. But now the kid, he milked good and he handled them good and took all kinds of chances, but he made it look too easy and he never got the attention the old man did. The kid never got the point that you can't make it look too easy.

So on the Fourth of July the stranger showed up, one of those long pale guys in a shiny blue suit too small for him, wearing shoes that were never meant for walking — the pointed kind that might have been yellow when they were new — and of course he had walked about a hundred miles. He stayed around the Cherokee's counter for about two hours until she told him to get the hell away from there. Then he hung back a little distance like a stray dog and just stared and waited. Then about noon he got some free ice water and hiked on and I just wrote him off my mind like a bad debt and patted myself on the back for having got a smart Indian out front like Lizzie, even if it did mean changing my handle a little bit. About four o'clock that afternoon he was back. He marched right up to the ticket window like he had money and asked Jerry, my wife, if the boss was around. He didn't need to explain that he was down on his luck. I guess the thing was that he had a Texas drawl and an unexpected soft voice. All of those fellows' voices will startle you, though. The voice never sounds like the guy looks. It's the road that does it. Jerry just pointed at the palisade gate with her thumb, and he slipped right on in on me. I could hear Lizzie swearing when he opened the gate. You would have thought some of the animals was loose. But Lizzie didn't have no use for white men in any form or fashion, especially his kind. They don't take too kindly to walking tourists up in the Smokies, for the walking ones never want to buy nothing and are always looking to put an honest Indian out of her job.

He come in and closed the gate behind him and give a sidelong glance at the cheetah, which was napping on his sawdust bed in one corner of his cage. I was just through with the three-thirty show and was trying to make a six-foot diamondback get on in his box. He was a new snake and was still hot as hell. I just kept coaxing him with my snake hook and holding that tail, and the other guy waited real polite till I had the diamondback in the box.

"Well?" I says. He was a pitiful sight. With everything else he had a blond mustache. It made him look like the next rain would dissolve him. But then he spoke up, brighter and more eager than I looked for.

"I need a stake," he says, waving one long hand like he was fending gnats away from his eyes. They were bright and yellow, like the Western sun, and Texas was right there in his voice so that he got to me fast, like remembering home and the old folks. But us show people are soft-hearted anyway.

"I found a little hick place over the ridge there," he went on, "talked them out of the high school auditorium for this evening to do a reptile show." The hand went hunting down into his pocket, the back pants pocket of the blue suit, and I couldn't hardly believe my eyes when it came out again. "I already collected fifty dollars in advance." He unfolded the bills one right after the other on top of the glass reptile case at his elbow. The snakes raised up and rattled a little and then laid right back down.They were the last of that original three hundred pounds, and they were getting wore out in a hurry. The most of them don't live over six weeks.

27

"Hey," I say, "I'd call that a pretty good stake already."

"Yeah," he says, "only I ain't got no snakes."

And there it was. He had located a school and store and a clump of houses up there on the edge of the park, and in three hours he had to be back up there ready to put on a full-feathered reptile show and he didn't have so much as a frog in his pocket. It wasn't any wonder to me at all, because if I've learned one thing after twenty-five years in show business, it's the fact that there ain't a single living American that ain't had a great-granddaddy or a stepuncle or some connection like that who was swallered whole by a rattler. Understand, they never *knew* him, but Granny told them about it, which makes the rattlesnake the surest moneymaker in American show business. They will pay to see what swallered Granddaddy everytime. Of course you have to expect the comments. If you have an eight-foot snake — it's another story, but me and my brothers did have one once, a Florida diamondback, and we was so scared of him that we would have almost rather been shot at than to work him. It took three of us to handle him, and never a show went by that some smart bastard didn't pipe up and remark how he killed 'em bigger than that with his bare feet every morning, right by his kitchen door. "You call *that* a snake?" they yell. But then that's part of why they pay, and in show business you got to roll with the punches.

So he just stood there with the money laid out on the glass over them dying snakes, and I finally says, "And they even let you leave with the money."

"Yeah, I told them my truck was broke down and I had to get it fixed before I could bring up my reptiles."

"When is the show for?" I says.

"Seven o'clock," he says, "in the Hartsville High auditorium."

"You handled reptiles much?" I says.

"You bet your boots. Hell, it's practically all I ever done."

"You want hot snakes?" I says. There was two kinds, the fresh hot ones, straight up from the Mexican border and feisty as a coon dog pup, and the old ones, so weak you couldn't hardly put them into a coil unless you just took and wound them up like a piece of old rope.

"Whatever you can spare. Snakes, lizards, anything you can lend

28

me. I'm willing to pay. The money's right there," he says, tossing his long sand-colored hair out away from those eyes where it had drooped while he was looking down.

The crowd was grouping up real nice about the arena next to us. I could see the glare of the white sand floor lighting their faces. I took a red balloon out of my pocket and blew it up and tied it. Then I stepped out into the middle of the arena and let it drift down onto the sand floor. Their eyes all went after it like a bunch of bees swarming with their mother queen. "Now folks, the show starts in just a few minutes," I says. Nothing can get quiet so quick as a crowd around a snake arena.

Then a kid yells: "Where are the snakes?"

"Now just be patient, Sonny. I'll be rounding up the stars of the show right away," I says, and this woman give a hysterical laugh, something like a coyote, and I ducked back into the reptile shed. The stranger had put one of the hot snakes into a coil, a four-foot Mexican green rattler.

"Now there's a hot one, ain't he?" I says, trying to cheer him up.

"Yeah," he says, "he's a jim-dandy." He turned his eyes on me and brushed his hair back from his forehead. "How much?" he says.

"I ain't going to charge you nothing," I says. "I know what it's like to be down."

"Well say, that's mighty swell. I ain't no begger, understand."

"Naw," I says, "I'm glad to do it. Only thing, I don't see how I could get anything over there to you much before seven thirty, daylight lasting like it does now. But if seven thirty won't be too late, I'll box up some stuff and hustle it over to the schoolhouse for you in my car. How's that sound?"

"I can hold them thirty minutes easy."

"Well, I got to get started. This here is a continuous show all afternoon, so I'll see you at half past seven."

"Couldn't be better," he says. "Mind if I watch your act?"

"Help yourself," I says. I saw him sticking his money back into that rear pants pocket as I picked up my snake box. I left him there in the shed and stepped back into the arena and put my box down. They were still watching the balloon. I took out my snakes and put them each one

29

in a coil by slapping my foot down at them, making a semicircle of coiled rattlers and starting my spiel. I looked up and saw he had elbowed his way to the rail. When I looked up the next time he was gone.

Before the milking act I took out one of my new iguana lizards. You got to be careful about how you hold an iguana because he's got a bite like a bulldog. The only difference is he don't give you no warning first, no growl, no frown, no hiss. He don't even quiver his eyes or show his tongue before he bites the very *bee*-devil right out of you. I held his head with all the iron I could get into my grip, and when I was done I took out a Gila monster. The old Gila was strong as a young steer. I held him the same way because a Gila is just like an iguana, only worse — once he gets his fangs into you he starts chewing like you was a plug of tobacco or something and you haven't got no alternative but to cut his head off to get him aloose. By then you're poisoned sure enough. So I was glad when I had worked the lizards and got them back in the box. I announced the milking act, and the old man came stumbling out with the kid right behind him and damned near scared the crowd to death. The kid brought the little milking table with the cocktail glass clamped to it, and I milked one and the old man did one, or made out like he did, and then I squirted a little stream of it right out in the air, just to prove to them it was real, squirted it right out of the snake's fang and got another coyote laugh out of the woman. I had just turned around when the old man started to howl and stuck his hand in his mouth. The crowd laughed some because they all thought it was a phony. They always think the real thing is phony, but I didn't even have to look at his hand to know it was real. The old man's face looked like a batch of cold grits at four A.M.

"Oscar," I says to the kid, quiet-like, "drive him to the hospital and don't worry about blowing out no tires." They went out and directly I heard the car take off outside and I had lost my best helper, probably for the rest of the season. I had it to myself for the rest of the afternoon, for when Oscar come back from the hospital he was too shaky to do nothing but stand around trembling like a tramp in January. He said the old man was in awful shape, that he was having a rigor and they had cut his arm open and all. "Don't tell me about it," I says. "I've been bit before." But he kept on, which is the trouble with them natives in the Smokies, that they can't shut up once they get shook. So finally I had to either tell him to go home or get my own self bit just to get away from him. So on the Fourth of July, like it will always happen in show business, I lost my extra help and had to clean out the cheetah's cage and tend to the armadillos all by myself and doctor the bear cub's paw where some tourist had give him a lighted cigar, until I was plumb whipped.

If Jerry, my wife, hadn't asked what that guy wanted I guess I would have forgotten him all the way. As it was I didn't start putting anything in the boxes until seven thirty, and then it was harum-scarum. I just grabbed up the first things I could lay my hands on and marked the cardboard boxes on the lids. Since I hadn't had no assistants to go behind the crowd and start them clapping, there hadn't been no applause all afternoon and Jerry could see I was whipped out. It's that applause that keeps you going in show business anyway. I went on marking the boxes, and Jerry says, "I hope he realizes what a favor you're doing him, after what all happened. You look wore out, Jake."

"Look," I says, "will you just start putting these here boxes in the car? I promised him seven-thirty. He's up there on the ridge now trying to hold his audience." I was in a hurry, so I just put on MG for Mexican green and TDB for Texas diamondback and G for Gila monster and so on, right on the top where he could read it before he took the lid off. I took the hottest stuff we had and piled it in the back seat and grabbed a snake hook and we took off, me and my wife, Jerry, fast as the old car would run. The last word the Cherokee yelled when we left was one I don't like to hear said around Jerry. I could tell that Indian squaw was against us giving any helping hand to a walking tourist. "He had a nice way of talking," Jerry said while we rolled up the mountain. "Texas," I said back to her and reached out for her little hand and gave it a big squeeze.

I guess it was eight o'clock anyway before we got to the school-house, and he had crowded more natives into it than I would have thought was staked out in all them hills. Not only that but they were

31

waiting just as faithful and polite as a bunch of treed house cats. A few had stood up and were jawing a little, but when Jerry and I came in they sneaked on back and sat down like they was trained that way.

The reason was right up there on the Hartsville High School auditorium stage, and when he opened his mouth it wasn't any wonder. If his spiel was a little wild, it was anyway one of the best I ever heard. Before Jerry and I could get the car unloaded and get the boxes on the stage, he had me believing I really was his "assistant," as he called me. Not only that, me and Jerry both hurried whenever we went out to the car for more boxes, so we wouldn't miss too much of what he said in his introduction. It wasn't any question but what he was good. And every time I took him a box onto the stage I tried to take him aside to explain about the markings on top, and every time he gave me the most elegant my-good-man treatment, waving me off and telling me where to set the box, until I just finally gave up.

I'll say this much for him. He did save us two seats down front which I appreciated, for I was in a notion to have a little nap during the show. In fact, if somebody had of told me anything could keep me awake, I would of laughed. But we hadn't sat down good and I hadn't closed my eyes quite shut, listening to him run on about Africa and Tibet and Peru and Norway and jungles and all, until Jerry's elbow, which is a sharp little thing, come into my side like a pool cue. I snapped open my eyes and started to say something rough to her, and then I looked at the stage and swallered my words whole. For he had put a Mexican green rattler into a coil and set a four-bit piece on its head. I heard him say it three times: "Now folks, I'm going to push that fifty cents off on the floor with my nose."

"Aw, why don't he *do* something," the woman on the other side of me says.

Jerry had hid her face against my shoulder. There just wasn't no way for the Mexican green to miss hitting him in the face. I figured we wouldn't get him outdoors until he'd be dead. And there his crowd was, already bitching and griping and him up on the stage like somebody bobbing apples without no tub, right over that snake's head, and it rattling so fast it was singing. He was doing a stunt that I had not seen or heard of, and which I knew I would not ever see again. In show business you always save your best stunt until last, and so I knew then what he was and where he had probably escaped from. It was the kind of stunt to end your life, instead of your act. I kept wondering if he had got the idea somewhere that their fangs had all been pulled out. The snake missed him three times and three times he put his four-bit piece back on its head. The last time he got his nose down and pushed the money off. By then it had sort of got through to the crowd what he was up to, and when that money hit the floor the last time, you could hear it roll. Then the snake struck and missed. It struck right through his hair, where it was hanging down, and I saw him brush it back with that quick flip of his head. He started up his spiel again, and I started wondering if maybe he used his hair that way on purpose. I didn't have to wait long. He was talking and opening boxes and the snakes were getting out mostly by themselves. Sometimes he stomped at them and put them into a coil, and other times he just let them come on out like they would or even dumped them. Then he reached in a box and hauled out the iguana by its tail. He held it up right in front of his face and laughed.

"Folks," he says, "I'm going to be honest with you. I don't know what this thing is." It was the truth, because he scratched it on the head. I kept waiting to hear him scream. But the iguana just hung there like he was in a tree at home and let that guy do anything he pleased.

Then he found the Gila monster. "Now," he says, "I do know what this here one is. This here is a Gila monster."

He handled it like it was stuffed and had its jaws wired. In fact he sort of waved it about while his spiel went on. I could feel my heart jumping, and Jerry's fingernails dug into my arm until it was starting to get numb. "You've heard lots of folks say Gila monsters is poison? Well, my friends, this little old lizard is not poison at all. People have told a lie on him all these years, and this evening I'm going to prove it to you. I'm going to show you he's ab-so-lute-ly harmless. Yes, friends and neighbors, I want you to watch me now. I'm going to stick my own tongue into this little feller's mouth."

"Anybody knows *they* ain't poison," the woman next to me says.

33

"He sure is a gyp, ain't he?"

"Well, what did you expect?" says her old man.

It's the only time I ever left Jerry alone like that since we been married, but I just took her fingers aloose. "You ain't leaving?" she says.

"Yes," I says. "I'll be just outside if you need me."

"I'll holler for you when the monster latches on," she says.

"No need," I says, "I ain't going more than a mile. I'll hear him okay."

There was several guffaws as I walked out and I turned just once to look, and sure enough, he had that lizard up and was trying to poke his tongue in its mouth. I just hurried on outside and leaned up against the wall of the school building, feeling dizzy. I felt to make sure that I had my pocketknife. Somebody would have to catch him and hold him while I cut the lizard's head off and then prized it off his tongue. I didn't know if I'd be up to it, and it was right there, the first time, that I wondered if I could stay on with show business. Inside they was busting gussets in all directions, laughing like a bunch of stooges. Then I heard his spiel again and risked a look inside the door. He had put the Gila monster up and was moving into something else. He had put a Texas diamondback around his neck like a scarf. I went on back in and sat down by Jerry.

"Everybody knows he's yanked the teeth out of every last one of them pore varmints," the woman by me says. "A fake, that's all in the world he is."

"What happened?" I says to Jerry.

"He couldn't make the lizard open its mouth," she says.

After a few more things, like milking venom straight into his mouth, he wound up his show and Jerry and I started the applause. It was kind of seedy. I didn't say anything. I just helped get everything off the stage and back into the boxes. Then we loaded the car and he crawled in the back seat instead of sitting up front like I asked him, and we started back down the mountain. I figured he wanted to get in the back so he could pet the iguana some more. Anyway I was too sore at him to say anything for a while. Finally I asked him what his name was.

"Doug," he says.

"Where did you say you worked reptiles before, Doug?" I says.

"I ain't going to lie to you," he says. I guess he thought it over then, for he paused before he finally said the truth. "Tonight was my first time," he says.

And then he told us he had worked around oil fields mostly and was just coming East when he saw our place there on the road and saw Lizzie behind the souvenir counter. I felt like stopping the car right there and kicking him off the side of the ridge, but in my business you can't always yield to temptation and make a go of it. I had to bear in mind that the old man was in the hospital snake-bit and Oscar was so shell-shocked over it there was no telling when *he* could go back to milking again. So I waited awhile until I could get a hold on myself. We passed the first one of our signs. It drifted by in the headlights. "Doug," I says, soft as I could manage, "how would you like to learn the reptile business?"

"By gummy, Mitch," he says, "I was hoping you would ask me that."

Tom Wolfe

The Last American Hero

TEN O'CLOCK SUNDAY morning in the hills of North Carolina. Cars, miles of cars, in every direction, millions of cars, pastel cars, aqua green, aqua blue, aqua beige, aqua buff, aqua dawn, aqua dusk, aqua Malacca, Malacca lacquer, Cloud lavender, Assassin pink, Rake-a-Cheek raspberry, Nude Strand coral, Honest Thrill orange, and Baby Fawn Lust cream-colored cars are all going to the stock car races, and that old mothering North Carolina sun keeps exploding off the windshields.

Seventeen thousand people, me included, all of us driving out Route 421, out to the stock car races at the North Wilkesboro Speedway, 17,000 going out to a five-eighths-mile stock car track with a Coca-Cola sign out front. This is not to say there is no preaching and shouting in the South this morning. There is preaching and shouting. Any of us can turn on the old automobile transistor radio and get all we want.

"They are greedy dogs. Yeah! They ride around in big cars. Unnh-hunh! And chase women. Yeah! And drink liquor. Unnh-hunh! And smoke cigars. Oh yes! And they are greedy dogs. Yeah! Unh-hunh! Oh yes! Amen!"

There are also some commercials on the radio for Aunt Jemima grits, which cost ten cents a pound. There are also the Gospel Harmonettes, singing: "If you dig a ditch, you better dig two. . . ."

There are also three fools in a panel discussion on the New South, which they seem to conceive of as General Lee running the new Dulcidreme Labial Cream factory down at Griffin, Georgia.

And suddenly my car is stopped still on Sunday morning in the middle of the biggest traffic jam in the history of the world. It goes for ten miles in every direction from the North Wilkesboro Speedway. And right there it dawns on me that as far as this situation is concerned, anyway, all the conventional notions about the South are confined to . . . the Sunday radio. The South has preaching and shouting, the South has grits, the South has country songs, old mimosa traditions, clay dust, Old Bigots, New Liberals — and all of it, all of that old mental cholesterol, is confined to the Sunday radio. What I was in the middle of — well, it wasn't anything one hears about in panels about the South today. Miles and miles of eye-busting pastel cars on the expressway, which roar right up into the hills, going to the stock car races. Fifteen years of stock car racing, and baseball — and the state of North Carolina alone used to have forty-four professional baseball teams — baseball is all over with in the South. We were all in the middle of a wild new thing, the Southern car world, and heading down the road on my way to see a breed such as sports never saw before, Southern stock car drivers, all lined up in these two-ton mothers that go over 175 m.p.h., Fireball Roberts, Freddie Lorenzen, Ned Jarrett, Richard Petty, and — the hardest of all the hard chargers, one of the fastest automobile racing drivers in history — yes! Junior Johnson.

The legend of Junior Johnson! In this legend, here is a country boy, Junior Johnson, who learns to drive by running whiskey for his father, Johnson, Senior, one of the biggest copper-still operators of all time, up in Ingle Hollow, near North Wilkesboro, in northwestern North Carolina, and grows up to be a famous stock car racing driver, rich, grossing $100,000 in 1963, for example, respected, solid, idolized in his hometown and throughout the rural South. There is all this about how good old boys would wake up in the middle of the night in the apple shacks and hear a supercharged Oldsmobile engine roaring over Brushy Mountain and say, "Listen at him — there he goes!" although that part is doubtful, since some nights there were so many good old boys taking off down the road in supercharged automobiles out of Wilkes County, and running loads to Charlotte, Salisbury, Greensboro, Winston-Salem, High Point, or wherever, it would be pretty hard to pick out one. It was Junior Johnson specifically, however, who was famous for the "bootleg turn" or "about-face," in which, if the Alcohol Tax agents had a roadblock up for you or were too close behind, you threw the car up into second gear, cocked the wheel, stepped on the accelerator and made the car's rear end skid around in a complete 180-degree arc, a complete about-face, and tore on back up the road exactly the way you came from. God! The Alcohol Tax agents used to burn over Junior Johnson. Practically every good old boy in town in Wilkesboro, the county seat, got to know the agents by sight in a very short time. They would rag them practically to their faces on the subject of Junior Johnson, so that it got to be an obsession. Finally, one night they had Junior trapped on the road up toward the bridge around Millersville, there's no way out of there, they had the barricades up and they could hear this souped-up car roaring around the bend, and here it comes — but suddenly they can hear a siren and see a red light flashing in the grille, so they think it's another agent, and boy, they run out like ants and pull those barrels and boards and sawhorses out of the way, and then — Ggghhzzzzzzzzhhhhhhgggggggzzzzzzzeeeeeong! — gawdam! there he goes again, it was him, Junior Johnson! with a gawdam agent's si-reen and a red light in his grille!

I wasn't in the South five minutes before people started making oaths, having visions, telling these hulking great stories, all on the subject of Junior Johnson. At the Greensboro, North Carolina, Airport there was one good old boy who vowed he would have eaten "a bucket of it" if that would have kept Junior Johnson from switching from a Dodge racer to a Ford. Hell yes, and after that — God-almighty, remember that 1963 Chevrolet of Junior's? Whatever happened to that car? A couple of more good old boys join in. A good old boy, I ought to explain, is a generic term in the rural South referring to a man, of any age, but more often young than not, who fits in with the status system of the region. It usually means he has a good sense of humor and enjoys ironic jokes, is tolerant and easygoing enough to get along in long conversations at places like on the corner, and has a reasonable amount of physical courage. The term is usually heard in some such form as: "Lud? He's a good old boy from over at Crozet." These good old boys in the airport, by the way, were in their twenties, except for one fellow who was a cabdriver and was about forty-five, I would say. Except for the cabdriver, they all wore neo-Brummellian clothes such as Lacoste tennis shirts, Slim Jim pants, windbreakers with the collars turned up, "fast" shoes of the winkle-picker genre, and so on. I mention these details just by way of pointing out that very few grits, Iron Boy overalls, clodhoppers or hats with ventilation holes up near the crown enter into this story. Anyway, these good old boys are talking about Junior Johnson and how he has switched to Ford. This they unanimously regard as some kind of betrayal on Johnson's part. Ford, it seems, they regard as the car symbolizing the established power structure. Dodge is kind of a middle ground. Dodge is at least a challenger, not a ruler. But the Junior Johnson they like to remember is the Junior Johnson of 1963, who took on the whole field of NASCAR (National Association For Stock Car Auto Racing) Grand National racing with a Chevrolet. All the other drivers, the drivers driving Fords, Mercurys, Plymouths, Dodges, had millions, literally millions when it is all added up, millions of dollars in backing from the Ford and Chrysler Corporations. Junior Johnson took them all on in a Chevrolet without one cent of backing from Detroit. Chevrolet had pulled out of stock car racing. Yet every race it was the same. It was never a question of whether anybody was going to *outrun* Junior Johnson. It was just a question of whether he was going to win or his car was going to break down, since, for one thing, half the time he had to make his own racing parts. God! Junior Johnson was like Robin Hood or Jesse James or Little David or something. Every time that Chevrolet, No. 3, appeared on the track, wild curdled yells, "Rebel" yells, they still have those, would rise up. At Daytona, at Atlanta, at Charlotte, at Darlington, South Carolina; Bristol, Tennessee; Martinsville, Virginia — Junior Johnson!

And then the good old boys get to talking about whatever happened to that Chevrolet of Junior's, and the cabdriver says he knows. He says Junior Johnson is using that car to run liquor out of Wilkes County. What does he mean? For Junior Johnson ever to go near another load of bootleg whiskey again — he would have to be insane. He has this huge racing income. He has two other businesses, a whole automated chicken farm with 42,000 chickens, a road-grading business — but the cabdriver says he has this dream Junior is still roaring down from Wilkes County, down through the clay cuts, with the Atlas Arc Lip jars full in the back of that Chevrolet. It is in Junior's blood — and then at this point he puts his right hand up in front of him as if he is groping through fog, and his eyeballs glaze over and he looks out in the distance and he describes Junior Johnson roaring over the ridges of Wilkes County as if it is the ghost of Zapata he is describing, bounding over the Sierras on a white horse to rouse the peasants.

A stubborn notion! A crazy notion! Yet Junior Johnson has followers who need to keep him, symbolically, riding through nighttime like a demon. Madness! But Junior Johnson is one of the last of those sports stars who is not just an ace at the game itself, but a hero a whole people or class of people can identify with. Other, older examples are the way Jack Dempsey stirred up the Irish or the way Joe Louis stirred up the Negroes. Junior Johnson is a modern figure. He is only thirty-three years old and still racing. He should be compared to two other sports heroes whose cultural impact is not too well known. One is Antonino Rocca, the professional wrestler, whose triumphs mean so much to New York City's Puerto Ricans that he can fill Madison Square Garden, despite the fact that everybody, the Puerto Ricans included, knows that wrestling is nothing but a crude form of folk theatre. The other is Ingemar Johanssen, who had a tremendous meaning to the Swedish masses — they were tired of that old king who played tennis all the time and all his friends who keep on drinking Cointreau behind the screen of socialism. Junior Johnson is a modern hero, all involved with car culture and car symbolism in the South. A wild new thing —

Wild — gone wild, Fireball Roberts' Ford spins out on the first turn at the North Wilkesboro Speedway, spinning, spinning, the spin seems almost like slow motion — and then it smashes into the wooden guardrail. It lies up there with the frame bent. Roberts is all right. There is a new layer of asphalt on the track, it is like glass, the cars keep spinning off the first turn. Ned Jarrett spins, smashes through the wood. "Now, boys, this ice ain't gonna get one goddamn bit better, so you can either line up and qualify or pack up and go home —"

I had driven from the Greensboro Airport up to Wilkes County to see Junior Johnson on the occasion of one of the two yearly NASCAR Grand National stock car races at the North Wilkesboro Speedway.

It is a long, very gradual climb from Greensboro to Wilkes County. Wilkes County is all hills, ridges, woods and underbrush, full of pin oaks, sweet-gum maples, ash, birch, apple trees, rhododendron, rocks, vines, tin roofs, little clapboard places like the Mount Olive Baptist Church, signs for things like Double Cola, Sherrill's Ice Cream, Eckard's Grocery, Dr. Pepper, Diel's Apples, Google's Place, Suddith's Place and — yes! — cars. Up onto the highway, out of a side road from a hollow, here comes a 1947 Hudson. To almost anybody it would look like just some old piece of junk left over from God knows when, rolling down a country road . . . the 1947 Hudson was one of the first real "hot" cars made after the war. Some of the others were the 1946 Chrysler, which had a "kick-down" gear for sudden bursts of speed, the 1955 Pontiac and a lot of the Fords. To a great many good old boys a hot car was a symbol of heating up life itself. The war! Money even for country boys! And the money bought cars. In California they suddenly found kids of all sorts involved in vast drag racing orgies and couldn't figure out what was going on. But in the South the mania for cars was even more intense, although much less publicized. To millions of good old boys, and girls, the automobile represented not only liberation from what was still pretty much a land-bound form of social organization but also a great leap forward into twentieth-century glamor, an idea that was being dinned in on the South like everywhere else. It got so that one of the typical rural sights, in addition to the red rooster, the gray split-rail fence, the Edgeworth Tobacco sign and the rusted-out harrow, one of the typical rural sights would be . . . you would be driving along the dirt roads and there beside the house would be an automobile up on blocks or something, with a rope over the tree for hoisting up the motor or some other heavy part, and a couple of good old boys would be practically disappearing into its innards, from below and from above, draped over the side under the hood. It got so that on Sundays there wouldn't be a safe straight stretch of road in the county, because so many wild country boys would be out racing or just raising hell on the roads. A lot of other kids, who weren't basically wild, would be driving like hell every morning and every night, driving to jobs perhaps thirty or forty miles away, jobs that were available only because of automobiles. In the morning they would be driving through the dapple shadows like madmen. In the hollows, sometimes one would come upon the most incredible tar-paper hovels, down near the stream, and out front would be an incredible automobile creation, a late-model car with aerials, Continental kit overhangs in the back, mudguards studded with reflectors, fender skirts, spotlights, God knows what all, with a girl and perhaps a couple of good old boys communing over it and giving you rotten looks as you drove by. On Saturday night everybody would drive into town and park under the lights on the main street and neck. Yes! There was something about being right there in town underneath the lights and having them reflecting off the baked enamel on the hood. Then if a good old boy insinuated his hands here and there on the front seat with a girl and began . . . necking . . . somehow it was all more *complete*. After the war there was a great deal of stout-burgher talk about people who lived in hovels and bought big-yacht cars to park out front. This was one of the symbols of a new, spendthrift age. But there was a great deal of unconscious resentment buried in the talk. It was resentment against (a) the fact that the good old boy had his money at all and (b) the fact that the car symbolized freedom, a slightly wild, careening emancipation from the old social order. Stock car racing got started about this time, right after the war, and it was immediately regarded as some kind of manifestation of the animal irresponsibility of the lower orders. It had a truly terrible reputation. It was — well, it looked *rowdy* or something. The cars were likely to be used cars, the tracks were dirt, the stands were rickety wood, the drivers were country boys, and they had regular feuds out there, putting each other "up against the wall" and "cutting tires" and everything else. Those country boys would drive into the curves full tilt, then slide maniacally, sometimes coming around the curve sideways, with red dirt showering up. Sometimes they would race at night, under those weak-eyed yellow-ochre lights they have at small tracks and baseball fields, and the clay dust would start showering up in the air, where the evening dew would catch it, and all evening long you would be sitting in the stands or standing out in the infield with a fine clay-mud drizzle coming down on you, not that anybody gave a damn — except for the Southern upper and middle classes, who never attended in those days, but spoke of the "rowdiness."

But mainly it was the fact that stock car racing was something that was welling up out of the lower orders. From somewhere these country boys and urban proles were getting the money and starting this hellish sport.

Stock car racing was beginning all over the country, at places like Allentown, Langhorne and Lancaster, Pennsylvania, and out in California and even out on Long Island, but wherever it cropped up, the Establishment tried to wish it away, largely, and stock car racing went on in a kind of underground world of tracks built on cheap stretches of land well out from the town or the city, a world of diners, drive-ins, motels, gasoline stations, and the good burghers might drive by from time to time, happen by on a Sunday or something, and see the crowd gathered from out of nowhere, the cars coming in, crowding up the highway a little, but Monday morning they would be all gone, and all would be as it was.

Stock car racing was building up a terrific following in the South during the early fifties. Here was a sport not using any abstract devices, any *bat* and *ball*, but the same automobile that was changing a man's own life, his own symbol of liberation, and it didn't require size, strength and all that, all it required was a taste for speed, and the guts. The newspapers in the South didn't seem to catch onto what was happening until late in the game. Of course, newspapers all over the country have looked backward over the tremendous rise in automobile sports, now the second-biggest type of sports in the country in terms of attendance. The sports pages generally have an inexorable lower-middle-class outlook. The sportswriter's "zest for life" usually amounts, in the end, to some sort of gruff Mom's Pie sentimentality at a hideously cozy bar somewhere. The sportswriters caught onto Grand Prix racing first because it had "tone," a touch of defrocked European nobility about it, what with a few counts racing here and there, although, in fact, it is the least popular form of racing in the United States. What finally put stock car racing onto the sports pages in the South was the intervention of the Detroit automobile firms. Detroit began putting so much money into the sport that it took on a kind of massive economic respectability and thereby, in the lower-middle-class brain, status.

What Detroit discovered was that thousands of good old boys in the South were starting to form allegiances to brands of automobiles, according to which were hottest on the stock car circuits, the way they used to have them for the hometown baseball team. The South was one of the hottest car-buying areas in the country. Cars like Hudsons, Oldsmobiles and Lincolns, not the cheapest automobiles by any means, were selling in disproportionate numbers in the South, and a lot of young good old boys were buying them. In 1955, Pontiac started easing into stock car racing, and suddenly the big surge was on. Everybody jumped into the sport to grab for themselves The Speed Image. Suddenly, where a good old boy used to have to bring his gasoline to the track in old fillng-station pails and pour it into the tank through a funnel when he made a pit stop, and change his tires with a hand wrench, suddenly, now, he had these "gravity" tanks of gasoline that you just jam into the gas pipe, and air wrenches to take the wheels off, and whole crews of men in white coveralls to leap all over a car when it came rolling into the pit, just like they do at Indianapolis, as if they are mechanical apparati *merging* with the machine as it rolls in, forcing water into the radiator, jacking up the car, taking off wheels, wiping off the windshield, handing the driver a cup of orange juice, all in one synchronized operation. And now, today, the *big money* starts descending on this little place, the North Wilkesboro, North Carolina, Speedway, a little five-eighths-of-a-mile stock car track with a Coca-Cola sign out by the highway where the road in starts.

The private planes start landing out at the Wilkesboro Airport.

Freddie Lorenzen, the driver, the biggest money winner last year in stock car racing, comes sailing in out of the sky in a twin-engine Aero Commander, and there are a few good old boys out there in the tall grass by the runway already with their heads sticking up watching this hero of the modern age come in and taxi up and get out of that twin-engine airplane with his blonde hair swept back as if by the mother internal combustion engine of them all. And then Paul Goldsmith, the driver, comes in in a 310 Cessna, and *he* gets out, all these tall, lanky hard-boned Americans in their thirties with these great profiles like a comic-strip hero or something, and then Glenn (Fireball) Roberts — Fireball Roberts! — Fireball is *hard* — he comes in in a Comanche 250, like a flying yacht, and then Ray Nichels and Ray Fox, the chief mechanics, who run big racing crews for the Chrysler Corporation, this being Fox's last race for Junior as his mechanic, before Junior switches over to Ford, they come in in two-engine planes. And even old Buck Baker — hell, Buck Baker is a middling driver for Dodge, but even he comes rolling in down the landing strip at two hundred miles an hour with his Southern-hero face at the window of the cockpit of a twin-engine Apache, traveling first class in the big status boat that has replaced the yacht in America, the private plane.

And then the Firestone and Goodyear vans pull in, huge mothers, bringing in huge stacks of racing tires for the race, big wide ones, 8.20's, with special treads, which are like a lot of bumps on the tire instead of grooves. They even have special tires for qualifying, soft tires, called "gumballs," they wouldn't last more than ten times around the track in a race, but for qualifying, which is generally three laps, one to pick up speed and two to race against the clock, they are great, because they hold tight on the corners. And on a hot day, when somebody like Junior Johnson, one of the fastest qualifying runners in the history of the sport, 170.777 m.p.h., in a one-hundred-mile qualifying race at Daytona in 1964, when somebody like Junior Johnson really pushes it on a qualifying run, there will be a ring of blue smoke up over the whole goddamned track, a ring like an oval halo over the whole thing from the gumballs burning, and some good old boy will say, "Great smokin' blue gumballs god almighty dog! There goes Junior Johnson!"

The thing is, each one of these tires costs fifty-five to sixty dollars, and on a track that is fast and hard on tires, like Atlanta, one car might go through ten complete tire changes, easily, forty tires, or almost $2500 worth of tires just for one race. And he may even be out of the money. And then the Ford van and the Dodge van and the Mercury van and the Plymouth van roll in with new motors, a whole new motor every few races, a 427-cubic-inch stock car racing motor, 600 horsepower, the largest and most powerful allowed on the track, that probably costs the company $1000 or more, when you consider that they are not mass produced. And still the advertising appeal. You can buy the very same car that these fabulous wild men drive every week at these fabulous wild speeds, and some of their power and charisma is yours. After every NASCAR Grand National stock car race, whichever company has the car that wins, this company will put big ads in the Southern papers, and papers all over the country if it is a very big race, like the Daytona 500, the Daytona Firecracker 400 or the Atlanta and Charlotte races. They sell a certain number of these 427-cubic-inch cars to the general public, a couple of hundred a year, perhaps, at eight or nine thousand dollars apiece, but it is no secret that these motors are specially reworked just for stock car racing. Down at Charlotte there is a company called Holman & Moody that is supposed to be the "garage" or "automotive-engineering" concern that prepares automobiles for Freddie Lorenzen and some of the other Ford drivers. But if you go by Holman & Moody out by the airport and Charlotte, suddenly you come upon a huge place that is a *factory*, for godsake, a big long thing, devoted mainly to the business of turning out stock car racers. A whole lot of other parts in stock car racers are heavier than the same parts on a street automobile, although they are made to the same scale. The shock absorbers are bigger, the wheels are wider and bulkier, the swaybars and steering mechanisms are heavier, the axles are much heavier, they have double sets of wheel bearings, and so forth and so on. The bodies of the cars are pretty much the same, except that they use lighter sheet metal, practically tinfoil. Inside, there is only the driver's seat and a heavy set of roll bars and diagonal struts that turn the inside of the car into a rigid cage, actually. That is why the drivers can walk away unhurt — most of the time — from the most spectacular crackups. The gearshift is the floor kind, although it doesn't make much difference, as there is almost no shifting gears in stock car racing. You just get into high gear and go. The dashboard has no speedometer, the main thing being the dial for engine revolutions per minute. So, anyway, it costs about $15,000 to prepare a stock car racer in the first place and another three or four thousand for each new race and this does not even count the costs of mechanics' work and transportation. All in all, Detroit will throw around a quarter of a million dollars into it every week while the season is on, and the season runs, roughly, from February to October, with a few big races after that. And all this turns up even out at the North Wilkesboro Speedway in the up-country of Wilkes County, North Carolina.

Sunday! Racing day! There is the Coca-Cola sign out where the road leads in from the highway, and hills and trees, but here are long concrete grandstands for about 17,000 and a paved five-eighths-mile oval. Practically all the drivers are out there with their cars and their crews, a lot of guys in white coveralls. The cars look huge . . . and curiously nude and blind. All the chrome is stripped off, except for the grilles. The headlights are blanked out. Most of the cars are in the pits. The so-called "pit" is a paved cutoff on the edge of the infield. It cuts off from the track itself like a service road off an expressway at the shopping center. Every now and then a car splutters, hacks, coughs, hocks a lunga, rumbles out onto the track itself for a practice run. There is a lot of esoteric conversation going on, speculation, worries, memoirs:

"What happened?"

"Mother —— condensed on me. Al brought it up here with him. Water in the line."

"Better keep Al away from a stable, he'll fill you up with horse manure."

". . . they told me to give him one, a creampuff, so I give him one, a creampuff. One goddamn race and the son of a bitch, he *melted* it. . . ."

". . . he's down there right now pettin' and rubbin' and huggin' that car just like those guys do a horse at the Kentucky Derby. . . ."

". . . They'll blow you right out of the tub. . . ."

". . . No, the quarter inch, and go on over and see if you can get Ned's blowtorch. . . ."

". . . Rear end's loose. . . ."

". . . I don't reckon this right here's got nothing to do with it, do you? . . ."

". . . Aw, I don't know, about yea big. . . ."

". . . Who the hell stacked them gumballs on the bottom? . . ."

". . . th'owing rocks. . . ."

". . . won't turn seven thousand. . . ."

". . . strokin' it. . . ."

". . . blistered. . . ."

". . . spun out. . . ."

". . . muvva. . . ."

Then, finally, here comes Junior Johnson. How he does come on. He comes tooling across the infield in a big white dreamboat, a brand-new white Pontiac Catalina four-door hard-top sedan. He pulls up and as he gets out he seems to get more and more huge. First his crew-cut head and then a big jaw and then a bigger neck and then a huge torso, like a wrestler's, all done up rather modish and California modern, with a red-and-white candy-striped sport shirt, white ducks and loafers.

"How you doing?" says Junior Johnson, shaking hands, and then he says, "Hot enough for ye'uns?"

Junior is in an amiable mood. Like most up-hollow people, it turns out, Junior is reserved. His face seldom shows an emotion. He has three basic looks: amiable, amiable and a little shy, and dead serious. To a lot of people, apparently, Junior's dead-serious look seems menacing. There are no cowards left in stock car racing, but a couple of drivers tell me that one of the things that can shake you up is to look into your rear-view mirror going around a curve and see Junior Johnson's car on your tail trying to "root you out of the groove," and then get a glimpse of Junior's dead-serious look. I think some of the sportswriters are afraid of him. One of them tells me Junior is strong, silent — and explosive. Junior will only give you three answers, "Uh-huh," "Uh-unh," and "I don't know," and so forth and so on. Actually, I found he handles questions easily. He has a great technical knowledge of automobiles and the physics of speed, including things he never fools with, such as Offenhauser engines. What he never does offer, however, is small talk. This gives him a built-in poise, since it deprives him of the chance to say anything asinine. "Ye'uns," "we'uns," "H'it" for "it," "growed" for "grew" and a lot of other unusual past participles — Junior uses certain older forms of English, not exactly "Elizabethan," as they are sometimes called, but older forms of English preserved up-country in his territory, Ingle Hollow.

Kids keep coming up for Junior's autograph and others are just hanging around and one little old boy comes up, he is about thirteen, and Junior says: "This boy here goes coon hunting with me."

One of the sportswriters is standing around, saying: "What do you shoot a coon with?"

"Don't shoot 'em. The dogs tree 'em and then you flush 'em out and the dogs fight 'em."

"Flush 'em out?"

"Yeah. This boy right here can flush 'em out better than anybody you ever did see. You go out at night with the dogs, and soon as they get the scent, they start barking. They go on out ahead of you and when they tree a coon, you can tell it, by the way they sound. They all start baying up at that coon — h'it sounds like, I don't know, you hear it once and you not likely to forget it. Then you send a little old boy up to flush him out and he jumps down and the dogs fight him."

"How does a boy flush him out?"

"Aw, he just climbs up there to the limb he's on and starts shaking h'it and the coon'll jump."

"What happens if the coon decides he'd rather come back after the boy instead of jumping down to a bunch of dogs?"

"He won't do that. A coon's afraid of a person, but he can kill a dog. A coon can take any dog you set against him if they's just the two of them fighting. The coon jumps down on the ground and he rolls right over on his back with his feet up, and he's *got* claws about like this. All he has to do is get a dog once in the throat or in the belly, and he can kill him, cut him wide open just like you took a knife and did it. Won't any dog even fight a coon except a coon dog."

"What kind of dogs are they?"

"*Coon* dogs, I guess. Black and tans they call 'em sometimes. They's bred for it. If his mammy and pappy wasn't coon dogs, he ain't likely to be one either. After you got one, you got to train him. You trap a coon, live, and then you put him in a pen and tie him to a post with a rope on him and then you put your dog in there and he has to fight him. Sometimes you get a dog just don't have any fight in him and he ain't no good to you."

Junior is in the pit area, standing around with his brother Fred, who is part of his crew, and Ray Fox and some other good old boys, in a general atmosphere of big stock car money, a big ramp truck for his car, a white Dodge, number 3, a big crew in white coveralls, huge stacks of racing tires, a Dodge P.R. man, big portable cans of gasoline, compressed air hoses, compressed water hoses, the whole business. Herb Nab, Freddie Lorenzen's chief mechanic, comes over and sits down on his haunches and Junior sits down on his haunches and Nab says:

"So Junior Johnson's going to drive a Ford."

Junior is switching from Dodge to Ford mainly because he hasn't been winning with the Dodge. Lorenzen drives a Ford, too, and the last year, when Junior was driving the Chevrolet, their duels were the biggest excitement in stock car racing.

"Well," says Nab, "I'll tell you, Junior. My ambition is going to be to outrun your ass every goddamned time we go out."

"That was your ambition last year," says Junior.

"I know it was," says Nab, "and you took all the money, didn't you? You know what my strategy was. I was going to outrun everybody else and outlast Junior, that was my strategy."

Setting off his California modern sport shirt and white ducks Junior has on a pair of twenty-dollar rimless sunglasses and a big gold Timex watch, and Flossie, his fiancée, is out there in the infield somewhere with the white Pontiac, and the white Dodge that Dodge gave Junior is parked up near the pit area — and then a little thing happens that brings

51

the whole thing right back there to Wilkes County, North Carolina, to Ingle Hollow and to hard muscle in the clay gulches. A couple of good old boys come down to the front of the stands with the screen and the width of the track between them and Junior, and one of the good old boys comes down and yells out in the age-old baritone raw-curdle yell of the Southern hills:

"Hey! Hog jaw!"

Everybody gets quiet. They know he's yelling at Junior, but nobody says a thing. Junior doesn't even turn around.

"Hey, hog jaw! . . ."

Junior, he does nothing.

"Hey, hog jaw, I'm gonna get me one of them fastback roosters, too, and come down there and get you!"

Fastback rooster refers to the Ford — it has a "fastback" design — Junior is switching to.

"Hey, hog jaw, I'm gonna get me one of them fastback roosters and run you right out of here, you hear me, hog jaw!"

One of the good old boys alongside Junior says, "Junior, go on up there and clear out those stands."

Then everybody stares at Junior to see what he's gonna do. Junior, he don't even look around. He just looks a bit dead serious.

"Hey, hog jaw, you got six cases of whiskey in the back of that car you want to let me have?"

"What you hauling in that car, hog jaw!"

"Tell him you're out of that business, Junior," one of the good old boys says.

"Go on up there and clean house, Junior," says another good old boy.

Then Junior looks up, without looking at the stands, and smiles a little and says, "You flush him down here out of that tree — and I'll take keer of him."

Such a howl goes up from the good old boys! It is almost a blood curdle —

"Goddam, he *will*, too!"

"Lord, he better know how to do an *about-face* hissef if he comes

52

down here!"

"Goddam, get him Junior!"

"Whooeeee!"

"Mother dog!"

— a kind of orgy of reminiscence of the old Junior before the Detroit money started flowing, wild *combats d'honneur* up-hollow — and, suddenly, when he heard that unearthly baying coming up from the good old boys in the pits, the good old boy retreated from the edge of the stands and never came back.

Later on Junior told me, sort of apologetically, "H'it used to be, if a fellow crowded me just a little bit, I was ready to crawl him. I reckon that was one good thing about Chillicothe.

"I don't want to pull any more time," Junior tells me, "but I wouldn't take anything in the world for the experience I had in prison. If a man needed to change, that was the place to change. H'it's not a waste of time there, h'it's good experience.

"H'it's that they's so many people in the world that feel that nobody is going to tell them what to do. I had quite a temper, I reckon. I always had the idea that I had as much sense as the other person and I didn't want them to tell me what to do. In the penitentiary there I found out that I could listen to another fellow and be told what to do and h'it wouldn't kill me."

Starting time! Linda Vaughn, with the big blonde hair and blossomy breasts, puts down her Coca-Cola and the potato chips and slips off her red stretch pants and her white blouse and walks out of the officials' booth in her Rake-a-Cheek red showgirl's costume with her long honeydew legs in net stockings and climbs up on the red Firebird float. The Life Symbol of stock car racing! Yes! Linda, every luscious morsel of Linda, is a good old girl from Atlanta who was made Miss Atlanta International Raceway one year and was paraded around the track on a float and she liked it so much and all the good old boys liked it so much, Linda's flowing hair and blossomy breasts and honeydew legs, that she became the permanent glamor symbol of stock car racing, and never mind this other modeling she was doing . . . this, she liked it. Right before practically every race on the Grand National circuit Linda

53

Vaughn puts down her Coca-Cola and potato chips. Her momma is there, she generally comes around to see Linda go around the track on the float, it's such a nice spectacle seeing Linda looking so lovely, and the applause and all. "Linda, I'm thirstin', would you bring me a Coca-Cola?" "A lot of them think I'm Freddie Lorenzen's girl friend, but I'm not any of 'em's girl friend, I'm real good friends with 'em all, even Wendell," he being Wendell Scott, the only Negro in big-league stock car racing. Linda gets up on the Firebird float. This is an extraordinary object, made of wood, about twenty feet tall, in the shape of a huge bird, an eagle or something, blazing red, and Linda, with her red showgirl's suit on, gets up on the seat, which is up between the wings, like a saddle, high enough so her long honeydew legs stretch down, and a new car pulls her — Miss Firebird! — slowly once around the track just before the race. It is more of a ceremony by now than the national anthem. Miss Firebird sails slowly in front of the stands and the good old boys let out some real curdle Rebel yells, "Yaaaaaaaaaaaaghhhhooooooo! Let me at that car!" "Honey, you sure do start my motor, I swear to God!" "Great God and Poonadingdong, I mean!"

And suddenly there's a big roar from behind, down in the infield, and then I see one of the great sights in stock car racing. That infield! The cars have been piling into the infield by the hundreds, parking in there on the clay and the grass, every which way, angled down and angled up, this way and that, where the ground is uneven, these beautiful blazing brand-new cars with the sun exploding off the windshields and the baked enamel and the glassy lacquer, hundreds, thousands of cars stacked this way and that in the infield with the sun bolting down and no shade, none at all, just a couple of Coca-Cola stands out there. And already the good old boys and girls are out beside the cars, with all these beautiful little buds in short shorts already spread-eagled out on top of the car roofs, pressing down on good hard slick automobile sheet metal, their little cupcake bottoms aimed up at the sun. The good old boys are lollygagging around with their shirts off and straw hats on that have miniature beer cans on the brims and buttons that read, "Girls Wanted — No Experience Required." And everybody, good old boys and girls of all ages, is out there with portable charcoal barbecue ovens set up, and folding tubular steel terrace furniture, deck chairs and things, and Thermos jugs and coolers full of beer — and suddenly it is not the up-country South at all but a concentration of the modern suburbs, all jammed into that one space, from all over America, with blazing cars and instant goodies, all cooking under the bare blaze — inside a strange bowl. The infield is like the bottom of a bowl. The track around it is banked so steeply at the corners and even on the straightaways, it is like the steep sides of a bowl. The wall around the track, and the stands and the bleachers are like the rim of a bowl. And from the infield, in this great incredible press of blazing new cars, there is no horizon but the bowl, up above only that cobalt-blue North Carolina sky. And then suddenly, on a signal, thirty stock car engines start up where they are lined up in front of the stands. The roar of these engines is impossible to describe. They have a simultaneous rasp, thunder and rumble that goes right through a body and fills the whole bowl with a noise of internal combustion. Then they start around on two build-up runs, just to build up speed, and then they come around the fourth turn and onto the straightaway in front of the stands at — here, 130 miles an hour, in Atlanta, 160 miles an hour, at Daytona, 180 miles an hour — and the flag goes down and everybody in the infield and in the stands is up on their feet going mad, and suddenly here is a bowl that is one great orgy of everything in the way of excitement and liberation the automobile has meant to Americans. An orgy!

The first lap of a stock car race is a horrendous, a wildly horrendous spectacle such as no other sport approaches. Twenty, thirty, forty automobiles, each of them weighing almost two tons, 3700 pounds, with 427-cubic-inch engines, 600 horsepower, are practically locked together, side to side and tail to nose, on a narrow band of asphalt at 130, 160, 180 miles an hour, hitting the curves so hard the rubber burns off the tires in front of your eyes. To the driver, it is like being inside a car going down the West Side Highway in New York City at rush hour, only with everybody going literally three to four times as fast, at speeds a man who has gone eighty-five miles an hour down a highway cannot conceive of, and with every other driver an enemy who is willing to cut inside of you, around you or in front of you, or ricochet off your side in the battle to get into a curve first.

The speeds are faster than those in the Indianapolis 500 race, the cars are more powerful and much heavier. The prize money in Southern stock car racing is far greater than that in Indianapolis-style or European Grand Prix racing, but few Indianapolis or Grand Prix drivers have the raw nerve required to succeed at it.

Although they will deny it, it is still true that stock car drivers will put each other "up against the wall" — cut inside on the left of another car and ram it into a spin — if they get mad enough. Crashes are not the only danger, however. The cars are now literally too fast for their own parts, especially the tires. Firestone and Goodyear have poured millions into stock car racing, but neither they nor anybody so far have been able to come up with a tire for this kind of racing at the current speeds. Three well-known stock car drivers were killed last year, two of them champion drivers, Joe Weatherly and Fireball Roberts, and another, one of the best new drivers, Jimmy Pardue, from Junior Johnson's own home territory, Wilkes County, North Carolina. Roberts was the only one killed in a crash. Junior Johnson was in the crash but was not injured. Weatherly and Pardue both lost control on curves. Pardue's death came during a tire test. In a tire test, engineers from Firestone or Goodyear try out various tires on a car, and the driver, always one of the top competitors, tests them at top speed, usually on the Atlanta track. The drivers are paid three dollars a mile and may drive as much as five or six hundred miles in a single day. At 145 miles an hour average that does not take very long. Anyway, these drivers are going at speeds that, on curves, can tear tires off their casings or break axles. They practically run off from over their own wheels.

Junior Johnson was over in the garden by the house some years ago, plowing the garden barefooted, behind a mule, just wearing an old pair of overalls, when a couple of good old boys drove up and told him to come on up to the speedway and get in a stock car race. They wanted some local boys to race, as a preliminary to the main race, "as a kind of side show," as Junior remembers it.

"So I just put the reins down," Junior is telling me, "and rode on over 'ere with them. They didn't give us seat belts or nothing, they just roped us in. H'it was a dirt track then. I come in second."

Junior was a sensation in dirt track racing right from the start. Instead of going into the curves and just sliding and holding on for dear life like the other drivers, Junior developed the technique of throwing himself into a slide about seventy-five feet before the curve by cocking the wheel to the left slightly and gunning it, using the slide, not the brake, to slow down, so that he could pick up speed again halfway through the curve and come out of it like a shot. This was known as his "power slide," and — yes! of course! — every good old boy in North Carolina started saying Junior Johnson had learned that stunt doing those goddamned *about-faces* running away from the Alcohol Tax agents. Junior put on such a show one night on a dirt track in Charlotte that he broke two axles, and he thought he was out of the race because he didn't have any more axles, when a good old boy came running up out of the infield and said, "Goddamn it, Junior Johnson, you take the axle off my car here, I got a Pontiac just like yours," and Junior took it off and put it on his and went out and broke *it* too. Mother dog! To this day Junior Johnson loves dirt track racing like nothing else in this world, even though there is not much money in it. Every year he sets new dirt track speed records, such as at Hickory, North Carolina, one of the most popular dirt tracks, last spring. As far as Junior is concerned, dirt track racing is not so much of a mechanical test for the car as those long five- and six-hundred-mile races on asphalt are. Gasoline, tire and engine wear aren't so much of a problem. It is all the driver, his skill, his courage — his willingness to mix it up with the other cars, smash and carom off of them at a hundred miles an hour or so to get into the curves first. Junior has a lot of fond recollections of mixing it up at places like Bowman Gray Stadium in Winston-Salem, one of the minor league tracks, a very narrow track, hardly wide enough for two cars. "You could always figure Bowman Gray was gonna cost you two fenders, two doors and two quarter panels," Junior tells me with nostalgia.

Anyway, at Hickory, which was a Saturday night race, all the good old boys started pouring into the stands before sundown, so they wouldn't miss anything, the practice runs or the qualifying or anything. And pretty soon, the dew hasn't even started falling before Junior Johnson and David Pearson, one of Dodge's best drivers, are out there on practice runs, just warming up, and they happen to come up alongside each other on the second curve, and — the thing is, here are two men, each of them driving $15,000 automobiles, each of them standing to make $50,000 to $100,000 for the season if they don't get themselves killed, and they meet on a curve on a goddamned practice run on a dirt track, and neither of them can resist it. Coming out of the turn they go into a wild-ass race down the backstretch, both of them trying to get into the third turn first, and all the way across the infield you can hear them ricocheting off each other and bouncing at a hundred miles an hour on loose dirt, and then they go into ferocious power slides, red dust all over the goddamned place, and then out of this goddamned red-dust cloud, out of the fourth turn, here comes Junior Johnson first, like a shot, with Pearson right on his tail, and the good old boys in the stands going wild, and the *qualifying* runs haven't started yet, let alone the race.

Junior worked his way up through the minor leagues, the Sportsman and Modified classifications, as they are called, winning championships in both, and won his first Grand National race, the big leagues, in 1955 at Hickory, on dirt. He was becoming known as "the hardest of the hard-chargers," power sliding, rooting them out of the groove, raising hell, and already the Junior Johnson legend was beginning.

He kept hard-charging, power sliding, going after other drivers as though there wasn't room on the track but for one, and became the most popular driver in stock car racing by 1959. The presence of Detroit and Detroit's big money had begun to calm the drivers down a little. Detroit was concerned about Image. The last great duel of the dying dog-eat-dog era of stock car racing came in 1959, when Junior and Lee Petty, who was then leading the league in points, had it out on the Charlotte raceway. Junior was in the lead, and Petty was right on his tail, but couldn't get by Junior. Junior kept coming out of the curves faster. So every chance he got, Petty would get up right on Junior's rear bumper and start banging it, gradually forcing the fender in to where the metal would cut Junior's rear tire. With only a few laps to go, Junior had a blowout and spun out up against the guardrail. That is Junior's version. Petty claimed Junior hit a pop bottle and spun out. The fans in Charlotte were always throwing pop bottles and other stuff onto the track late in the race, looking for blood. In any case, Junior eased back into the pits, had the tire changed, and charged out after Petty. He caught him on a curve and — well, whatever really happened, Petty was suddenly "up against the wall" and out of the race, and Junior won.

What a howl went up. The Charlotte chief of police charged out onto the track after the race, according to Petty, and offered to have Junior arrested for "assault with a dangerous weapon," the hassling went on for weeks —

"Back then," Junior tells me, "when you got into a guy and racked him up, you might as well get ready, because he's coming back for you. H'it was dog eat dog. That straightened Lee Petty out right smart. They don't do stuff like that anymore, though, because the guys don't stand for it."

Anyway, the Junior Johnson legend kept building up and building up, and in 1960 it got hotter than ever when Junior won the biggest race of the year, the Daytona 500, by discovering a new technique called "drafting." That year stock car racing was full of big powerful Pontiacs manned by top drivers, and they would go like nothing else anybody ever saw. Junior went down to Daytona with a Chevrolet.

"My car was about ten miles an hour slower than the rest of the cars, the Pontiacs," Junior tells me. "In the preliminary races, the warmups and stuff like that, they was smoking me off the track. Then I remember once I went out for a practice run, and Fireball Roberts was out there in a Pontiac and I got in right behind him on a curve, right on his bumper. I knew I couldn't stay with him on the straightaway, but I came out of the curve fast, right in behind him, running flat out, and then I noticed a funny thing. As long as I stayed right in behind him, I noticed I picked up speed and stayed right with him and my car was going faster than it had ever gone before. I could tell on the tachometer. My car wasn't turning no more than 6000 before, but when I got into this drafting position, I was turning 6800 to 7000. H'it felt like the car was plumb off the ground, floating along."

"Drafting," it was discovered at Daytona, created a vacuum behind the lead car and both cars would go faster than they normally would. Junior "hitched rides" on the Pontiacs most of the afternoon, but was still second to Bobby Johns, the lead Pontiac. Then, late in the race, Johns got into a drafting position with a fellow Pontiac that was actually one lap behind him and the vacuum got so intense that the rear window blew out of Johns' car and he spun out and crashed and Junior won.

This made Junior the Lion Killer, the Little David of stock car racing, and his performance in the 1963 season made him even more so.

Junior raced for Chevrolet at Daytona in February, 1963, and set the all-time stock car speed record in a hundred-mile qualifying race, 164.083 miles an hour, twenty-one miles an hour faster than Parnelli Jones's winning time at Indianapolis that year. Junior topped that at Daytona in July of 1963, qualifying at 166.005 miles per hour in a five-mile run, the fastest that anyone had ever averaged that distance in a racing car of any type. Junior's Chevrolet lasted only twenty-six laps in the Daytona 500 in 1963, however. He went out with a broken push rod. Although Chevrolet announced they were pulling out of racing at this time, Junior took his car and started out on the wildest perform-ance in the history of stock car racing. Chevrolet wouldn't give him a cent of backing. They wouldn't even speak to him on the telephone. Half the time he had to have his own parts made. Plymouth, Mercury, Dodge and Ford, meantime, were pouring more money than ever into stock car racing. Yet Junior won seven Grand National races out of the thirty-three he entered and led most others before mechanical trouble forced him out.

All the while, Junior was making record qualifying runs, year after year. In the usual type of qualifying run, a driver has the track to himself and makes two circuits, with the driver with the fastest average time getting the "pole" position for the start of the race. In a way this presents stock car danger in its purest form. Driving a stock car does not require much handling ability, at least not as compared to Grand Prix racing, because the tracks are simple banked ovals and there is almost no shifting of gears. So qualifying becomes a test of raw nerve — of how fast a man is willing to take a curve. Many of the top drivers in competition are poor at qualifying. In effect, they are willing to calculate their risks only against the risks the other drivers are taking. Junior takes the pure risk as no other driver has ever taken it.

"Pure" risk or total risk, whichever, Indianapolis and Grand Prix drivers have seldom been willing to face the challenge of Southern stock car drivers. A. J. Foyt, last year's winner at Indianapolis, is one exception. He has raced against the Southerners and beaten them. Parnelli Jones has tried and fared badly. Driving "Southern style" has a quality that shakes a man up. The Southerners went on a tour of northern tracks last fall. They raced at Bridgehampton, New York, and went into the corners so hard the marshals stationed at each corner kept radioing frantically to the control booth: "They're going off the track. They're all going off the track."

But this, Junior Johnson's last race in a Dodge, was not his day, neither for qualifying nor racing. Lorenzen took the lead early and won the 250-mile race a lap ahead of the field. Junior finished third, but was never in contention for the lead.

"Come on, Junior, do my hand —"

Two or three hundred people come out of the stands and up out of the infield and onto the track to be around Junior Johnson. Junior is signing autographs in a neat left-handed script he has. It looks like it came right out of the Locker book. The girls! Levis, stretch pants, sneaky shorts, stretch jeans, they press into the crowd with lively narbs and try to get their hands up in front of Junior and say:

"Come on, Junior, do my hand!"

In order to do a hand, Junior has to hold the girl's hand in his right hand and then sign his name with a ball-point on the back of her hand.

"Junior, you got to do mine, too!"

"Put it on up here."

All the girls break into . . . smiles. Junior Johnson does a hand. Ah, sweet little cigarette-ad blonde! She says:

"Junior, why don't you ever call me up?"

"I 'spect you get plenty of calls 'thout me."

"Oh, Junior! You call me up, you hear now?"

But also a great many older people crowd in, and they say:

"Junior, you're doing a real good job out there, you're driving real good."

"Junior, when you get in that Ford, I want to see you pass that Freddie Lorenzen, you hear now?"

"Junior, you like that Ford better than that Dodge?"

And:

"Junior, here's a young man that's been waiting some time and wanting to see you —" and the man lifts up his little boy in the middle of the crowd and says: "I told you you'd see Junior Johnson. This here's Junior Johnson!"

The boy has a souvenir racing helmet on his head. He stares at Junior through a buttery face. Junior signs the program he has in his hand, and then the boy's mother says:

"Junior, I tell you right now, he's beside you all the way. He can't be moved."

And then:

"Junior, I want you to meet the meanest little girl in Wilkes County."

"She don't look mean to me."

Junior keeps signing autographs and over by the pits the other kids are all over his car, the Dodge. They start pulling off the decals, the ones saying Holly Farms Poultry and Autolite and God knows what all. They fight over the strips, the shreds of decal, as if they were totems.

All this homage to Junior Johnson lasts about forty minutes. He must be signing about 250 autographs, but he is not a happy man. By and by the crowd is thinning out, the sun is going down, wind is blowing the Coca-Cola cups around, all one can hear, mostly, is a stock car engine starting up every now and then as somebody drives it up onto a truck or something, and Junior looks around and says:

"I'd rather lead one lap and fall out of the race than stroke it and finish in the money."

"Stroking it" is driving carefully in hopes of outlasting faster and more reckless cars. The opposite of stroking it is "hard-charging." Then Junior says:

"I hate to get whipped up here in Wilkes County, North Carolina."

Wilkes County, North Carolina! Who was it tried to pin the name on Wilkes County, "The bootleg capital of America?" This fellow Vance Packard. But just a minute. . . .

The night after the race Junior and his fiancée, Flossie Clark, and myself went into North Wilkesboro to have dinner. Junior and Flossie came by Lowes Motel and picked us up in the dreamboat white Pontiac. Flossie is a bright, attractive woman, *saftig*, well-organized. She and Junior have been going together since they were in high school. They are going to get married as soon as Junior gets his new house built. Flossie has been doing the decor. Junior Johnson, in the second-highest income bracket in the United States for the past five years, is moving out of his father's white frame house in Ingle Hollow at last. About three hundred yards down the road. Overlooking a lot of good green land and Anderson's grocery. Junior shows me through the house, it is almost finished, and when we get to the front door, I ask him, "How much of this land is yours?"

Junior looks around for a minute, and then back up the hill, up past his three automated chicken houses, and then down into the hollow over the pasture where his $3100 Santa Gertrudis bull is grazing, and then he says:

"Everything that's green is mine."

Junior Johnson's house is going to be one of the handsomest homes in Wilkes County. Yes. And — such complicated problems of class and status. Junior is not only a legendary figure as a backwoods boy with guts who made good, he is also popular personally, he is still a good old boy, rich as he is. He is also respected for the sound and sober way he has invested his money. He also has one of the best business connections in town, Holly Farms Poultry. What complicates it is that half the county, anyway, reveres him as the greatest, most fabled night-road driver in the history of Southern bootlegging. There is hardly a living soul in the hollows who can conjure up two seconds' honest moral indignation over "the whiskey business." That is what they call it, "the whiskey business." The fact is, it has some positive political overtones, sort of like the I.R.A. in Ireland. The other half of the county — well, North Wilkesboro itself is a prosperous, good-looking town of 5,000, where a lot of hearty modern business burghers are making money the modern way, like everywhere else in the U.S.A., in things like banking, poultry processing, furniture, mirror, and carpet manufacture, apple growing, and so forth and so on. And one thing these men are tired of is Wilkes County's reputation as a center of moonshining. The U.S. Alcohol and Tobacco Tax agents sit over there in Wilkesboro, right next to North Wilkesboro, year in and year out, and they have been there since God knows when, like an Institution in the land, and every day that they are there, it is like a sign saying, Moonshine County. And even that is not so *bad* — it has nothing to do with it being immoral and only a little to do with it being illegal. The real thing is, it is — raw and hillbilly. And one thing thriving modern Industry is not is hillbilly. And one thing the burghers of North Wilkesboro are not about to be is hillbilly. They have split-level homes that would knock your eyes out. Also swimming pools, white Buick Snatchwagons, flagstone *terrasse*-porches enclosed with louvered glass that opens wide in the summertime, and built-in brick barbecue pits and they give parties where they wear Bermuda shorts and Jax stretch pants and serve rum collins and play twist and bossa nova records on the hi-fi and tell Shaggy Dog jokes about strange people ordering martinis. Moonshining . . . just a minute — the truth is, North Wilkesboro. . . .

So we are all having dinner at one of the fine new restaurants in North Wilkesboro, a place of suburban plate-glass elegance. The manager knows Junior and gives us the best table in the place and comes over and talks to Junior a while about the race. A couple of men get up and come over and get Junior's autograph to take home to their sons and so forth. Then toward the end of the meal a couple of North Wilkesboro businessmen come over ("Junior, how are you, Junior. You think you're going to like that fast-backed Ford?") and Junior introduces them to me.

"You're not going to do like that fellow Vance Packard did, are you?"

"Vance Packard?"

"Yeah, I think it was Vance Packard wrote it. He wrote an article and called Wilkes County the bootleg capital of America. Don't pull any of that stuff. I think it was in *American* magazine. The bootleg capital of America. Don't pull any of that stuff on us."

I looked over at Junior and Flossie. Neither one of them said anything. They didn't even change their expressions.

The next morning I met Junior down in Ingle Hollow at Anderson's Store. That's about fifteen miles out of North Wilkesboro on County Road No. 2400. Junior is known in a lot of Southern newspapers as "the wild man from Ronda" or "the lead-footed chicken farmer from Ronda," but Ronda is only his post-office-box address. His telephone exchange, with the Wilkes Telephone Membership Corporation, is Clingman, North Carolina, and that isn't really where he lives either. Where he lives is just Ingle Hollow, and one of the communal centers of Ingle Hollow is Anderson's Store. Anderson's is not exactly a grocery store. Out front there are two gasoline pumps under an overhanging roof. Inside there are a lot of things like a soda-pop cooler filled with ice, Coca-Colas, Nehi drinks, Dr. Pepper, Double Cola, and a gumball machine, a lot of racks of Red Man chewing tobacco, Price's potato chips, OKay peanuts, cloth hats for working outdoors in, dried sausages, cigarettes, canned goods, a little bit of meal and flour, fly swatters, and I don't know what all. Inside and outside of Anderson's there are good old boys. The young ones tend to be inside, talking, and the old ones tend to be outside, sitting under the roof by the gasoline pumps, talking. And on both sides, cars; most of them new and pastel.

Junior drives up and gets out and looks up over the door where there is a row of twelve coon tails. Junior says:

"Two of them gone, ain't they?"

One of the good old boys says, "Yeah," and sighs.

A pause, and the other one says, "Somebody stole 'em."

The the first one says, "Junior, that dog of yours ever come back?"

Junior says, "Not yet."

The second good old boy says, "You looking for her to come back?"

Junior says, "I reckon she'll come back."

The good old boy says, "I had a coon dog went off like that. They don't ever come back. I went out 'ere one day, back over yonder, and there he was, cut right from here to here. I swear if it don't look like a coon got him. Something. H'it must of turned him every way but loose."

Junior goes inside and gets a Coca-Cola and rings up the till himself, like everybody who goes into Anderson's does, it seems like. It is dead quiet in the hollow except for every now and then a car grinds over the dirt road and down the way. One coon dog missing. But he still has a lot of the black and tans, named Rock. . . .

. . . Rock, Whitey, Red, Buster are in the pen out back of the Johnson house, the old frame house. They have scars all over their faces from fighting coons. Gypsy has one huge gash in her back from fighting something. A red rooster crosses the lawn. That's a big rooster. Shirley, one of Junior's two younger sisters, pretty girls, is out by the fence in shorts, pulling weeds. Annie May is inside the house with Mrs. Johnson. Shirley has the radio outside on the porch aimed at her, The Four Seasons! "Dawn! — ahhh, ahhhhh, ahhhhhh!" Then a lot of electronic wheeps and lulus and a screaming disc jockey, yessss! WTOB, the Vibrant Mothering Voice of Winston-Salem, North Carolina. It sounds like WABC in New York. Junior's mother, Mrs. Johnson, is a big, good-natured woman. She comes out and says, "Did you ever see anything like that in your life? Pullin' weeds listenin' to the radio." Junior's father, Robert Glenn Johnson, Sr. — he built this frame house about thirty-five years ago, up here where the gravel road ends and the woods starts. The road just peters out into the woods up a hill. The house has a living room, four bedrooms and a big kitchen. The living room is full of Junior's racing trophies, and so is the piano in Shirley's room. Junior was born and raised here with his older brothers, L. P., the oldest, and Fred, and his older sister, Ruth. Over yonder, up by that house, there's a man with a mule and a little plow. That's L. P. The Johnsons still keep that old mule around to plow the vegetable gardens. And all around, on all sides, like a rim are the ridges and the woods. Well, what about those woods, where Vance Packard said the agents come stealing over the ridges and good old boys go crashing through the underbrush to get away from the still and the women start "calling the cows" up and down the hollows as the signal *they were coming*. . . .

Junior motions his hand out toward the hills and says, "I'd say nearly everybody in a fifty-mile radius of here was in the whiskey business at one time or another. When we growed up here, everybody seemed to be more or less messing with whiskey, and myself and my two brothers did quite a bit of transporting. H'it was just a business, like any other business, far as we was concerned. H'it was a matter of survival. During the Depression here, people either had to do that or starve to death. H'it wasn't no gangster type of business or nothing. They's nobody that ever messed with it here that was ever out to hurt anybody. Even if they got caught, they never tried to shoot anybody or anything like that. Getting caught and pulling time, that was just part of it. H'it was just a business, like any other business. Me and my brothers, when we went out on the road at night, h'it was just like a milk run, far as we was concerned. They was certain deliveries to be made and. . . ."

A milk run — yes! Well, it was a business, all right. In fact, it was a regional industry, all up and down the Appalachian slopes. But never mind the Depression. It goes back a long way before that. The Scotch-Irish settled the mountains from Pennsylvania down to Alabama, and they have been making whiskey out there as long as anybody can remember. At first it was a simple matter of economics. The land had a low crop yield, compared to the lowlands, and even after a man struggled to grow his corn, or whatever, the cost of transporting it to the markets from down out of the hills was so great, it wasn't worth it. It was much more profitable to convert the corn into whiskey and sell that. The trouble started with the Federal Government on that score almost the moment the Republic was founded. Alexander Hamilton put a high excise tax on whiskey in 1791, almost as soon as the Constitution was ratified. The "Whiskey Rebellion" broke out in the mountains of western Pennsylvania in 1794. The farmers were mad as hell over the tax. Fifteen thousand Federal troops marched out to the mountains and suppressed them. Almost at once, however, the trouble over the whiskey tax became a symbol of something bigger. This was a general enmity between the western and eastern sections of practically every seaboard state. Part of it was political. The eastern sections tended to control the legislatures, the economy and the law courts, and the western sections felt short-changed. Part of it was cultural. Life in the western sections was rougher. Religions, codes and styles of life were sterner. Life in the eastern capitals seemed to give off the odor of Europe and decadence. Shay's Rebellion broke out in the Berkshire hills of western Massachusetts in 1786 in an attempt to shake off the yoke of Boston, which seemed as bad as George III's. To this day people in western Massachusetts make proposals, earnestly or with down-in-the-mouth humor, that they all ought to split off from "Boston." Whiskey — the mountain people went right on making it. Whole sections of the Appalachians were a whiskey belt, just as sections of Georgia, Alabama and Mississippi were a cotton belt. Nobody on either side ever had any moral delusions about why the Federal Government was against it. It was always the tax, pure and simple. Today the price of liquor is 60 per cent tax. Today, of course, with everybody gone wild over the subject of science and health, it has been much easier for the Federals to persuade people that they crack down on moonshine whiskey because it is dangerous, it poisons, kills and blinds people. The statistics are usually specious.

Moonshining was *illegal*, however, that was also the unvarnished truth. And that had a side effect in the whiskey belt. The people there were already isolated, geographically, by the mountains and had strong clan ties because they were all from the same stock, Scotch-Irish. Moonshining isolated them even more. They always had to be careful who came up there. There are plenty of hollows to this day where if you drive in and ask some good old boy where so-and-so is, he'll tell you he never heard of the fellow. Then the next minute, if you identify yourself and give some idea of why you want to see him, and he believes you, he'll suddenly say, "Aw, you're talking about *so-and-so*. I thought you said —" With all this isolation, the mountain people began to take on certain characteristics normally associated, by the diffident civilizations of today, with tribes. There was a strong sense of family, clan and honor. People would cut and shoot each other up over honor. And physical courage! They were almost like Turks that way.

In the Korean War, there were seventy-eight Medal of Honor winners. Thirty-two of them were from the South, and practically all of the thirty-two were from small towns in or near the Appalachians. The New York metropolitan area, which has more people than all these towns put together, had three Medal of Honor winners, and one of them had just moved to New York from the Appalachian region of West Virginia. Three of the Medal of Honor winners came from within fifty miles of Junior Johnson's side porch.

Detroit has discovered these pockets of courage, almost like a natural resource, in the form of Junior Johnson and about twenty other drivers. There is something exquisitely ironic about it. Detroit is now engaged in the highly sophisticated business of offering the illusion of Speed for Everyman — making their cars go 175 miles an hour on racetracks — by discovering and putting behind the wheel a breed of mountain men who are living vestiges of a degree of physical courage that became extinct in most other sections of the country by 1900. Of course, very few stock car drivers have ever had anything to do with the whiskey business. A great many always lead quiet lives off the track. But it is the same strong people among whom the whiskey business developed who produced the kind of men who could drive the

69

stock cars. There are a few exceptions, Freddie Lorenzen, from Elmhurst, Illinois, being the most notable. But, by and large, it is the rural Southern code of honor and courage that has produced these, the most daring men in sports.

Cars and bravery! The mountain-still operators had been running white liquor with hopped-up automobiles all during the thirties. But it was during the war that the business was so hot out of Wilkes County, down to Charlotte, High Point, Greensboro, Winston-Salem, Salisbury, places like that; a night's run, by one car, would bring anywhere from $500 to $1000. People had money all of a sudden. One car could carry twenty-two to twenty-five cases of white liquor. There were twelve half-gallon fruit jars full per case, so each load would have 132 gallons or more. It would sell to the distributor in the city for about ten dollars a gallon, when the market was good, of which the driver would get two dollars, as much as $300 for the night's work.

The usual arrangement in the white liquor industry was for the elders to design the distillery, supervise the formulas and the whole distilling process and take care of the business end of the operation. The young men did the heavy work, carrying the copper and other heavy goods out into the woods, building the still, hauling in fuel — and driving. Junior and his older brothers, L. P. and Fred, worked that way with their father, Robert Glenn Johnson, Sr.

Johnson, Senior, was one of the biggest individual copper-still operators in the area. The fourth time he was arrested, the agents found a small fortune in working corn mash bubbling in the vats.

"My Daddy was always a hard worker," Junior is telling me. "He always wanted something a little bit better. A lot of people resented that and held that against him, but what he got, he always got h'it by hard work. There ain't no harder work in the world than making whiskey. I don't know of any other business that compels you to get up at all times of night and go outdoors in the snow and everything else and work. H'it's the hardest way in the world to make a living, and I don't think anybody'd do it unless they had to."

Working mash wouldn't wait for a man. It started coming to a head when it got ready to and a man had to be there to take it off, out there in the woods, in the brush, in the brambles, in the muck, in the snow. Wouldn't it have been something if you could have just set it all up inside a good old shed with a corrugated metal roof and order those parts like you want them and not have to smuggle all that copper and all that sugar and all that everything out here in the woods and be a coppersmith and a plumber and a cooper and a carpenter and a pack horse and every other goddamned thing God ever saw in this world, all at once.

And live decent hours — Junior and his brothers, about two o'clock in the morning they'd head out to the stash, the place where the liquor was hidden after it was made. Sometimes it would be somebody's house or an old shed or some place just out in the woods, and they'd make their arrangements out there, what the route was and who was getting how much liquor. There wasn't anything ever written down. Everything was cash on the spot. Different drivers liked to make the run at different times, but Junior and his brother always liked to start out from 3 to 4 A.M. But it got so no matter when you started out you didn't have those roads to yourself.

"Some guys liked one time and some guys liked another time," Junior is saying, "but starting about midnight they'd be coming out of the woods from every direction. Some nights the whole road was full of bootleggers. It got so some nights they'd be somebody following you going just as fast as you were and you didn't know who h'it was, the law or somebody else hauling whiskey."

And it was just a business, like any other business, just like a milk route — but this funny thing was happening. In those wild-ass times, with the money flush and good old boys from all over the country running that white liquor down the road ninety miles an hour and more than that if you try to crowd them a little bit — well, the funny thing was, it got to be competitive in an almost aesthetic, a pure sporting way. The way the good old boys got to hopping up their automobiles — it got to be a science practically. Everybody was looking to build a car faster than anybody ever had before. They practically got into industrial espionage over it. They'd come up behind one another on those wild-ass nights on the highway, roaring through the black gulches between the clay cuts and the trees, pretending like they were officers, just to challenge them, test them out, race . . . *pour le sport*, you mothers, careening through the darkness, old Carolina moon. All these cars were registered in phony names. If a man had to abandon one, they would find license plates that traced back to . . . nobody at all. It wasn't anything, particularly, to go down to the Motor Vehicle Bureau and get some license plates, as long as you paid your money. Of course, it's rougher now, with compulsory insurance. You have to have your insurance before you can get your license plates, and that leads to a lot of complications. Junior doesn't know what they do about that now. Anyway, all these cars with the magnificent engines were plain on the outside, so they wouldn't attract attention, but they couldn't disguise them altogether. They were jacked up a little in the back and had 8.00 or 8.20 tires, for the heavy loads, and the sound —

"They wasn't no way you could make it sound like an ordinary car," says Junior.

God-almighty, that sound in the middle of the night, groaning, roaring, humming down into the hollows, through the clay gulches — yes! And all over the rural South, hell, all over the South, the legends of wild-driving whiskey running got started. And it wasn't just the plain excitement of it. It was something deeper, the symbolism. It brought into a modern focus the whole business, one and a half centuries old, of the country people's rebellion against the Federals, against the seaboard establishment, their independence, their defiance of the outside world. And it was like a mythology for that and for something else that was happening, the whole wild thing of the car as the symbol of liberation in the postwar South.

"They was out about every night, patroling, the agents and the State Police was," Junior is saying, "but they seldom caught anybody. H'it was like the dogs chasing the fox. The dogs can't catch a fox, he'll just take 'em around in a circle all night long. I was never caught for transporting. We never lost but one car and the axle broke on h'it."

The fox and the dogs! Whiskey running certainly had a crazy

gamelike quality about it, considering that a boy might be sent up for two years or more if he were caught transporting. But these boys were just wild enough for that. There got to be a code about the chase. In Wilkes County nobody, neither the good old boys nor the agents, ever did anything that was going to hurt the other side physically. There was supposed to be some parts of the South where the boys used smoke screens and tack buckets. They had attachments in the rear of the cars, and if the agents got too close they would let loose a smoke screen to blind them or a slew of tacks to make them blow a tire. But nobody in Wilkes County ever did that because that was a good way for somebody to get killed. Part of it was that whenever an agent did get killed in the South, whole hordes of agents would come in from Washington and pretty soon they would be tramping along the ridges practically inch by inch, smoking out the stills. But mainly it was — well, the code. If you got caught, you went along peaceably, and the agents never used their guns. There were some tense times. Once was when the agents started using tack belts in Iredell County. This was a long strip of leather studded with nails that the agents would lay across the road in the dark. A man couldn't see it until it was too late and he stood a good chance of getting killed if it got his tires and spun him out. The other was the time the State Police put a roadblock down there at that damned bridge at Millersville to catch a couple of escaped convicts. Well, a couple of good old boys rode up with a load, and there was the roadblock and they were already on the bridge, so they jumped out and dove into the water. The police saw two men jump out of their car and dive in the water, so they opened fire and they shot one good old boy in the backside. As they pulled him out, he kept saying:

"What did you have to shoot at me for? What did you have to shoot at me for?"

It wasn't pain, it wasn't anguish, it wasn't anger. It was consternation. The bastards had broken the code.

Then the Federals started getting radio cars.

"The radios didn't do them any good," Junior says. "As soon as the officers got radios, then *they* got radios. They'd go out and get the same radio. H'it was an awful hard thing for them to radio them down.

They'd just listen in on the radio and see where they're setting up the roadblocks and go a different way."

And such different ways. The good old boys knew back roads, dirt roads, up people's backlanes and every which way, and an agent would have to live in the North Carolina hills a lifetime to get to know them. There wasn't hardly a stretch of road on any of the routes where a good old boy couldn't duck off the road and into the backcountry if he had to. They had wild detours around practically every town and every intersection in the region. And for tight spots — the legendary devices, the "bootleg slide," the siren and the red light. . . .

It was just a matter of keeping up with the competition. You always have to have the latest equipment. It was a business thing, like any other business, you have to stay on top — "They was some guys who was more dependable, they done a better job" — and it may have been business to Junior, but it wasn't business to a generation of good old boys growing up all over the South. The Wilkes County bootleg cars started picking up popular names in a kind of folk hero worship — "The Black Ghost," "The Grey Ghost," which were two of Junior's, "Old Mother Goose," "The Midnight Traveler," "Old Faithful."

And then one day in 1955 some agents snuck over the ridges and caught Junior Johnson at his daddy's still. Junior Johnson, the man couldn't *any*body catch!

The arrest caught Junior just as he was ready to really take off in his career as a stock car driver. Junior says he hadn't been in the whiskey business in any shape or form, hadn't run a load of whiskey for two or three years, when he was arrested. He says he didn't need to fool around with running whiskey after he got into stock car racing, he was making enough money at that. He was just out there at the still helping his daddy with some of the heavy labor, there wasn't a good old boy in Ingle Hollow who wouldn't help his daddy lug those big old cords of ash wood, it doesn't give off much smoke, out in the woods. Junior was sentenced to two years in the Federal reformatory in Chillicothe, Ohio.

"If the law felt I should have gone to jail, that's fine and dandy," Junior tells me. "But I don't think the true facts of the case justified the sentence I got. I never had been arrested in my life. I think they was punishing me for the past. People get a kick out of it because the officers can't catch somebody, and this angers them. Soon as I started getting publicity for racing, they started making it real hot for my family. I was out of the whiskey business, and they knew that, but they was just waiting to catch me on something. I got out after serving ten months and three days of the sentence, but h'it was two or three years I was set back, about half of fifty-six and every bit of fifty-seven. H'it takes a year to really get back into h'it after something like that. I think I lost the prime of my racing career. I feel that if I had been given the chance I feel I was due, rather than the sentence I got, my life would have got a real boost."

But, if anything, the arrest only made the Junior Johnson legend hotter.

And all the while Detroit kept edging the speeds up, from 150 m.p.h. in 1960 to 155 to 165 to 175 to 180 flat out on the longest straightaway, and the good old boys of Southern stock car racing stuck right with it. Any speed Detroit would give them they would take right with them into the curve, hard-charging even though they began to feel strange things such as the rubber starting to pull right off the tire casing. And God! Good old boys from all over the South roared together after the Stanchion — Speed! Guts! — pouring into Birmingham, Daytona Beach, Randleman, North Carolina; Spartanburg, South Carolina; Weaverville, Hillsboro, North Carolina; Atlanta, Hickory, Bristol, Tennessee; Augusta, Georgia; Richmond, Virginia; Asheville, North Carolina; Charlotte, Myrtle Beach — tens of thousands of them. And still upper- and middle-class America, even in the South, keeps its eyes averted. Who cares! They kept on heading out where we all live, after all, out amongst the Drive-ins, white-enameled filling stations, concrete aprons, shopping-plaza apothecaries, show-window steak houses, Burger-Ramas, Bar-B-Cubicles and Miami aqua-swimming-pool motor inns, on out the highway . . . even outside a town like Darlington, a town of 10,000 souls, God, here they come, down route 52, up 401, on 340, 151 and 34, on through the South Carolina lespedeza fields. By Friday night already the good old boys are pulling the infield of the Darlington raceway with those blazing pastel dream-boats stacked this way and that on the clay flat and the tubular terrace furniture and the sleeping bags and the Thermos jugs and the brown whiskey bottles coming on out. By Sunday — the race! — there are 65,000 piled into the racetrack at Darlington. The sheriff, as always, sets up the jail right there in the infield. No use trying to haul them out of there. And now — the *sound* rises up inside the raceway, and a good old boy named Ralph goes mad and starts selling chances on his Dodge. Twenty-five cents and you can take the sledge he has and smash his car anywhere you want. How they roar when the windshield breaks! The police could interfere, you know, but they are busy chasing a good old girl who is playing Lady Godiva on a hogbacked motorcy-cle, naked as sin, hauling around and in and out of the clay ruts.

Eyes averted, happy burghers. On Monday the ads start appearing — for Ford, for Plymouth, for Dodge — announcing that we gave it to you, speed such as you never saw. There it was! At Darlington, Daytona, Atlanta — and not merely in the Southern papers but in the albino pages of the suburban women's magazines, such as *The New Yorker*, in color — the Ford winners, such as Fireball Roberts, grin-ning with a cigar in his mouth in *The New Yorker* magazine. And somewhere, some Monday morning, Jim Pascal of High Point, Ned Jarrett of Boykin, Cale Yarborough of Timmonsville and Curtis Crider from Charlotte, Bobby Isaac of Catawba, E. J. Trivette of Deep Gap, Richard Petty of Randleman, Tiny Lund of Cross, South Carolina; Stick Elliott of Shelby — and from out of Ingle Hollow —

And all the while, standing by in full Shy, in alumicron suits — there is Detroit, hardly able to believe itself what it has discovered, a breed of good old boys from the fastnesses of the Appalachian hills and flats — a handful from this rare breed — who have given Detroit . . . speed . . . and the industry can present it to a whole generation as . . . yours. And the Detroit P.R. men themselves come to the tracks like folk worshipers and the millions go giddy with the thrill of speed. Only Junior Johnson goes about it as if it were . . . the usual. Junior goes on down to Atlanta for the Dixie 400 and drops by the Federal penitentiary to see his Daddy. His Daddy is in on his fifth illegal distillery conviction; in the whiskey business that's just part of it; an able craftsman, an able businessman, and the law kept hounding him, that was all. So Junior drops by and then goes on out to the track and gets in his new Ford and sets the qualifying speed record for Atlanta Dixie 400, 146.301 m.p.h.; later on he tools on back up the road to Ingle Hollow to tend to the automatic chicken houses and the road-grading operation. Yes.

Yet how can you tell that to . . . anybody . . . out on the bottom of that bowl as the motor thunder begins to lift up through him like a sigh and his eyeballs glaze over and his hands reach up and there, riding the rim of the bowl, soaring over the ridges, is Junior's yellow Ford . . . which is his white Chevrolet . . . which is a White Ghost, forever rousing the good old boys . . . hard-charging! . . . up with the automobile into their America, and the hell with arteriosclerotic old boys trying to hold onto the whole pot with arms of cotton seersucker. Junior!

Mark Twain

Journalism in Tennessee

The editor of the Memphis *Avalanche* swoops thus mildly down upon a correspondent who posted him as a Radical: — "While he was writing the first word, the middle, dotting his i's, crossing his t's, and punching his period, he knew he was concocting a sentence that was saturated with infamy and reeking with falsehood." — *Exchange*.

I WAS TOLD BY the physician that a Southern climate would improve my health, and so I went down to Tennessee, and got a berth on the *Morning Glory and Johnson County War-Whoop* as associate editor. When I went on duty I found the chief editor sitting tilted back in a three-legged chair with his feet on a pine table. There was another pine table in the room and another afflicted chair, and both were half buried under newspapers and scraps and sheets of manuscript. There was a wooden box of sand, sprinkled with cigar stubs and "old soldiers," and a stove with a door hanging by its upper hinge. The chief editor had a long-tailed black cloth frock coat on, and white linen pants. His boots were small and neatly blacked. He wore a ruffled shirt, a large seal ring, a standing collar of obsolete pattern, and a checkered neckerchief with the ends hanging down. Date of costume about 1848. He was smoking a cigar, and trying to think of a word, and in pawing his hair he had rumpled his locks a good deal. He was scowling fearfully, and I judged that he was concocting a particularly knotty editorial. He told me to take the exchanges and skim through them and write up the "Spirit of the Tennessee Press," condensing into the article all of their contents that seemed of interest.

I wrote as follows:

"SPIRIT OF THE TENNESSEE PRESS.

"The editors of the *Semi-Weekly Earthquake* evidently labor under a misapprehension with regard to the Ballyhack railroad. It is not the object of the company to leave Buzzardville off to one side. On the contrary, they consider it one of the most important points along the line, and consequently can have no desire to slight it. The gentlemen of the *Earthquake* will, of course, take pleasure in making the correction.

"John W. Blossom, Esq., the able editor of the Higginsville *Thunderbolt and Battle Cry of Freedom,* arrived in the city yesterday. He is stopping at the Van Buren House.

"We observe that our contemporary of the Mud Springs *Morning Howl* has fallen into the error of supposing that the election of Van Werter is not an established fact, but he will have discovered his mistake before this reminder reaches him, no doubt. He was doubtless misled by incomplete election returns.

"It is pleasant to note that the city of Blathersville is endeavoring to contract with some New York gentlemen to pave its well-nigh impassable streets with the Nicholson pavement. The *Daily Hurrah* urges the measure with ability, and seems confident of ultimate success."

I passed my manuscript over to the chief editor for acceptance, alteration, or destruction. He glanced at it and his face clouded. He ran his eye down the pages, and his countenance grew portentous. It was easy to see that something was wrong. Presently he sprang up and said:

"Thunder and lightning! Do you suppose I am going to speak of those cattle that way? Do you suppose my subscribers are going to stand such gruel as that? Give me the pen!"

I never saw a pen scrape and scratch its way so viciously, or plow through another man's verbs and adjectives so relentlessly. While he was in the midst of his work, somebody shot at him through the open window, and marred the symmetry of my ear.

"Ah," said he, "that is that scoundrel Smith, of the *Moral Volcano* — he was due yesterday." And he snatched a navy revolver from his belt and fired. Smith dropped, shot in the thigh. The shot spoiled Smith's aim, who was just taking a second chance, and he crippled a stranger. It was me. Merely a finger shot off.

Then the chief editor went on with his erasures and interlineations. Just as he finished them a hand-grenade came down the stove pipe, and the explosion shivered the stove into a thousand fragments. However, it did no further damage, except that a vagrant piece knocked a couple of my teeth out.

"That stove is utterly ruined," said the chief editor.

I said I believed it was.

"Well, no matter — don't want it this kind of weather. I know the man that did it. I'll get him. Now, *here* is the way this stuff ought to be written."

I took the manuscript. It was scarred with erasures and interlineations till its mother wouldn't have known it if had had one. It now read as follows:

"SPIRIT OF THE TENNESSEE PRESS.

"The inveterate liars of the *Semi-Weekly Earthquake* are evidently endeavoring to palm off upon a noble and chivalrous people another of their vile and brutal falsehoods with regard to that most glorious conception of the nineteenth century, the Ballyhack railroad. The idea that Buzzardville was to be left off at one side originated in their own fulsome brains — or rather in the settlings which *they* regard as brains. They had better swallow this lie if they want to save their abandoned reptile carcasses the cowhiding they so richly deserve.

"That ass, Blossom, of the Higginsville *Thunderbolt and Battle Cry of Freedom,* is down here again sponging at the Van Buren.

"We observe that the besotted blackguard of the Mud Spring *Morning Howl* is giving out, with his usual propensity for lying, that Van Werter is not elected. The heaven-born mission of journalism is to disseminate truth; to eradicate error; to educate, refine, and elevate the tone of public morals and manners, and make all men more gentle, more virtuous, more charitable, and in all ways better, and holier, and happier; and yet this black-hearted scoundrel degrades his great office persistently to the dissemination of falsehood, calumny, vituperation, and vulgarity.

"Blathersville wants a Nicholson pavement — it wants a jail and a poorhouse more. The idea of a pavement in a one-horse town composed of two gin mills, a blacksmith shop, and that mustard-plaster of a newspaper, the *Daily Hurrah!* The crawling insect, Buckner, who edits the *Hurrah,* is braying about this business with his customary imbecility, and imagining that he is talking sense."

"Now *that* is the way to write — peppery and to the point. Mush-and-milk journalism gives me the fan-tods."

About this time a brick came through the window with a splintering crash, and gave me a considerable of a jolt in the back. I moved out of range — I began to feel in the way.

The chief said, "That was the Colonel, likely. I've been expecting him for two days. He will be up now right away."

He was correct. The Colonel appeared in the door a moment afterward with a dragoon revolver in his hand.

He said, "Sir, have I the honor of addressing the poltroon who edits this mangy sheet?"

"You have. Be seated, sir. Be careful of the chair, one of its legs is gone. I believe I have the honor of addressing the putrid liar, Colonel Blatherskite Tecumseh?"

"Right, sir. I have a little account to settle with you. If you are at leisure we will begin."

"I have an article on the 'Encouraging Progess of Moral and Intellectual Development in America' to finish, but there is no hurry. Begin."

Both pistols rang out their fierce clamor at the same instant. The chief lost a lock of his hair, and the Colonel's bullet ended its career in the fleshy part of my thigh. The Colonel's left shoulder was clipped a little. They fired again. Both missed their men this time, but I got my share, a shot in the arm. At the third fire both gentlemen were wounded slightly, and I had a knuckle chipped. I then said, I believed I would go out and take a walk, as this was a private matter, and I had a delicacy about participating in it further. But both gentlemen begged me to keep my seat, and assured me that I was not in the way.

They then talked about the elections and the crops while they reloaded, and I fell to tying up my wounds. But presently they opened fire again with animation, and every shot took effect — but it is proper to remark that five out of the six fell to my share. The sixth one mortally wounded the Colonel, who remarked, with fine humor, that he would have to say good morning now, as he had business up town. He then inquired the way to the undertaker's and left.

The chief turned to me and said, "I am expecting company to dinner, and shall have to get ready. It will be a favor to me if you will read proof and attend to the customers."

I winced a little at the idea of attending to the customers, but I was too bewildered by the fusillade that was still ringing in my ears to think of anything to say.

He continued, "Jones will be here at 3 — cowhide him. Gillespie will call earlier, perhaps — throw him out of the window. Ferguson will be along about 4 — kill him. That is all for to-day, I believe. If you have any odd time, you may write a blistering article on the police — give the chief inspector rats. The cowhides are under the table; weapons in the drawer — ammunition there in the corner — lint and bandages up there in the pigeonholes. In case of accident, go to Lancet, the surgeon, downstairs. He advertises — we take it out in trade."

He was gone. I shuddered. At the end of the next three hours I had been through perils so awful that all peace of mind and all cheerfulness were gone from me. Gillespie had called and thrown *me* out of the window. Jones arrived promptly, and when I got ready to do the cowhiding he took the job off my hands. In an encounter with a stranger, not in the bill of fare, I had lost my scalp. Another stranger, by the name of Thompson, left me a mere wreck and ruin of chaotic rags. And at last, at bay in the corner, and beset by an infuriated mob of editors, blacklegs, politicians, and desperadoes, who raved and swore and flourished their weapons about my head till the air shimmered with glancing flashes of steel, I was in the act of resigning my berth on the paper when the chief arrived, and with him a rabble of charmed and enthusiastic friends. Then ensued a scene of riot and carnage such as no human pen, or steel one either, could describe. People were shot, probed, dismembered, blown up, thrown out of the window. There was a brief tornado of murky blasphemy, with a confused and frantic war-dance glimmering through it, and then all was over. In five minutes there was silence, and the gory chief and I sat alone and surveyed the sanguinary ruin that strewed the floor around us.

He said, "You'll like this place when you get used to it."

I said, "I'll have to get you to excuse me; I think maybe I might write to suit you after a while; as soon as I had had some practice and learned the language I am confident I could. But, to speak the plain truth, that sort of energy of expression has its inconveniences, and a man is liable to interruption. You see that yourself. Vigorous writing is calculated to elevate the public, no doubt, but then I do not like to attract so much attention as it calls forth. I can't write with comfort when I am interrupted so much as I have been to-day. I like this berth well enough, but I don't like to be left here to wait on the customers. The experiences are novel, I grant you, and entertaining, too, after a fashion, but they are not judiciously distributed. A gentleman shoots at you through the window and cripples *me;* a bomb-shell comes down the stove-pipe for your gratification and sends the stove door down *my* throat; a friend drops in to swap compliments with you, and freckles *me* with bullet-holes till my skin won't hold my principles; you go to dinner, and Jones comes with his cowhide, Gillespie throws me out of the window, Thompson tears all my clothes off, and an entire stranger takes my scalp with the easy freedom of an old acquaintance; and in less than five minutes all the blackguards in the country arrive in their war-paint, and proceed to scare the rest of me to death with their tomahawks. Take it altogether, I never had such a spirited time in all my life as I have had to-day. No; I like you, and I like your calm unruffled way of explaining things to the customers, but you see I am not used to it. The Southern heart is too impulsive; Southern hospitality is too lavish with the stranger. The paragraphs which I have written to-day, and into whose cold sentences your masterly hand has infused the fervent spirit of Tennessean journalism, will wake up another nest of hornets. All that mob of editors will come — and they will come hungry, too, and want somebody for breakfast. I shall have to bid you adieu. I decline to be present at these festivities. I came South for my health, I will go back on the same errand, and suddenly. Tennesseean journalism is too stirring for me."

After which we parted with mutual regret, and I took apartments at the hospital.

Martha Lacy Hall

The Man Who Gave Brother Double Pneumonia

I READ SOMETHING IN Sunday's paper about a Mississippi girl getting married, a Barbara Dickey Becker, and right then I thought of Mama. I couldn't ever see the name Becker without remembering Mr. Dickey and Mama and Brother and all the rest.

Not long before Mama died somebody asked her, "You remember Mr. Dickey Becker . . . ?" And she interrupted, "Remember him? I reckon I do remember him. He's the one who gave Brother double pneumonia." By that time Daddy was no longer there to stand up for Mr. Dickey, as he had for years, with, "Now, Ellen, you know Dickey wasn't responsible for that. Nobody was to blame." And I always felt like the *nobody* included me.

Mr. Dickey Becker was a barber — one of two in Sweet Bay. Mr. Dickey's was the one with the barber pole that actually turned, its red and white stripes coiling endlessly in its glass cylinder. He didn't even turn it off Sundays. We would drive down Main Street after church, and the only thing moving on the whole street would be Mr. Dickey Becker's barber pole. Mr. Dud Lewis's across the street between the post office and Willey's Feed and Seed had a barber pole, but it was just a painted column of wood, and the paint was flaking off. He didn't ever paint it that I can remember, but he was called a good barber.

During the year when Brother and I were seven Daddy asked Mama to start taking us to Mr. Dickey for our haircuts. Brother had been going to Mr. Lewis, and Mama usually took me with her to Miss Ella B. Jones's Beauty Shoppe. Mama didn't want to take us to Mr.

87

Dickey's, but we were deep in the Depression, and Mr. Dickey owed Daddy some money and couldn't pay it right then. He asked Daddy to trade it out in haircuts for himself and us two. Daddy and Mama argued, but she finally gave in. I pouted and fussed about going to a man's barber shop, where scarcely another female ever showed her face except for mothers who brought their little boys in. Mama came in with us the first time and gave Mr. Dickey instructions. After that she would drop us off and go on to the library or the grocery store or somewhere until time to pick us up. We always had to wait, and if Mama pulled up to the curb out front and saw that we were not through, she would either sit there and read or drive on off for one more errand.

Mr. Dickey's shop was long and narrow like most barber shops. He had three chairs, with a big white porcelain lavatory behind each chair. Several long benches for waiting customers sat along the opposite wall. Mirrors lined both walls, and large milk glass lighting fixtures hung down the center, two with ceiling fans attached. There were lots of jars and bottles behind Mr. Dickey and a stack of white towels, and under the lavatory a white wicker hamper where he threw wet towels.

Brother and I had haircuts every three weeks or so. At twenty-five cents a cut, Mama said, Mr. Dickey would never on this earth retire his debt in his lifetime. We went there only through the summer and halfway through the winter of 1933 — until Brother got double pneumonia.

One afternoon in early January, Mama bundled us up to go down to Mr. Dickey's — with me protesting. Daddy was at home.

"Why don't you like Mr. Dickey?" Daddy finally asked me.

"He teases me."

"How does he tease you, Sister?"

"He calls me a boy. He says I don't have long curls like other girls. He says my bangs and my short bob are for boys, and I hate him."

"No, now, you don't hate anybody. Mr. Dickey's not a bad fellow. He and I are good friends from way back."

"I don't care. I do hate him."

"Ah, Sister." Then Daddy laughed. "I'll tell you what you do. If he teases you today, tell him he's a ring-tailed tooter."

"Thad!" Mama whirled around.

"Tell him that. You tell him your daddy says he's a ring-tailed tooter."

"No," I said. "I'm not telling him anything. What is a ring-tailed tooter?"

"Doesn't matter what it is. Just call him that. You can tell him that he's the only barber you ever heard of who barbers all week, bootlegs on Saturday night, and preaches on Sunday."

"Thaddeus!"

"Does he do all that?" I asked.

"Sure he does. You don't think he supports that big family of his cutting hair for two bits a head, do you?"

"Thad, I want this stopped this minute. You cannot talk to a seven-year-old child like that. It's one thing for you and him to keep up this foolishness between the two of you, but I will not have Sister going down there speaking disrespectfully to Mr. Dickey. I don't care what he does with his weekends."

I was trying to count up how many children Mr. Dickey had to feed and clothe on haircutting. "Well," I said, "he sells bottles of hair tonic and other stuff."

"Now stop right there, Sister. There'll be no impudence to Mr. Becker or to anyone else," said Mama. "But I do want you to remind him not to put a drop of anything on Brother's hair. Not one drop. I've told him time and again not to use hair tonic on Brother, but he forgets, I reckon, and does it anyway. Every time. But this is pneumonia weather, and I don't want Brother coming out of there with a wet head. Will you remember to tell him?" She was pulling Brother's leather helmet over his blond softly curling hair and snapping the tabs under his chin.

"Yes'm, I'll tell him. But I don't want to go in there." I had on brown cotton stockings that fastened to my short union suit — a getup nobody else's mother made them wear no matter how cold it got. I decided I was already so tacky that having my hair cut in a man's barber shop couldn't add much to my misery. Brother and I got into Mama's car arguing over who would ride in the front seat with her, and

of course Brother won. He always did. He was frail, and Mama had to
let him have his own way because she was afraid he would have one of
his tantrums and throw up.

I got onto the backseat and slipped down so that my neck bent up
against the back and so my feet could push hard against the back of
Brother's seat. "Mama, tell her to stop," he whined.

"Mercy sakes, Sister, sit up like a lady. The idea."

I sat up and watched the houses go by, most of them white, with the
rocking chairs turned over against the wall on the cold front porches. It
was five blocks to the barber shop, and Mama stopped at each corner to
look every which way, even when she had the right-of-way. She was
like that. Daddy would say, "Ellen, caution is your middle name."
And she would say, "Well, mark my word, Thaddeus, I'd rather be a
live monkey than a dead heroine." She had picked that up from Daddy,
only he said *hero*.

There were hardly any other cars on the streets that day. There
weren't all that many cars in Sweet Bay. There weren't all that many
people. And on cold days they mostly stayed in around the fire. You
won't find long winters in south Mississippi, but there are always a few
freezing days.

Mama wore a hat every time she went anywhere, and that day she
had on a little hat made of curly fur, shaped like a soufflé dish, with a
coat collar to match. She wore black kid gloves that had little rows of
stitching on the backs, and the way she gripped the steering wheel
made the gloves shine and look as tight as her skin.

She pulled up along the curb in front of Mr. Dickey's. *Becker's
Barber Shop* was painted in big red letters on the window, arched like a
rainbow and with white shadings painted along the right side of each
red letter. The sign kept you from seeing everything in the shop, but I
could see Mr. Dickey flipping his razor back and forth on the leather
strop that hung off the back of his chair. He had the first chair, near the
window, and I saw him looking out at us. He had a big fat customer in
his chair.

Mama made Brother crawl over her so he wouldn't have to get out in
the street and maybe get run over. There was hardly a car moving but,

as I said, she never took any chances. He just stepped all over her and she said, "Well, for heaven's sake, Brother. I think you could be a little more careful. Now, trot straight in there and stay till I come back for you."

I got out of the back, sulking, as she said, "Sister, remember I'm depending on you. Don't you dare let Mr. Dickey put hair tonic on Brother's head. As sure as I'm sitting here that child will come out in this pneumonia weather and catch his death."

"I'll tell him," I said, slamming the door so hard that I spun myself all the way around. I caught my scarf in the door, and Mama was about to drive away with it pulling right off my neck till I called, "Mama, wait!" She shoved her foot down quickly and stopped. She really hadn't moved two feet, but she rolled her window down while I opened the back door and got my scarf loose.

"I declare to my soul, Sister, I don't know what I'm going to do with you! Now that was careless. If I hadn't been paying attention to what I was doing, no telling what might have happened to you. Now go on in there while I sit here and see you in. March!" I went into the barber shop.

"Hurry up, Ellen. Hurry that door closed. You'll blow us out of here," said Mr. Dickey. I shut his old door carefully. I say old because it was *old,* a big old tall door with glass and carving and a funny big brass handle shaped like a swan. I rattled it good when I shut it.

"Just have a seat there by Brother and I'll get to you-all directly, Sister." Mr. Dickey would call me *Sister* one minute and *Ellen* the next.

I took off my cap, coat, gloves, scarf, and balled them up on the bench beside me.

"You better take off your helmet," I said to Brother. "And your jacket, too. If you sit in here by the stove in them, they won't feel as warm when you go back out in the cold." I'm twenty-five minutes older than he is, and I was taller than he was then, and Mama held me accountable for whatever happened to either one of us. He had the Bible stories, just turning the pages. I knew he was looking for the colored pictures. He couldn't read except in his reader and only about the front half of that.

"You better," I said.

"I am not. You can't tell me what to do. You're not my boss."

Mr. Dickey looked over at us and said, "Which one of you-all is the boy and which one is the girl? I never can tell." He looked at me and squinted his eyes like he couldn't see the difference perfectly well and said, "Oh, now I see, you're the girl — Miss Ellen Warner. Little Miss Warner. Ain't that right?"

I guess I looked at him kind of dumb. I thought he sounded silly. But since I had his attention I blurted, "Mr. Dickey, don't put hair tonic on Brother's head. Mama said to tell you. She said don't dare do it or he'll catch his death."

"Aw. Did your mama say that, Brother? You got that real leather helmet, fleece lined, and she's ascairt of a little tonic wetting your head?"

"You better do what my mama said," I said louder. "She *told* me to tell you."

Brother dropped the book and slid way down to the other end of his bench and kind of fell over to one side like an idiot and didn't say a word. He just looked at Mr. Dickey and down at the other barbers. Brother was plenty smart, but a lot of the time he liked to act like he didn't have a brain in his head. He wasn't any distance from that stove, which was red hot, and he still had on his helmet and jacket. Just because I told him to take them off. I just hushed up about it. Let him sweat.

I could see us in the mirror behind Mr. Dickey. And I could see what was in our mirror in Mr. Dickey's mirror, and it went on like that, everything just reflecting itself over and over again across the narrow shop. I figured the only way to stop that was to wait till it was night and turn off the lights to make it pitch black.

Finally Brother took his helmet off, and his jacket, and let them fall on the floor. Cubby came along with his broom and his dustpan with the long handle, sweeping up hair around the chairs, and he picked up Brother's things and hung them on the pegs by the door.

"Here, let me hang yo's up, too, Miss Sister," he said. I thanked him, aware of how much better my manners were than Brother's. That's what came of being a girl, I thought. Boys just naturally didn't have any manners.

"So you are a little girl, after all," Mr. Dickey started up again. He talked that way, smiling at me like he was doing me a favor to tell the whole room what everybody in town knew. I didn't look up. I picked up the Bible stories and opened them to a drawing of a man in a long gown looking out over the ocean. A fisher of men, it said. But I was listening to Mr. Dickey, who was talking to me at the same time he was talking to his customer.

It was Old Man Duff Willey. I wouldn't have called him Old Man Willey out loud, of course, but that's what I'd heard him called. I hadn't recognized him at first because Mr. Dickey had his face covered with a hot towel, and his body, which was stretched out like he was in bed, was almost covered by the sheet Mr. Dickey put over you for a haircut. Old Man Willey had a huge stomach and black hightops. His ankles were crossed on the silver metal prop that grown people could rest their feet on. His shoes were shiny, and I figured Cubby had been there popping his shoeshine rag on them before we came in.

When Mr. Dickey took off the towel Old Man Willey came up like a whale, and Mr. Dickey pulled off the sheet and raised the back of the chair and lowered the footrest — all at one time. Then he turned and popped the sheet like a whip. Pow! Brother sat up. He liked a big racket. He started laughing like he was crazy, and Mr. Dickey winked at him and began laughing big like it was funny, like it was something only he and Brother knew about. That's the kind of thing I didn't like about going to a man's barber shop.

Old Man Willey's face was red as a beet. He had red, white, and blue eyes that sat in puffy bags. His eyebrows were white and bushy, and his hair was just a white circle around his bald head. His head was as red as his face. He reached down in his pocket and got some change to pay Mr. Dickey and then got his coat off the wall peg. Old Man Willey smiled big and walked over, all bundled up, and snapped his big pink fingers back of Brother's ear, like a magician.

"Well, will you looka there, boy. Look what I found ahint your ear." And he gave Brother a whole dime. Then he patted Brother on the head and said, "Pretty little fellow. Look at them eyelashes. You sure oughta been a girl, son." Then he walked on past me without so much as a kiss my foot and rattled the old door closed behind him.

Brother closed his fist around the dime. I knew from the way he did it I would never see a penny of it. Not that it mattered. I had a nickel at home under Mama's dresser scarf, and Daddy would always give me another if I asked him, even with the Depression on him.

Mr. Dickey shook his sheet again, only this time he didn't pop it. "All righty," he said, looking first at Brother, then at me, "who's next?" Brother just sat there clutching his dime. "Ladies first?" Mr. Dickey bowed toward me.

Of course that waked Brother up. "No, I want to be first," he said, and jumped off the bench. Mr. Dickey was getting his children's board that he kept leaning against the wall under the lavatory. Brother climbed up to the footrest and onto the black leather seat, standing there tall as anything while Mr. Dickey laid the board across the arms. "All righty, little feller, just set it down right there."

When Brother sat, Mr. Dickey flipped the big sheet over him and fastened it behind his neck with a safety pin. The sheet hung over Brother and the whole chair like a white tent, and his head looked like a little round babydoll with blonde curls and big blue eyes. Mama cried the first time Brother's curls were cut. Daddy cut them off himself because he was afraid people would think Brother was a girl. That wasn't a bad idea because Brother was pretty, I had to admit. I didn't get nearly so much chin-chuckling and cheek-pinching as he did. Brother could smile like an angel. And he was right sweet on occasion.

Mr. Dickey began snipping, and the soft pale hair fell over the sheet and onto the floor. Some fell over Brother's face, and when he tried to blow it off his own face he made a loud noise. He and I began to giggle and we couldn't stop. Finally Mr. Dickey just left the comb sticking in Brother's hair and held the scissors down by his side. "Now you younguns got to stop this foolishness. I can't cut hair if you don't behave yourselves. You don't want me to cut your ear off, do you, Brother? You wanta see red blood running down all over that white sheet?"

Brother got still. But I kept on giggling.

"What's that boy giggling about over there, Brother? That boy in that dress with them brown stockings? Ain't that a boy just giggling to beat the band over there on my bench?"

Brother said, "Yeah," just the way Mama told us not to say it to grown folks. But I knew he wasn't thinking about a thing in this world but getting out of that chair and down to Mr. Claude Corbett's drugstore, just as fast as his legs would carry him, to get a double-dip with his dime. I could just see it, chocolate in one side and vanilla in the other. And not one lick for me. He would make himself sick and throw up all over himself before he would give me a lick. And who would get blamed for his ruining his supper? He didn't hear a word Mr. Dickey was saying.

"You know what you are?"

At first Mr. Dickey thought I was talking to Brother. Then he caught on to me talking to him. He smiled friendly and said, "What am I, little Miss?" I think he was expecting me to say *he* was a girl.

"You are — you are a ring-tailed tooter."

Well, I wish you could have seen him. He just stood there for a minute and I knew I had, as Daddy would say, fired a big gun. I didn't know what I was talking about, and in fact I do not to this day.

"Well, now, where'd you pick up such talk? Shame on you! Shame on you!" Mr. Dickey didn't like it. I could tell. I began to figure I had been too sassy, and I started wondering just how bad a ring-tailed tooter was. I tried to smile pretty big and looked right at Mr. Dickey Becker. Brother wasn't even listening; I knew where his mind was. Then Mr. Dickey began to laugh again.

"But that's right. You're a boy, ain't you? And that's boy talk." He laughed.

"I am not a boy."

"Sure you are. Look at that straight hair. How come you don't have them big eyes and long eyelashes like a girl ought to? Wouldn't you say that was a boy, Brother?"

His teasing fired me up again. I took a deep breath and said, "And you are a barber today. But Saturday you will be a bootlegger selling whiskey to the ignoramuses. And Sunday you will preach hell and thunderation to the multitude in that Baptist church out by Hickson's cotton gin." I tucked my chin and looked sideways to the back of the shop. Everybody began laughing.

Mr. Dickey had been putting powder on Brother's neck and dusting it off like clouds of smoke with his soft round brush. He held still a little bit. Then he laughed and shook his head. "I'll be dawged. If that ain't Thad Warner talking, I'm a monkey's uncle. Your daddy put you up to that, young lady."

"Lady?" yelled Brother, like somebody who suddenly had come to his senses. "How can she be a young lady if she's a boy?" See? That's what I mean about him acting like he had good sense sometimes. But then he began to laugh like crazy. He did that every now and then, just began laughing real loud, hollering really. His best friend, Junior Henderson, did the same thing, so I figured it wasn't unnatural.

Everybody was so jolly over my big joke that I felt better, until all of a sudden I realized Mr. Dickey had that narrow-necked bottle upside down over Brother's head, shaking it like he was trying to get catsup out. Before I knew it Brother's head was sopping wet.

"Mr. Dickey Becker! Mr. Dickey Becker! You've put hair tonic on my brother's head."

"Oh, law me," he said, like he really had not meant to do something wrong. Well, I had told him. He grabbed a huck towel and began rubbing Brother's hair. He rubbed it and rubbed it. When he took the towel off, Brother looked like a doll that had fallen in the washtub. His hair stuck out every which way, and it was still wet.

"Aw, it's almost dry, Sister," said Mr. Dickey. He combed it forward like bangs over Brother's forehead. Then he parted it straight as an arrow on one side and combed the sides down straight. He combed the top to one side and whipped a neat cowlick back over Brother's forehead. "Now, just looka there. That's a pretty child." He was talking to the mirror over my head. "And by the time Mrs. Warner drives up out there, that hair will be as dry as a bone." He took the sheet off and popped it.

In a wink Brother slid down off the board, onto the seat, down to the footrest, and off onto the floor. He made a beeline for the door. I couldn't even scream, "Brother, come back here!" before he was out in that pneumonia weather with his wet head, flying down the street to the drugstore for a double-dip. I just knew Mama would drive up right then. But she didn't.

I grabbed my things and Brother's helmet and jacket and tore out after him. Mr. Claude Corbett already had his scoop down in the chocolate when I ran in through the back door where children weren't even allowed. Brother was up on the stool, leaning on his elbows way over the marble counter so he could see down into the ice cream cans.

"Brother, what'd you do that for? Are you just plain crazy? Mama's going to die, just plain die. Put on your jacket and helmet this minute before she comes and sees you." He got his cone and laid Old Man Willey's dime on the counter. Then he got down and let me put the jacket and helmet on him. He never missed a lick on his cone, just switched it from one hand to the other while he put his arms into the sleeves. Ice cream was all over his face by the time I dragged him back up to the barber shop.

We had no more than gotten inside when there was Mama's car.

"Here, now, Sister," said Mr. Dickey. "What about your haircut?"

"I'll have to come back," I said to the ring-tailed tooter, who was just sitting there in his own barber chair perfectly unconcerned over what had happened. I didn't want him to have a chance to speak to Mama again and tell her I'd been impudent.

Mama hadn't turned the engine off; because of the cold she might have had trouble starting up again. She was just sitting there sort of daydreaming, looking straight ahead. She didn't notice the ice cream on Brother's chin and cheeks, or that my hair wasn't trimmed under my cap. She had library books all over the front seat, so Brother had to get on the backseat with me. I accidentally stepped on his foot, and he hit me on my arm and made it hurt. "Mama," he hollered, "she made me drop my ice cream." He picked up all he could off the seat and tried to stuff it back in the cone.

"Ice cream? Where on earth did you get ice cream? Don't you know it will give you the sorest kind of throat to eat ice cream in weather like

.

this? What are we coming to when a druggist, a graduate pharmacist from the University of Mississippi, will sell ice cream to children in 40-degree weather and snow threatened all over Mississippi tonight? My soul and body!"

By the time she had said all that, we were under the porte cochere. Brother crawled all over me getting out of the car, so he could beat me up the steps.

Mama and I followed him, with her saying, "Lord have mercy, Sister, what have you let him get into?"

Once inside the house she seemed to notice everything at once — chocolate and vanilla ice cream on Brother's face, hands, and clothes, my hair not cut, Brother's helmet hanging crooked, not snapped. Then she looked thunderstruck, and she pulled off the helmet like she feared the worst.

"Sister! What did I tell you? Would you look? For pity's sake, his nose is already running." It was, too. She pulled off his coat. "Oleander!" I almost said *Mama hollered*, but of course Mama didn't holler, not like Brother and I hollered. But she kind of shrieked this time. Oleander came running.

"Draw us a hot tub of water, Oleander. Quickly!"

"What done happen to our boy, Miss Ellen?"

"That old . . . Mr. Dickey Becker wet his head with hair tonic and sent him out in the cold."

"Well, you ain't about to put him in no water after such exposin', are you?"

"Of course not. I want to keep him in there in the steam so he won't stop up. Get a blanket and the Vicks and bring them in there. Then don't let a soul dare open that door." As she led Brother into the bathroom he began to sneeze. They stayed in there a long time, Mama's and Oleander's voices rising and falling, Brother's voice breaking over theirs, cranky and mad.

Brother got pneumonia. It took him two days to really get it, but he got sick that night after the haircut and he got sicker all the next day, when Mama called Dr. Butler. He came right then, like he always did, and his little black coupé was in our driveway twice a day for about a week. Mama hardly ever left Brother. Daddy tiptoed in and out. They got Miss Ruby Burris, the trained nurse, to come, and she stayed day and night taking Brother's temperature and helping to hold the mustard poultices up to the fireplace so they could lay them hot on Brother's chest.

Mama closed the piano and turned off the radio. She didn't even come to the table. She talked about "sending for the girls," our two sisters who were away at school. Daddy's sister, who didn't even like Mama, came from down the street with a tureen of gumbo "for the family." Mama happened to be in the hall, and she kissed Aunt Minnie and said kindly, "Thank you, Minnie." Now I was sure Brother was going to die.

"Is it really *double* pneumonia, Ellen?"

"Yes, Minnie. Both lungs."

I spent a lot of time sitting on the footstool in the living room. Nobody accused me of anything, but I felt pretty sure that if Brother didn't get well they would think it was my fault. And it would be true. I could have stood at the door and stopped him. I had known he was going to head out for that ice cream. The minute Old Man Willey gave him the dime, I knew it. Why hadn't I stopped him? Why hadn't I watched Mr. Dickey when he picked up the bottle?

Then on about the seventh day Dr. Butler came out of Mama and Daddy's room, which was the sickroom, and he said to Daddy, "Well, Thad, he's passed the crisis." And Daddy put his arm across Doctor's shoulders and said, "Thank God, Henry. Thank God." Doctor came in the living room, stretching and sort of grunting like he was relieved and thinking about some rest now. He saw me sitting in Mama's chair by the fire.

"Sister, you're looking a little peaked yourself. Are you feeling well?"

"Yes, sir."

"Well, don't look so unhappy. Your brother is going to be all right. You ought to cheer up. You're sure you aren't feeling poorly? Stick out your tongue." He came over and held my wrist and peered down at me through his bifocals. "No, you're fine. Cool as a cucumber."

"I'm the one that made him sick."

"You're what?"

"I let him out in the cold with his head wet after he got his hair cut."

"Sister!" He dropped into Daddy's chair and pulled me against his knee, and I cried and cried and told him the whole thing.

"Sister Warner, your brother's pneumonia had nothing to do with Mr. Dickey's hair tonic. I want you to promise me you'll forget such nonsense." He took out a clean handkerchief and patted my eyes, then he shook the folds out and put it under my nose. "Here, now, blow!" Then he stood up and stuffed his handkerchief in his coat pocket. He wrinkled his nose to push his glasses up higher. He did that all the time. It was funny. He would make that quick funny little face, and it would push his glasses up, but then they would slip right down again on his thin straight nose. I wanted to hug his neck, but I didn't.

In a few days I was allowed to go in and play on the bed with Brother. He had so many new toys there was hardly any room. Oleander made him a big vanilla milkshake every day to build him up, and she made me one, too, even though I didn't need any building up. Brother liked the milkshake and drank every drop till I told him it had a raw egg in it. Then he wouldn't touch it. He threw a fit if anybody even brought it in the room. Mama was outdone with me for telling him about the raw egg, but she didn't make much of it.

And one day she just up and told me it wasn't my fault at all that Brother got pneumonia. Daddy said good gracious no. Never in a million years. He said it was nobody's fault. But Mama believed to her dying day that Mr. Dickey Becker gave Brother double pneumonia. We never had to go back to his barber shop. Brother started going over to Lewis's again. He told me Mr. Lewis didn't use a nice soft brush to dust the powder off his neck like Mr. Dickey. "He blows it off," said Brother, "and when it gets in your face, he blows right in your face." Brother stretched his mouth down in the corners and held his nose.

Mama began taking me with her again to Miss Ella B.'s Beauty Shoppe, where I had a wonderful time watching ladies get their hair dipped in blueing or get hooked up to the electrical permanent wave machines. Miss Ella B. even talked Mama into letting my hair grow long to plait.

Daddy kept going to Mr. Dickey's for his haircuts and his shoe-shines. He said it gave Mr. Dickey a painless way to make a payment on his loan, and besides, Daddy didn't want him to get his feelings hurt about the double pneumonia.

Walker Percy

from Lost in the Cosmos: The Last Self-Help Book

THE PROMISCUOUS SELF: *Why is it that One's Self often not only does not Prefer Sex with one's Chosen Mate, Chosen for His or Her Attractiveness and Suitability, even when the Mate is a Person well known to one, knowing of one, loved by one, with a Life, Time, and Family in common, but rather prefers Sex with a New Person, even a Total Stranger, or even Vicariously through Pornography*

A RECENT SURVEY in a large city reported that 95 percent of all video tapes purchased for home consumption were *Insatiable*, a pornographic film starring Marilyn Chambers.

Of all sexual encounters on soap opera, only 6 percent occur between husband and wife.

In some cities of the United States, which now has the highest divorce rate in the world, the incidence of divorce now approaches 60 percent of married couples.

A recent survey showed that the frequency of sexual intercourse in married couples declined 90 percent after three years of marriage.

"A female sexologist reported . . ." that a favorite fantasy of American women, second only to oral sex, was having sex with two strange men at once.

According to the president of the North American Swing Club Association, only 3 percent of married couples who are swingers get divorces, as compared with over 50 percent of non-swinging couples.

Walker Percy

In large American cities, lunch-break liaisons between business men and women have become commonplace.

Sexual activity and pregnancy in teenagers have increased dramatically in the last twenty years, in both those who have received sex education in schools and those who have not. In some cities, more babies are born to single women than to married women.

A radio psychotherapist reported that nowadays many young people who disdain marriage, preferring "relationships" and "commitments," speak of entering into simultaneous relationships with a second or third person as a growth experience.

In San Francisco's Buena Vista Park, to the outrage of local middle-class residents, homosexuals cruise and upon encountering a sexual prospect, always a stranger, exchange a word or a sign and disappear into the bushes. In a series of interviews, Buena Vista homosexuals admitted to sexual encounters with an average of more than 500 strangers.

A survey by a popular magazine reported that the incidence of homosexuality in the United States had surpassed that of the Weimar Republic and is approaching that of England.

Question: Do Americans, as well as other Westerners, prefer sexual variety, both heterosexual and homosexual, because

(a) The sexual revolution has occurred, which is nothing else but the overthrow of the unnatural repressions and taboos of 1,900 years of Christianity and the exploration of the free and healthy practices of a sexually liberated society.

(b) Humans are biologically as promiscuous as chimpanzees. It is only the cultural constraints of society, probably imposed by the economic necessities of an agricultural society, which required a monogamous union and children as a reliable labor source.

(c) No, man is by nature monogamous, as ethnologists have demonstrated in most cultures. It is Western society which is disintegrating, to a degree remarkably similar to the decline of the Roman Empire in the fifth century, when similar practices were reported.

(d) No, Western man is promiscuous because promiscuous sexuality is the obverse or flip side of Christianity and is in fact specified by Christianity as its opposite. Thus, pornography is something new in the world, having no parallel in ancient, so-called pagan cultures. Accordingly, there is little if any difference between present-day promiscuity and that of, say, the Victorian era. The so-called sexual revolution is nothing but the legitimizing of the secret behavior of the Victorians and its extension to women.

(e) Western man is promiscuous because something unprecedented has happened. As a consequence of the scientific and technological revolution, there has occurred a displacement of the real as a consequence of which genital sexuality has come to be seen as the substratum of all human relationships, of friendship, love, and the rest. This displacement has come to pass as a consequence of a lay misperception of the physicist's quest for establishing a molecular or energic basis for all interactions and of what is perceived as Freud's identification of genital sexuality as the ground of all human relationships.

A letter to Dear Abby:

I am a twenty-three-year-old liberated woman who has been on the pill for two years. It's getting pretty expensive and I think my boyfriend should share half the cost, but I don't know him well enough to discuss money with him.*

(f) The Self since the time of Descartes has been stranded, split off from everything else in the Cosmos, a mind which professes to understand bodies and galaxies but is by the very act of understanding marooned in the Cosmos, with which it has no connection. It therefore needs to exercise every option in order to reassure itself that it is not a ghost but is rather a self among other selves. One such option is a sexual encounter. Another is war. The pleasure of a sexual encounter derives not only from physical gratification but also from the demon-

---

* Abigail Van Buren, *The Best of Dear Abby* (New York: Andrews and McMeel, 1981), p. 242.

stration to oneself that, despite one's own ghostliness, one is, for the moment at least, a sexual being. Amazing! Indeed, the most amazing of all the creatures of the Cosmos: a ghost with an erection! Yet not really amazing, for only if the abstracted ghost has an erection can it, like Jove spying Europa on the beach, enter the human condition.

(g) It's not that complicated. It's simply that people nowadays have too much money and time to spend and don't know what to do with themselves and so will try anything out of boredom.

(h) Why go further than the orthodox Judaeo-Christian belief that monogamous marriage was ordained by God for man's happiness, that the devil goes about like a roaring lion seeking whom he may devour, and that as a consequence modern man has lost his way, has not the faintest notion who he is or what he is doing, and nothing short of catastrophe will bring him to his senses. At the height of a hurricane, husbands come to themselves and can even embrace their wives. During hurricane Camille, one Biloxi couple, taking refuge in a tree house, reported that, during the passage of the eye, they had intercourse for the first time in years.

(i) No, the explanation is biological. Man is undergoing a mutation in sexual behavior which will in the end, like the tooth of the saber-toothed tiger, render him extinct. Since most of the emerging varieties of sexual expression — homosexuality, anal and oral sex — do not reproduce the species and therefore have no survival value, the species will become extinct.

(j) None of the above. It has always been so. That is to say, the sexual behavior of humans has not changed. Therefore, there is nothing to explain.

(CHECK ONE OR MORE)

Thought Experiment

THE LAST DONAHUE SHOW

The Donahue Show is in progress on what appears at first to be an ordinary weekday morning.

The theme of this morning's show is Donahue's favorite, sex, the extraordinary variety of sexual behavior — "sexual preference," as Donahue would call it — in the country and the embattled attitudes toward it. Although Donahue has been accused of appealing to prurient interest, with a sharp eye cocked on the ratings, he defends himself by saying that he presents these controversial matters in "a mature and tasteful manner" — which he often does. It should also be noted in Donahue's defense that the high ratings of these sex-talk shows are nothing more nor less than an index of the public's intense interest in such matters.

The guests today are:

Bill, a homosexual and habitué of Buena Vista Park in San Francisco

Allen, a heterosexual businessman, married, and a connoisseur of the lunch-hour liaison

Penny, a pregnant fourteen-year-old

Dr. Joyce Friday, a well-known talk-show sex therapist, or in media jargon: a psych jockey

BILL'S STORY: Yes, I'm gay, and yes, I cruise Buena Vista. Yes, I've probably had over five hundred encounters with lovers, though I didn't keep count. So what? Whose business is it? I'm gainfully employed by a savings-and-loan company, am a trustworthy employee, and do an honest day's work. My recreation is Buena Vista Park and the strangers I meet there. I don't molest children, rape women, snatch purses. I contribute to United Way. Such encounters that I do have are by mutual consent and therefore nobody's business — except my steady live-in friend's. Naturally, he's upset, but that's our problem.

DONAHUE (*striding up and down, mike in hand, boyishly inarticulate*): C'mon, Bill. What about the kids who might see you? You know what I mean. I mean — (*Opens his free hand to the audience, soliciting their understanding*)

BILL: Kids don't see me. Nobody sees me.

DONAHUE (*coming close, on the attack but good-naturedly, spoofing himself as prosecutor*): Say, Bill. I've always been curious. Is there

107

some sort of signal? I mean, how do you and the other guy know —
help me out —

BILL: Eye contact, or we show a bit of handkerchief here.
(*Demonstrates*)

STUDIO AUDIENCE: (*Laughter*)

DONAHUE (*shrugging [Don't blame me, folks], pushes up nose-
bridge of glasses, swings mike over to Dr. J.F. without looking at her*):
How about it, Doc?

DR. J.F. (*in her not-mincing-words voice*): I think Bill's behavior is
immature and depersonalizing. (*Applause from audience*) I think he
ought to return to his steady live-in friend and work out a mature,
creative relationship. You might be interested to know that studies have
shown that stable gay couples are more creative than straights.
(*Applause again, but more tentative*)

DONAHUE (*eyes slightly rolled back, swings mike to Bill*): How
about it, Bill?

BILL: Yeah, right. But I still cruise Buena Vista.

DONAHUE (*pensive, head to one side, strides backward, forward,
then over to Allen*): How about you, Allen?

ALLEN'S STORY: I'm a good person, I think. I work hard, am
happily married, love my wife and family, also support United Way,
served in the army. I drink very little, don't do drugs, have never been
to a porn movie. My idea of R & R — maybe I got it in the army — is
to meet an attractive woman. What a delight it is, to see a handsome
mature woman, maybe in the secretarial pool, maybe in a bar, restaurant, anywhere, exchange eye contact, speak to her in a nice way,
respect her as a person, invite her to join me for lunch (no sexual
harassment in the office — I hate that!), have a drink, two drinks, enjoy
a nice meal, talk about matters of common interest — then simply ask
her — by now, both of you know whether you like each other. What
a joy to go with her up in the elevator of the downtown Holiday
Inn, both of you silent, relaxed, smiling, anticipating — The door of
the room closes behind you. You look at her, take her hand. There's
champagne already there. You stand at the window with her, touch
glasses, talk — there's nothing vulgar. No closed-circuit TV. Do you

know what we did last time? We turned on *La Bohème* on the FM. She loves Puccini.

DONAHUE: C'mon, Allen. What are ya handing me? What d'ya mean you're happily married? You mean *you're* happy.

ALLEN: No, no. Vera's happy, too.

AUDIENCE (*mostly women, groaning*): Nooooooo.

DONAHUE: Okay-okay, ladies, hold it a second. What do you mean, Vera's happy? I mean how do you manage — help me out, I'm about to get in trouble — hold the letters, folks —

ALLEN: Well, actually, Vera has a low sex drive. We've always been quite inactive, even at the beginning —

AUDIENCE: (*groans, jumbled protests*): Nooooo.

DONAHUE (*backing away, holding up placating free hand, backing around to Dr. J.F.*): It's all yours, Doc.

DR. J.F.: Studies have shown that open marriages can be growth experiences for both partners. However — (*groans from audience*) — *However*: it seems to me that Vera may be getting the short end here. I mean, I don't know Vera's side of it. But could I ask you this? Have you and Vera thought about reenergizing your sex life?

ALLEN: Well, ah —

DR. J.F.: Studies have shown, for example, that more stale marriages have been revived by oral sex than any other technique —

DONAHUE: Now, Doc —

DR. J.F.: Other studies have shown that mutual masturbation —

DONAHUE (*eyes rolled back*): We're running long folks, we'll be right back after this — don't go away. Oh boy. (*Lets mike slide to the hilt through his hand, closes eyes, as camera cuts away to a Maxithins commercial*)

DONAHUE: We're back. Thank the good Lord for good sponsors. (*Turns to Penny, a thin, inattentive, moping teen-ager, even possibly a pre-teen*): Penny?

PENNY (*chewing something*): Yeah?

DONAHUE (*solicitous, quite effectively tender*): What's with you, sweetheart?

PENNY: Well, I liked this boy a lot and he told me there was one way

I could prove it —

DONAHUE: Wait a minute, Penny. Now this, your being here, is okay with your parents, right? I mean let's establish that.

PENNY: Oh, sure. They're right over there — you can ask them. (*Camera pans over audience, settling on a couple with mild, pleasant faces. It is evident that on the whole they are not displeased with being on TV*)

DONAHUE: Okay. So you mean you didn't know about taking precautions —

DR. J.F. (*breaking in*): Now, that's what I mean, Phil.

DONAHUE: What's that, Doc?

DR. J.F.: About the crying need for sex education in our schools. Now if this child —

PENNY: Oh, I had all that stuff at Ben Franklin.

DONAHUE: You mean you knew about the pill and the other, ah —

PENNY: I had been on the pill for a year.

DONAHUE (*scratching head*): I don't get it. Oh, you mean you slipped up, got careless?

PENNY: No, I did it on purpose.

DONAHUE: Did what on purpose? You mean —

PENNY: I mean I wanted to get pregnant.

DONAHUE: Why was that, Penny?

PENNY: My best friend was pregnant.

AUDIENCE: (*Groans, laughter*)

DR. J.F.: You see, Phil, that's just what I mean. This girl is no more equipped with parenting skills than a child. She is a child. I hope she realizes she still has viable options.

DONAHUE: How about it, Penny?

PENNY: No, I want to have my baby.

DONAHUE: Why?

PENNY: I think babies are neat.

DONAHUE: Oh boy.

DR. J.F.: Studies have shown that unwanted babies suffer 85 percent more child abuse and 150 percent more neuroses later in life.

DONAHUE (*striding*): Okay, now what have we got here? Wait.

What's going on?

There is an interruption. Confusion at the rear of the studio. Heads turn. Three strangers, dressed outlandishly, stride down the aisle.

DONAHUE (*smacks his forehead*): What's this? What's this? Holy smoke!

Already the audience is smiling, reassured both by Donahue's comic consternation and by the exoticness of the visitors. Clearly, the audience thinks, they are part of the act.

The three strangers are indeed outlandish.

One is a tall, thin, bearded man dressed like a sixteenth-century reformer. Indeed, he could be John Calvin, in his black cloak, black cap with short bill, and snug earflaps.

The second wears the full-dress uniform of a Confederate officer. Though he is a colonel, he is quite young, surely no more than twenty-five. Clean-shaven and extremely handsome, he looks for all the world like Colonel John Pelham, Jeb Stuart's legendary artillerist. Renowned both for his gallantry in battle and for his chivalry toward women, the beau ideal of the South, he engaged in sixty artillery duels, won them all, lost not a single piece. With a single Napoleon, he held off three of Burnside's divisions in front of Fredericksburg before being ordered by Stuart to retreat.

The third is at once the most ordinary-looking and yet the strangest of all. His dress is both modern and out-of-date. In his light-colored double-breasted suit and bow tie, his two-tone shoes of the sort known in the 1940s as "perforated wing-tips," his neat above-the-ears haircut, he looks a bit like the clean old man in the Beatles movie *A Hard Day's Night*, a bit like Lowell Thomas or perhaps Harry Truman. It is as if he were a visitor from the Cosmos, from a planet ten or so light-years distant, who had formed his notion of earthlings from belated transmissions of 1950 TV, from watching the Ed Sullivan Show, old Chester Morris movies, and Morey Amsterdam. Or, to judge from his speaking voice, he could have been an inveterate listener during the Golden Age of radio and modeled his speech on that of Harry Von Zell.

DONAHUE (*backpedaling, smacking his head again*): Holy smoke! Who are these guys? (*Beseeching the audience with a slow comic pan around*)

The audience laughs, not believing for a moment that these latecomers are not one of Donahue's surprises. And yet —

DONAHUE (*snapping his fingers*): I got it. Wait'll I get that guy. It's Steve Allen, right? Refugees from the Steve Allen Show, *Great Conversations*? Famous historical figures? You know, folks, they do that show in the studio down the hall. Wait'll I get that guy.

General laughter. Everybody remembers it's been done before, an old show-biz trick, like Carson barging in on Rickles during the C.P.O. Sharkey taping.

DONAHUE: Okay already. Okay, who we got here? This is Moses? General Robert E. Lee? And who is this guy? Harry Truman? Okay, fellas, let's hear it. (Donahue, an attractive fellow, is moving about as gracefully as a dancer)

THE STRANGER (*speaks first, in his standard radio-announcer's voice, which is not as flat as the Chicagoans who say, Hyev a hyeppy New Year*): I don't know what these two are doing here, but I came to give you a message. We've been listening to this show.

DONAHUE (*winking at the audience*): And where were you listening to us?

STRANGER: In the green room.

DONAHUE: Where else? Okay. Then what do you think? Let's hear it first from the reverend here. What did you say your name was, Reverend?

STRANGER: John Calvin.

DONAHUE: Right. Who else? Okay, we got to break here for these messages. Don't go 'way, folks. We're coming right back and sort this out, I promise.

Cut to Miss Clairol, Land O Lakes margarine, Summer's Eve, and Alpo commercials.

But when the show returns, John Calvin, who does not understand commercial breaks, has jumped the gun and is in mid-sentence.

CALVIN (*speaking in a thick French accent, not unlike Charles Boyer*): — of his redemptive sacrifice? What I have heard is licentious talk about deeds which are an abomination before God, meriting eternal damnation unless they repent and throw themselves on God's mercy. Which they are predestined to do or not to do, so why bother to discuss it?

DONAHUE (*gravely*): That's pretty heavy, Reverend.

CALVIN: Heavy? Yes, it's heavy.

DONAHUE (*mulling, scratching*): Now wait a minute, Reverend. Let's check this out. You're entitled to your religious beliefs. But what if others disagree with you in all good faith? And aside from *that* (*prosecutory again, using mike like forefinger*) what's wrong with two consenting adults expressing their sexual preference in the privacy of their bedroom or, ah, under a bush?

CALVIN: Sexual preference? (*Puzzled, he turns for help to the Confederate officer and the Cosmic stranger. They shrug*)

DONAHUE (*holding mike to the officer*): How about you, sir? Your name is —

CONFEDERATE OFFICER: Colonel John Pelham, C.S.A., commander of the horse artillery under General Stuart.

PENNY: He's cute.

AUDIENCE: (*Laughter*)

DONAHUE: You heard it all in the green room, Colonel. What 'dya think?

COLONEL PELHAM (*in a soft Alabama accent*): What do I think of what, sir?

DONAHUE: Of what you heard in the green room.

PELHAM: Of the way these folks act and talk? Well, I don't think much of it, sir.

DONAHUE: How do you mean, Colonel?

PELHAM: That's not the way people should talk or act. Where I come from, we'd call them white trash. That's no way to talk if you're a man or a woman. A gentleman knows how to treat women. He knows because he knows himself, who he is, what his obligations are. And he discharges them. But after all, you won the war, so if that's the way you want to act, that's your affair. At least, we can be sure of one thing.

DONAHUE: What's that, Colonel?

PELHAM: We're not sorry we fought.

DONAHUE: I see. Then you agree with the reverend, I mean Reverend Calvin here.

PELHAM: Well, I respect his religous beliefs. But I never thought much about religion one way or the other. In fact, I don't think religion has much to do with whether a man does right. A West Point man is an officer and a gentleman, religion or no religion. I have nothing against religion. In fact, when we studied medieval history at West Point, I remember admiring Richard Coeur de Lion and his recapturing Acre and the holy places. I remember thinking: I would have fought for him, just as I fought for Lee and the South.

Applause from the audience. Calvin puts them off, but this handsome officer reminds them of Rhett Butler — Clark Gable, or rather Ashley Wilkes — Leslie Howard.

DONAHUE (*drifting off, frowning; something is amiss but he can't put his finger on it. What is Steve Allen up to? He shakes his head, blinks*): You said it, Colonel. Okay. Where were we? (*Turning to Cosmic stranger*) We're running a little long. Can you make it brief, Harry — Mr. President, or whoever you are? Oh boy.

THE COSMIC STRANGER (*stands stiffly, hands at his sides, and begins speaking briskly, very much in the style of the late Raymond Gram Swing*): I will be brief. I have taken this human form through a holographic technique unknown to you in order to make myself understood to you.

Hear this. I have a message. Whether you heed it or not is your affair.

I have nothing to say to you about God or the Confederacy, whatever that is — I assume it is not the G2V Confederacy in this arm of the galaxy — though I could speak about God, but it is too late for you, and I am not here to do that.

We are not interested in the varieties of your sexual behavior, except as a symptom of a more important disorder.

It is this disorder which concerns us and which we do not fully understand.

As a consequence of this disorder, you are a potential threat to all civilizations in the G2V region of the galaxy. Throughout G2V you are known variously and jokingly as the Ds or the DDs or the DLs, that is, the ding-a-lings or the death-dealers or the death-lovers. Of all the species here and in all of G2V, you are the only one which is by nature sentimental, murderous, self-hating, and self-destructive.

You are two superpowers here. The other is hopeless, has already succumbed, and is a death society. It is a living death and an agent for the propagation of death.

You are scarcely better — there is a glimmer of hope for you — but that is of no interest to me.

If the two of you destroy each other, as appears likely, it is of no consequence to us. To tell you the truth, G2V will breathe a sigh of relief.

The danger is that you may not destroy each other and that your present crude technology may constitute a threat to G2V in the future.

I am here to tell you three things: what is going to happen, what I am going to do, and what you can do.

Here's what will happen. Within the next twenty-four hours, your last war will begin. There will occur a twenty-megaton airburst one mile above the University of Chicago, the very site where your first chain reaction was produced. Every American city and town will be hit. You will lose plus-minus 160 million immediately, plus-minus 50 million later.

Here's what I am going to do. I have been commissioned to collect a specimen of DD and return with it so that we can study it toward the end of determining the nature of your disorder. Accordingly, I propose to take this young person referred to as Penny — for two reasons. One, she is perhaps still young enough not to have become hopeless. Two, she is pregnant and so we will have a chance to rear a DD in an environment free of your noxious influence. Then perhaps we can determine whether your disorder is a result of some peculiar earth environmental factor or whether you are a malignant sport, a genetic accident, the consequence of what you would have called, quite accurately, in an earlier time an MD — *mutatio diabolica*, a diabolical mutation.

Finally, here's what you can do. It is of no consequence to us whether you do it or not, because you will no longer be a threat to anyone. This is only a small gesture of goodwill to a remnant of you who may survive and who may have the chance to start all over — though you will probably repeat the same mistake. We have been students of your climatology for years. I have here a current read-out and prediction of the prevailing wind directions and fallout patterns for the next two weeks. It so happens that the place nearest you which will escape all effects of both blast and fallout is the community of Lost Cove, Tennessee. We do not anticipate a stampede to Tennessee. Our projection is that very few of you here and you out there in radio land will attach credibility to this message. But the few of you who do may wish to use this information. There is a cave there, corn, grits, collard greens, and smoked sausage in abundance.

That is the end of my message. Penny —

DONAHUE: We're long! We're long! Heavy! Steve, I'll get you for this. Oh boy. Don't forget, folks, tomorrow we got surrogate partners and a Kinsey panel — come back — you can't win 'em all — 'bye! Grits. I dunno.

AUDIENCE: (*Applause*)

Cut to station break, Secure Card 65 commercial, Alpo, Carefree Panty Shields, and Mentholatum, then *The Price Is Right*.

Question: If you heard this Donahue Show, would you head for Lost Cove, Tennessee?

(*a*) Yes

(*b*) No

(CHECK ONE)

Augustus Baldwin Longstreet

The Horse-Swap

D URING THE SESSION of the Supreme Court, in the village of
____, about three weeks ago, where a number of people were
collected in the principal street of the village, I observed a young man
riding up and down the street, as I supposed, in a violent passion. He
galloped this way, then that, and then the other; spurred his horse to one
group of citizens, then to another, then dashed off at half speed, as if
fleeing from danger; and, suddenly checking his horse, returned first in
a pace, then in a trot, and then in a canter. While he was performing these
various evolutions, he cursed, swore, whooped, screamed, and tossed
himself in every attitude which man could assume on horseback. In
short, he *cavorted* most magnanimously (a term which, in our tongue,
expresses all that I have described, and a little more), and seemed to be
setting all creation at defiance. As I like to see all that is passing, I
determined to take a position a little nearer to him, and to ascertain, if
possible, what it was that affected him so sensibly. Accordingly, I
approached a crowd before which he had stopped for a moment, and
examined it with the strictest scrutiny. But I could see nothing in it that
seemed to have anything to do with the cavorter. Every man appeared to
be in good humour, and all minding their own business. Not one so much
as noticed the principal figure. Still he went on. After a semicolon
pause, which my appearance seemed to produce (for he eyed me closely
as I approached), he fetched a whoop, and swore that he could out-swap
"any live man, woman, or child that ever walked these hills, or that ever
straddled horseflesh since the days of old daddy Adam."

"Stranger," said he to me, "did you ever see the *Yellow Blossom*
from Jasper?"

"No," said I, "but I have often heard of him."

"I'm the boy," continued he; "perhaps a *leetle*, jist a *leetle*, of the best man at a horse-swap that ever trod shoe-leather."

I began to feel my situation a little awkward, when I was relieved by a man somewhat advanced in years, who stepped up and began to survey the "Yellow Blossom's" horse with much apparent interest. This drew the rider's attention, and he turned the conversation from me to the stranger.

"Well, my old coon," said he, "do you want to swap *hosses*?"

"Why, I don't know," replied the stranger; "I believe I've got a beast I'd trade with you for that one, if you like him."

"Well, fetch up your nag, my old cock; you're jist the lark I wanted to get hold of. I am perhaps a *leetle*, jist a *leetle*, of the best man at a horse-swap that ever stole *cracklins* out of his mammy's fat gourd. Where's your *hoss*?"

"I'll bring him presently; but I want to examine your horse a little."

"Oh! look at him," said the Blossom, alighting and hitting him a cut; "look at him. He's the best piece of *hoss*flesh in the thirteen united universal worlds. There's no sort o' mistake in little Bullet. He can pick up miles on his feet, and fling 'em behind him as fast as the next man's *hoss*, I don't care where he comes from. And he can keep at it as long as the sun can shine without resting."

During this harangue, little Bullet looked as if he understood it all, believed it, and was ready at any moment to verify it. He was a horse of goodly countenance, rather expressive of vigilance than fire; though an unnatural appearance of fierceness was thrown into it by the loss of his ears, which had been cropped pretty close to his head. Nature had done but little for Bullet's head and neck; but he managed, in a great measure, to hide their defects by bowing perpetually. He had obviously suffered severely for corn, but if his ribs and hip bones had not disclosed the fact, *he* never would have done it; for he was in all respects as cheerful and happy as if he commanded all the corn-cribs and fodder-stacks in Georgia. His height was about twelve hands; but as his shape partook somewhat of that of the giraffe, his haunches stood much lower. They were short, strait, peaked, and concave. Bullet's tail, however, made amends for all his defects. All that the artist could do to beautify it had been done; and all that horse could do to compliment the artist, Bullet did. His tail was nicked in superior style, and exhibited the line of beauty in so many directions, that it could not fail to hit the most fastidious taste in some of them. From the root it dropped into a graceful festoon; then rose in a handsome curve; then resumed its first direction; and then mounted suddenly upward like a cypress knee to a perpendicular of about two and a half inches. The whole had a careless and bewitching inclination to the right. Bullet obviously knew where his beauty lay, and took all occasions to display it to the best advantage. If a stick cracked, or if any one moved suddenly about him, or coughed, or hawked, or spoke a little louder than common, up went Bullet's tail like lightning; and if the *going up* did not please, the *coming down* must of necessity, for it was as different from the other movement as was its direction. The first was a bold and rapid flight upward, usually to an angle of forty-five degrees. In this position he kept his interesting appendage until he satisfied himself that nothing in particular was to be done; when he commenced dropping it by half inches, in second beats, then in triple time, then faster and shorter, and faster and shorter still, until it finally died away imperceptibly into its natural position. If I might compare sights to sounds, I should say its *settling* was more like the note of a locust than anything else in nature.

Either from native sprightliness of disposition, from uncontrollable activity, or from an unconquerable habit of removing flies by the stamping of the feet, Bullet never stood still; but always kept up a gentle fly-scaring movement of his limbs, which was peculiarly interesting.

"I tell you, man," proceeded the Yellow Blossom, "he's the best live hoss that ever trod the grit of Georgia. Bob Smart knows the hoss. Come here, Bob, and mount this hoss, and show Bullet's motions." Here Bullet bristled up, and looked as if he had been hunting for Bob all day long, and had just found him. Bob sprang on his back. "Boo-oo-oo!" said Bob, with a fluttering noise of the lips; and away went Bullet, as if in a quarter race, with all his beauties spread in handsome style.

"Now fetch him back," said Blossom. Bullet turned and came in pretty much as he went out.

"Now trot him by." Bullet reduced his tail to *customary*; sidled to the right and left airily, and exhibited at least three varieties of trot in the short space of fifty yards.

"Make him pace!" Bob commenced twitching the bridle and kicking at the same time. These inconsistent movements obviously (and most naturally) disconcerted Bullet; for it was impossible for him to learn, from them, whether he was to proceed or stand still. He started to trot, and was told that wouldn't do. He attempted a canter, and was checked again. He stopped, and was urged to go on. Bullet now rushed into the wide field of experiment, and struck out a gait of his own, that completely turned the tables upon his rider, and certainly deserved a patent. It seemed to have derived its elements from the jig, the minuet, and the cotillion. If it was not a pace, it certainly had *pace* in it, and no man would venture to call it anything else, so it passed off to the satisfaction of the owner.

"Walk him!" Bullet was now at home again; and he walked as if money was staked on him.

The stranger, whose name, I afterward learned, was Peter Ketch, having examined Bullet to his heart's content, ordered his son Neddy to go and bring up Kit. Neddy soon appeared upon Kit; a well-formed sorrel of the middle size, and in good order. His *tout ensemble* threw Bullet entirely in the shade, though a glance was sufficient to satisfy any one that Bullet had the decided advantage of him in point of intellect.

"Why, man," said Blossom, "do you bring such a hoss as that to trade for Bullet? Oh, I see you're no notion of trading."

"Ride him off, Neddy!" said Peter. Kit put off at a handsome lope.

"Trot him back!" Kit came in at a long, sweeping trot, and stopped suddenly at the crowd.

"Well," said Blossom, "let me look at him; maybe he'll do to plough."

"Examine him!" said Peter, taking hold of the bridle close to the mouth; "he's nothing but a tacky. He an't as *pretty* a horse as Bullet, I know; but he'll do. Start 'em together for a hundred and fifty *mile*; and if Kit an't twenty mile ahead of him at the coming out, any man may take Kit for nothing. But he's a monstrous mean horse, gentleman; any man may see that. He's the scariest horse, too, you ever saw. He won't do to hunt on, no how. Stranger, will you let Neddy have your rifle to shoot off him? Lay the rifle between his ears, Neddy, and shoot at the blaze in that stump. Tell me when his head is high enough."

Ned fired, and hit the blaze; and Kit did not move a hair's breadth.

"Neddy, take a couple of sticks, and beat on that hogshead at Kit's tail."

Ned made a tremendous rattling, at which Bullet took fright, broke his bridle, and dashed off in grand style; and would have stopped all farther negotiations by going home in disgust, had not a traveller arrested him and brought him back; but Kit did not move.

"I tell you, gentlemen," continued Peter, "he's the scariest horse you ever saw. He an't as gentle as Bullet, but he won't do any harm if you watch him. Shall I put him in a cart, gig, or wagon for you, stranger? He'll cut the same capers there he does here. He's a monstrous mean horse."

During all this time Blossom was examining him with the nicest scrutiny. Having examined his frame and limbs, he now looked at his eyes.

"He's got a curious look out of his eyes," said Blossom.

"Oh yes, sir," said Peter, "just as blind as a bat. Blind horses always have clear eyes. Make a motion at his eyes, if you please, sir."

Blossom did so, and Kit threw up his head rather as if something pricked him under the chin than as if fearing a blow. Blossom repeated the experiment, and Kit jerked back in considerable astonishment.

"Stone blind, you see, gentlemen," proceeded Peter; "but he's just as good to travel of a dark night as if he had eyes."

"Blame my buttons," said Blossom, "if I like them eyes."

"No," said Peter, "nor I neither. I'd rather have 'em made of diamonds; but they'll do, if they don't show as much white as Bullet's."

"Well," said Blossom, "make a pass at me."

"No," said Peter; "you made the banter, now make your pass."

"Well, I'm never afraid to price my hosses. You must give me twenty-five dollars boot."

"Oh, certainly; say fifty, and my saddle and bridle in. Here, Neddy, my son, take away Daddy's horse."

"Well," said Blossom, "I've made my pass, now you make yours."

"I'm for short talk in a horse-swap, and therefore always tell a gentleman at once what I mean to do. You must give me ten dollars."

Blossom swore absolutely, roundly, and profanely, that he never would give boot.

"Well," said Peter, "I didn't care about trading; but you cut such high shines, that I thought I'd like to back you out, and I've done it. Gentlemen, you see I've brought him to a hack."

"Come, old man," said Blossom, "I've been joking with you. I begin to think you do want to trade; therefore, give me five dollars and take Bullet. I'd rather lose ten dollars any time than not make a trade, though I hate to fling away a good hoss."

"Well," said Peter, "I'll be as clever as you are. Just put the five dollars on Bullet's back, and hand him over; it's a trade."

Blossom swore again, as roundly as before, that he would not give boot; and, said he, "Bullet wouldn't hold five dollars on his back, no how. But, as I bantered you, if you say an even swap, here's at you."

"I told you," said Peter, "I'd be as clever as you, therefore, here goes two dollars more, just for trade sake. Give me three dollars, and it's a bargain."

Blossom repeated his former assertion; and here the parties stood for a long time, and the by-standers (for many were now collected) began to taunt both parties. After some time, however, it was pretty unanimously decided that the old man had backed Blossom out.

At length Blossom swore he "never would be backed out for three dollars after bantering a man;" and, accordingly, they closed the trade.

"Now," said Blossom, as he handed Peter the three dollars, "I'm a man that, when he makes a bad trade, makes the most of it until he can make a better. I'm for no rues and after-claps."

"That's just my way," said Peter; "I never goes to law to mend my bargains."

"Ah, you're the kind of boy I love to trade with. Here's your hoss, old man. Take the saddle and bridle off him, and I'll strip yours; but lift up the blanket easy from Bullet's back, for he's a mighty tender-backed hoss."

The old man removed the saddle, but the blanket stuck fast. He attempted to raise it, and Bullet bowed himself, switched his tail, danced a little, and gave signs of biting.

"Don't hurt him, old man," said Blossom, archly; "take it off easy. I am, perhaps, a leetle of the best man at a horse-swap that ever catched a coon."

Peter continued to pull at the blanket more and more roughly, and Bullet became more and more *cavortish*: insomuch that, when the blanket came off, he had reached the *kicking* point in good earnest.

The removal of the blanket disclosed a sore on Bullet's back-bone that seemed to have defied all medical skill. It measured six full inches in length and four in breadth, and had as many features as Bullet had motions. My heart sickened at the sight; and I felt that the brute who had been riding him in that situation deserved the halter.

The prevailing feeling, however, was that of mirth. The laugh became loud and general at the old man's expense, and rustic witticisms were liberally bestowed upon him and his late purchase. These Blossom continued to provoke by various remarks. He asked the old man if he thought Bullet would "let five dollars lie on his back." He declared most seriously that he had owned that horse three months, and had never discovered before that he had a sore back, or he "never should have thought of trading him," &c., &c.

The old man bore it all with the most philosophic composure. He evinced no astonishment at his late discovery, and made no replies. But his son Neddy had not disciplined his feelings quite so well. His eyes opened wider and wider from the first to the last pull of the blanket; and, when the whole sore burst upon his view, astonishment and fright seemed to contend for the mastery of his countenance. As the blanket disappeared, he stuck his hands in his breeches pockets, heaved a deep sigh, and lapsed into a profound revery, from which he was only roused by the cuts at his father. He bore them as long as he could; and, when he could contain himself no longer, he began, with a certain wildness of expression which gave a peculiar interest to what he uttered: "His back's mighty bad off; but dod drot my soul if he's put it to Daddy as bad as he thinks he has, for old Kit's both blind and *deef*, I'll be dod drot if he eint."

"The devil he is," said Blossom.

"Yes, dod drot my soul if he *eint*. You walk him, and see if he *eint*. His eyes don't look like it; but he'd *jist as leve go agin* the house with you, or in a ditch, as any how. Now you go try him." The laugh was now turned on Blossom; and many rushed to test the fidelity of the little boy's report. A few experiments established its truth beyond controversy.

"Neddy," said the old man, "you oughtn't to try and make people discontented with their things. Stranger, don't mind what the little boy says. If you can only get Kit rid of them little failings, you'll find him all sorts of a horse. You are a *leetle* the best man at a horse-swap that ever I got hold of; but don't fool away Kit. Come, Neddy, my son, let's be moving; the stranger seems to be getting snappish."

Clyde Edgerton

from Raney

LISTRE, NORTH CAROLINA

APRIL 18, 1975

FROM THE *Hansen County Pilot:*

BETHEL — Mr. and Mrs. Thurman A. Bell announce the engagement of their daughter, Raney, to Charles C. Shepherd of Atlanta, Georgia. Mr. Bell owns the Hope Road General Store and the family attends Bethel Free Will Baptist Church. Raney graduated from Chester F. Knowles High School where she was in the school band and various other activities. She attended Listre Community College.

Charles Shepherd, the son of Dr. and Mrs. William Shepherd of Atlanta, is the assistant librarian at Listre Community College. Dr. Shepherd is a college professor, while Mrs. Shepherd is a public school teacher.

A June 7th wedding is planned at Bethel Free Will Baptist Church. A reception will follow in the education building.

The couple plans to honeymoon at Myrtle Beach and live in Listre at 209 Catawba Drive.

Clyde Edgerton

I

We get married in two days: Charles and me.

Charles's parents are staying at the Ramada — wouldn't stay with any of us — and today me, Mama, Aunt Naomi, and Aunt Flossie ate lunch with Charles's mother, Mrs. Shepherd. And found out that she's, of all things, a vegetarian.

We ate at the K and W. Mrs. Shepherd wanted to eat at some place we could sit down and order — like a restaurant — but Aunt Naomi strongly suggested the K and W. She said the K and W would be more reasonable and the line wouldn't be long on a Thursday. So we ate at the K and W.

I got meatloaf, Mama got meatloaf (they have unusually good meatloaf — not bready at all), Aunt Naomi got turkey, Aunt Flossie got roast beef, and Mrs. Shepherd, Mrs. Shepherd didn't get any meat at all. She got the vegetable plate.

When we got seated Mama said, "I order the vegetable plate every once in a while myself."

"Oh, did you get the vegetable plate?" says Aunt Naomi to Mrs. Shepherd.

"Sure did," says Mrs. Shepherd. "I've stopped eating meat."

We all looked at her.

"I got involved in a group in Atlanta which was putting together programs on simple living and after a few programs I became convinced that being a vegetarian — me, that is — made sense."

Somehow I thought people were *born* as vegetarians. I never thought about somebody just *changing over*.

"What kind of group was that?" asks Mama.

"Several Episcopal women. I'm originally Methodist, but —"

"Naomi!" says this woman walking by holding her tray. "Good gracious, is this all your family?" Her husband went ahead and sat down about three tables over — picked a chair with arms.

"It sure is," says Aunt Naomi. "Let me introduce you. Opal Register, this is my sister-in-law, Doris Bell." (That's Mama.) "You know Doris, don't you?"

"Oh, yes. I think we met in here one time. Right over there."

"And this is her daughter, Raney, who's getting married Saturday."

"Mercy me," says Mrs. Register. She had on big glasses with a chain, little brown curls on the top of her head, and too much lipstick. "You're at the start of a wonderful journey, honey," she says. "It was thirty-seven years for me and Carl the twenty-first of last month. I hope your journey is as happy and fulfilling as ours."

"And this is Mrs. Millie Shepherd, the groom's — groom-to-be's — mother. She's up from Atlanta, Georgia."

"Atlanta!" says Mrs. Register.

"And this is Flossie Purvis, Doris's sister. And ya'll, this is Opal and Carl Register," said Aunt Naomi, pointing toward Mr. Register who had started eating over at his table. He smiled, with food in his mouth. You couldn't see any though.

"Atlanta!" said Mrs. Register again. "You don't know C. C. Lawrence, do you?"

"No, I don't think I do," said Mrs. Shepherd.

"C. C. works at one of the big banks in Atlanta. He got a law degree and a business degree — one right after the other. His mama and daddy didn't think he'd ever finish — and them working at Liggett and Myers. He went —"

"Opal," Mr. Register calls out. "Sit down and eat."

"Well, nice to have met you," said Mrs. Register. "Good luck on that wonderful journey, honey," she says to me.

When Mrs. Register was out of hearing distance, Mama says, "Mr. Register just had a prostrate operation and I don't think he's recovered."

"Prostate," says Aunt Flossie.

"Is it?" says Mama. "Prostate? Oh. You know, I've always liked him better than her. She always makes so much out of every little thing."

The conversation went from the Registers to prostrate operations back around to eating meat.

"You know," says Aunt Naomi, "once in a while I've gone without meat, but I got so weak I thought I'd pass out."

"Well, that happens a bit at first," Mrs. Shepherd says. "But after a few days that usually goes away. It's a matter of what you get used to, I think. The body adjusts."

"I'd be afraid I couldn't get enough proteins," says Mama.

"Oh, no," says Mrs. Shepherd. "There are many protein substitutes for meat. Beans — soybeans, for example — are excellent."

"My next door neighbor, Lillie Cox, brought me some hamburger with soybean in it," said Aunt Naomi, "when I had the flu last winter, and it tasted like cardboard. She's always trying out the latest thing."

"I couldn't do without my meat," says Mama. She was fishing through her tossed salad for cucumber — and putting it on her plate. "I'd be absolutely lost without sausage for breakfast. Cole's sausage. The mild, not the hot. Do they have Cole's in Atlanta?"

"I don't think so. I really don't know."

"Do you get the patties or the links?" Aunt Naomi asks Mama.

"The patties — Thurman don't like the links; they roll off his plate."

We all laughed. Even Mrs. Shepherd, so Mama stretched it out. "Every time we go to Kiwanis for the pancake supper he'll lose one or two links. Because of the way he eats his pancakes — pushes them all around in the syrup. Last time one rolled up under the edge of Sam Lockamy's plate, and for a minute there we couldn't find it. Then Sam swore it was his."

"I guess you have less cholesterol if you don't eat meat," says Aunt Naomi.

"There are health advantages," said Mrs. Shepherd. "And also our women's group has been concentrating on how eating less meat can help curtail hunger in the third world."

"On another *planet?*" says Aunt Naomi.

"Oh, no. Developing nations," says Mrs. Shepherd. She finished chewing and swallowed. "Developing nations."

"What I don't understand," says Aunt Naomi, "is that if they don't eat their own cows, like in India, then why should we send them ours? They wouldn't eat ours, would they? Or maybe they *would* eat American meat."

"We wouldn't send meat to India, of course; we'd send grain and other staple goods. The fewer cows we eat the less grain we'll need to feed cows, so there will be a greater grain surplus."

Aunt Naomi blew her nose on this Kleenex she had been fumbling with. She had a cold. She can get more nose blows on one Kleenex than anybody I ever saw. She always ends up with this tiny corner which she slowly spreads out, then blows her nose into.

We'd finished eating so I said, "Aunt Naomi, you get more nose blows out of one Kleenex than anybody I've ever seen in my life."

"I probably won't be able to sing Sunday," she said. She sings in the church choir. "This cold just drags on and on and on."

"Ain't it nice the way Raney and Charles play music together," says Mama to Mrs. Shepherd. I was relieved to get off the meat subject.

"Yes, it is," says Mrs. Shepherd.

"I think it's wonderful," says Aunt Naomi.

"They sound real good together," says Aunt Flossie.

Music is what brought me and Charles together. He plays banjo and collects old songs from the mountains. When I sang for the faculty at the college Christmas dinner he was there — he's the assistant librarian — and he came up afterward and complimented my singing. He was real nice about it. And has been ever since. Charles is the kind of person who is real natural around people — and is smart as he can be.

Then I met him again when I went to the library to check out a record. They have a good collection, thanks to Charles. One thing led to another and the first thing you know we're playing music together. We've had three or four performances. Kiwanis and such. Charles calls them gigs.

"Charles sent me a tape," says Mrs. Shepherd. "You two sound really good together. You have a beautiful voice, Raney."

I thanked her.

Charles is learning to sing too. We harmonize on two or three songs. He's improving gradually. He plays good banjo. He don't *look* like a banjo picker, but he sounds good.

"I don't know what I'm going to do without Raney singing around the house, and helping out with Norris and Mary Faye," says Mama, looking at me.

"Mama, I'm twenty-four years old," I said.

There's a big gap between me and my little brother, Norris, and sister, Mary Faye. Norris is eight and Mary Faye is eleven. Mary Faye picks on Norris all the time, but sometimes he deserves it.

"How many children do you have, Mrs. Shepherd?" says Aunt Flossie.

"One," says Aunt Naomi.

"Please call me Millie," says Mrs. Shepherd. "All of you," she says, and smiles. "You too, Raney, if you're comfortable with that. I have only one," she says. "Charles is the only one."

II

You would think a man could get married without getting drunk, especially after I explained that nobody in my family drunk alcohol except Uncle Nate, who was in the Navy in World War II, but got burned in combat on over fifty percent of his body, and caught pneumonia and had to be discharged from the Pacific. He had to stay in the hospital for three and a half months. Now he has asthma spells.

Uncle Nate comes to our house in a taxi at any hour of the day or night, drunk, cussing his former wife, who's dead — Joanne. And when I say drunk, I mean so drunk he can't get up the front steps without me and Mama and sometimes the taxi driver helping him. And smell? — Uncle Nate I'm talking about — whew. A sweat-whisky smell that lingers in the house as solid as flower smells at a funeral — lingers long after Mama's undressed him, got him in the tub, and piled his clothes on the back porch. And the thing is, he don't ever get asthma when he's drunk.

Mary Faye and Norris have to stand there in the middle of all that, being influenced in no telling what ways.

When Uncle Nate's sober he's my favorite uncle. I love his stories about when he was growing up with Mama and Aunt Flossie and Uncle Norris (who lives in Charlotte) and their Uncle Pugg. And he always gives me presents and says I'm his favorite niece.

He's always lived with us and worked at Daddy's store part time. His lung troubles make him disabled, so he gets a check every month from the government. They think he inhaled so much smoke he'll never recover. The scars are mostly on his body under his clothes so you can't ever see them except on his left wrist and under his left ear. He never talks about it except to Uncle Newton, who was in the war, too. Sometimes his asthma gets so bad he has to sit perfectly still for three or four hours. So he can't get a job anywhere, of course — except helping Daddy out at the store. Daddy says he makes a big difference and is very dependable — unless he's drunk.

I don't know what Mama will do about getting him out of the taxi and up the steps since I'll be living here in Listre. Mary Faye and Norris will have to help. But Mama hates for them to be exposed to such.

Charles *knew* all about Uncle Nate and how I — how my whole family — feels about drinking.

So at the rehearsal Friday night everything was going fine except Mama caught Norris hiding in the baptism place and made him sit on the front row. She'd already caught him once. I told him the water would flow in there and drown him if he didn't watch out. Mary Faye was one of my attendants and being as smart as she could be.

I'm standing in the back of the church with Daddy and Flora, my cousin, who directed the wedding, and I notice that Charles's friend, Buddy Shellar, from Maryland, who I had never met until that night, keeps going outside. And Charles keeps following him. Phil, Jim, Dale, and Crafton — my cousins — were of course staying in their places like they were supposed to. Flora gives me a little push and I start down the aisle with Daddy. Charles is standing with this red-faced grin. When Preacher Gordon says you may kiss the bride, I turned to Charles and there were three little red blood vessels in his left eye that looked like red thread and all of a sudden I caught a whiff of you-know-what. It hit me. It all suddenly fell together. I thought they had been going outside to *talk*.

The thing you won't believe is: Charles's daddy looked lit too.

I did not kiss Charles. I kept my lips clamped. I grabbed him by the arm and led him right up the aisle and out the front door. Madora Bryant, my maid of honor, and some of the other girls were clapping as hard as they could. They couldn't tell what was really happening. When I got him out on the front porch — right beside the bell rope — I said: (now I was really tore up) "Charles, I have told you for months about the condition Uncle Nate has put our family in with alcohol, and you promised me you would not have a bachelor party and get drunk and here you are, drunk, under the nose of Preacher Gordon, Mama, Daddy, Flora and Aunt Naomi and Aunt Flossie and my bridesmaids and Mary Faye and Norris and I will never forget this as long as I live."

"Raney," he says, "first of all, I am not having a bachelor party, and second of all, I am not drunk. I am not doing anybody any harm. I —"

"Not doing any harm? Charles, I —"

"Raney, Buddy drove all the way down here from Baltimore, Maryland, and he has one little pint of something in his car, and we were in the *war* together and if you will just relax. And he's the *only* one of my close friends in the wedding. All these damn cousins of yours."

"Charles, please do not start cussing right here on church property. And if you are mad about my cousins being in the wedding I would have appreciated you saying something about that before now — like while I was spending all my time getting this whole thing planned."

Charles's daddy, Dr. Shepherd, walks up. I could not believe what was happening, yet I dared not make a scene in front of him. I was thinking that if Mama and Aunt Naomi and Aunt Flossie found out about all this drinking I would die.

"Raney, honey," Dr. Shepherd says, "you look adorable." He's a big man and wears those glasses without any rims — shaped like stop signs. He's a math professor, of all things. A doctor. And Mrs. Shepherd is a school teacher. They use these long words I know Mama and Daddy don't know. And they should know Mama and Daddy don't know them. But they'll go on back down to Atlanta after the wedding and we won't see them except maybe a few times a year. Charles says they belong to a country club and all that. What gets me is that Charles said he explained to them about us being Christians and not drinking which I didn't even know we *had* to explain until Madora told me that

Charles's parents would probably be used to drinking spiked punch at weddings and what were we going to do?

I hadn't thought about it. I've never been to a wedding where they drink liquor in the punch. I mean there's usually a preacher at a wedding and it's usually at a church. But Madora explained how rich people — or at least Episcopalians and Catholics and sometimes Methodists — will get married in church and then ride over to a country club or someplace where they all drink up a storm.

Dr. Shepherd stands there kind of flushed and glassy-eyed and tells me how proud he is — and he laughs at everything he says, funny or not — and I'll be durn if he didn't reach up right then and there and pull the church bell rope and ring the bell. I could just see old Mrs. Bledsoe, down the road, figure it was not Friday night at all, but Wednesday night — prayer meeting night — instead, and get all upset and maybe grab *Mr.* Bledsoe, who can't hear, and cart him off to a prayer meeting which don't exist. Not to mention all the other people in hearing distance.

The rehearsal dinner was in the education building around behind the church. I walked down the church steps between Charles and his daddy — their arms locked through mine — not able to say a word, and hot behind my ears with embarassment at the prospect of a scandal.

When we got to the education building there was Mrs. Shepherd — Millie — standing at the door, smiling.

"Smooth as could be," she said, and kissed Dr. Shepherd on the lips — right there in the door to the education building.

Inside, there were two long tables and a head table. Aunt Naomi was in charge. She had got Betty Winnberry to cater. Steaks. T-bone steaks. French fries. The works. I had hoped all along it wouldn't be tacky — like paper tablecloths, which Aunt Naomi was talking about along at first. I'm certainly not going to be cow-tied to any fancy ways of the Shepherds, but I did want things to be proper for everybody concerned.

On the tables were about twelve or thirteen red-checkered, overlapped tablecloths that Aunt Flossie had borrowed from Penny's Grill (and had to wash and dry later that night in order to get them back to the grill in time for Penny to serve breakfast. They open at six A.M.). And over in the corner Mack Lumley was sitting on a bale of hay playing his guitar. He didn't charge but ten dollars, and furnished the hay, too. Somebody suggested me and Charles sing, but I think singing at your own wedding wouldn't be right.

Aunt Flossie had put together the prettiest flower arrangement — right in the middle of the head table; roses, daisies, and Queen Anne's lace, and pittosporum and nandina for greenery.

Just before supper, Charles and Buddy went out for you-know-what, I guess. I had to keep smiling and be as nice as I could to everybody. The supper *was* meaningful, but while I was cutting a piece of T-bone steak I bent over to Charles and whispered: "Charles, I will never forget this." But Charles just turned to Daddy and started talking about the Braves. They always talk about the Braves. As soon as they see one another they start talking about the Braves. I wanted to say, "Daddy, don't you see what Charles is doing? How can you sit there and talk about the Braves while Charles is doing what he's doing?" But I didn't say anything. Lord knows, there was disturbance enough.

I had spent all that time working out the arrangements and Charles wrote all the invitations by hand — he has this beautiful handwriting — and we had talked all about his new library job and our house and our future and how everything was going to work out, and he had been so good about running little errands. Then this.

Charles is very intelligent, and good looking in his own way — his head is slightly large, but I think it just seems that way because his shoulders are narrow — and, oh, we had one or two little fusses getting ready for the wedding, but no more than you'd shake a stick at. And we've been playing music at different gatherings right along through all this — getting better and better and having lots of fun. Charles learns real fast and we like the same music mostly.

Then I end up sitting at my own wedding rehearsal dinner fussing at Charles for doing the one thing I was hoping against hope wouldn't happen ever since Madora explained about how some people get drunk at weddings. We had talked about drinking several times, and I had this feeling of not being able to get a clear picture of how Charles felt. He talks a lot about "psychology."

The actual wedding itself went off without a hitch. It was the most wonderful day of my life. Charles was perfect. Dr. and Mrs. Shepherd were perfect. Mary Faye and Norris were perfect. Mama and Daddy were perfect. Mama wore a long dress — pink — and she was real pretty, except her hair-do was a little tight. Daddy looked the way he always does at church: out of place in a suit, and his head white where his hat goes, and his face red. (He *looks* like he has high blood pressure, but it's normal and always has been.) Right before we walked down the aisle, he said, "Honey, I'm real happy for you. Charles is a good man." His chin was quivering, and two tears rolled down his cheeks. He was holding my hand, which was something I don't remember him doing since I was a little girl. Daddy don't show much emotion.

A bunch of people said it was the nicest wedding they had ever been to. I was just flushed throughout the whole thing. It went exactly according to plans. Charles was handsomer than I've ever seen him. The shoulders in his tux were padded.

The wedding was fairly short and we all went straight to the reception in the education building *without* getting our pictures made, so people wouldn't have to wait. Mama was real worried about us not getting a photographer, but Mack Lumley did it for only ten dollars over cost.

Mama and Mrs. Shepherd — Millie — cried several times each, and so did Flora and Aunt Naomi and Aunt Flossie, and two or three times Dr. Shepherd gave Millie a long hug right in front of everybody. Charles's friend, Buddy Shellar, spent some time talking to Mary Faye and Norris. I thought that was nice. Buddy and my cousins fixed up our car with tin cans and shaving cream; we changed clothes; Sylvia Curtis caught the bouquet; we ran to Charles's Dodge Dart under all that rice, and headed for Myrtle Beach.

Now. The honeymoon. I do not have the nerve to explain everything that happened on the first night there in the Holiday Inn. We had talked about it some before — or Charles had talked about it. And we had, you know, necked the same as any engaged couple. And I had told Charles way back, of course, that I wanted my marriage consumed *after* I was married. Not before. Because if it was consumed before, then I would have to carry the thought of that throughout my entire life and it's hard to undo that which has already been done.

I've read books. I've had talks with my mama. And I've read the Bible. You'd think that would prepare a woman for her wedding night.

It didn't. First of all, Charles had rib-eye steaks rolled into our room on this metal table with drawers which could keep the steaks warm. And there in the middle of the table was a dozen red roses. All that was nice.

But in this silver bucket with ice and a white towel was, of all things, a bottle of champagne.

It was a predicament for me, because on the one hand it was all so wonderful, and Charles had planned it all out like the man is supposed to do — I mean, my dream was being fulfilled. Charles was getting things right. But on the other hand, there in the middle of the table rearing its ugly head, as they say, was a bottle of champagne. I've seen enough bottles of champagne after the World Series on TV (when the ballplayers make fools out of themselves and cuss over the airways) to know one when I see it.

Well, I'm not a prude. Getting drunk at your wedding is one thing, but I can understand a little private celebrating, maybe — as a symbol of something wonderful happening. Something symbolic. So I didn't say anything about the champagne. It's very hard to find fault on your wedding night with a dozen red roses staring you full in the face — even though a still, small voice was warning me.

Charles poured me a glass and I said to myself, Why not just a sip, like medicine, and I tried a sip, but that's all. It tasted like Alka Seltzer with honey in it. I politely refused anymore. And didn't think Charles would drink over a glass. (I figured you couldn't buy it except in the bottle, and that's why he got it that way.)

We finished eating and Charles pushed the table, with the dishes, out into the hall. I said excuse me, went into the bathroom, put on my negligee and got ready, you know, and came back out to find Charles standing there in his Fruit of the Loom, drinking champagne out of a plastic cup. It was a terrible scene to remember.

I was planning to do what Mama explained to me: get in the bed and let Charles carry out his duties. And I was thinking that's what Charles would be planning to do. But. He had a different idea which I do not have the nerve to explain. It turned into an argument which finally turned into a sort of Chinese wrestling match with my nerves tore all to pieces. Charles kept saying nothing was in the Bible about what married people could or couldn't do. I finally cried, and Charles said he was sorry. It was awful. I cried again the next morning and Charles said he was sorry again. This may be something I can forgive but I don't think I'll ever forget it. Not for a long time.

On the second day, we didn't say much at breakfast, or after. We went to the beach for a while, ate hot dogs for lunch, and then came back to change clothes. Charles asked the manager about us playing music in the motel lounge that night. (We took our instruments in case we got a chance to play.) When he found out we'd do it free the manager said fine.

So on the second night, rather than going to this country music show like we'd planned, we met the manager in the lounge. Charles wore bluejeans and I wore my blue-checkered blouse, jeans, and cowgirl hat. The manager came in and lit all the candles in these orange candle vases. There were only three or four people there. The only thing I didn't like about it was that they served beer. But the bartender went out of his way to be nice.

We decided to play half an hour and see if we could draw an audience. We started with several banjo pieces and then I sang "This World Is Not My Home" and "I'll Fly Away." I like the way those two songs fit together. It gives me something to talk about when I introduce them. Charles is good about letting me talk about the songs. I have played with people who hog it all.

A crowd gathered, and sure enough they liked the music and clapped and somebody requested "Your Cheating Heart" and Charles tried it.

He's been learning it for the last month or so. He forgets words pretty easy. Nobody noticed but he sang the same verse twice. He looked at me and I managed to wink in spite of the fact I was still in turmoil from the night before.

We had told the manager we couldn't play past nine-thirty that night. We told him it was our honeymoon and all. The truth is we only know about two hours worth of songs. But I did want to get back up to our bed and start our marriage in the proper manner. It's something I had been thinking about since I was sixteen or seventeen years old and the night before had *not* worked out at all like I thought it would. It had made me a bundle of nerves and I had discovered something in Charles I didn't know existed — something corroded, and him drinking a whole bottle of champagne brought it out. He still hasn't taken serious my principles about drinking. That first night was a awful experience which I can't bring myself to talk about, but I must say things went better on the second night. I was able to explain to Charles how I was supposed to come out of the bathroom in my negligee, go get in the bed, get under the cover, and then he was supposed to go to the bathroom, come out, come get under the cover, and accomplish what was supposed to be accomplished. It all worked the way it was supposed to, and was wonderful, I must say.

Next morning when I came out of the shower, before we went down for breakfast, Charles was talking on the phone to his other main friend besides Buddy Shellar: Johnny Dobbs, who lives in New Orleans. They were all three in the army together.

"She has a great voice," he was saying. "Raney, get your guitar. Wait a minute, Johnny."

Charles put the phone receiver on the bed, got out his banjo, hit a couple of licks and said to me, "Do 'This World Is Not My Home.' Wait a minute, let me introduce you to Johnny." So he did, over the phone, and Johnny sounded real nice.

"Charles," I whispered, "do you know how much this is costing?"

"I'll pay for it," he said. "I've been telling Johnny about your voice."

So I sang "This World Is Not My Home," and Charles asked Johnny if he could hear it clear over the phone and he said he could and then Charles wanted me to do my chicken song — the one I wrote. Charles thinks it's the funniest thing he's ever heard. It *is* a good song, and since Charles was paying. . . . It goes like this:

The town council chairman came by late last May.
Said we're sorry, Mr. Oakley, 'bout what we must say.
But the airport's expanding, we mean you no harm.
The new north-south runway's gonna point toward your farm.

My chicken's ain't laying; my cow has gone dry,
'Cause the airplanes keep flying to the sweet by and by,
To the lights of the city, to the Hawaiian shore,
While I rock on my front porch and tend to get poor.

I talked to the governor, and told him my desire:
Could you please make them airplanes fly a little bit higher.
"My chickens ain't laying," I tried to explain.
But my words were going north on a south-bound train.

My chickens ain't laying; my cow has gone dry,
'Cause the airplanes keep flying to the sweet by and by,
To the lights of the city, to the Hawaiian shore,
While I rock on my front porch and tend to get poor.

I talked to a doctor; he gave me a pill.
I talked to a lawyer; you should have seen the bill.
I talked to a librarian; he grinned and winked his eye.
And he gave me a little book called, "Chickens Can Fly."
(Charles says the book is by B. F. Skinner)

I read the little book. Taught my chickens to fly,
To aim at the intakes as the jet planes flew by.
My chickens are gone now, but the answer is found:
My kamakazi chickens closed the new runway down.
My kamakazi chickens closed the new runway down.

When I finished, Charles said Johnny really liked it. They talked about another fifteen minutes before Charles finally hung up.

I hugged Charles and said something about the night before. Charles said we ought to *talk* about our "sexual relationship" sometime, and I said okay, but Lord knows I won't be able to *talk* about it. It's something you're supposed to do in a natural manner, not *talk* about. That's why you don't find it talked about in church and school — or at least you shouldn't: it's not supposed to be talked about. It's something which is supposed to stay in the privacy of your own bedroom.

Next morning when we left, the manager was at the desk and he gave us an envelope with a twenty dollar bill in it. Said it was some of the best entertainment they ever had and would we please come back and that he once worked in a hotel in Reno, and he'd heard some better, but he'd sure heard a lot worse.

Erskine Caldwell

The Fly in the Coffin

THERE WAS POOR old Dose Muffin, stretched out on the corn-crib floor, dead as a frostbitten watermelon vine in November, and a pesky housefly was walking all over his nose.

Let old Dose come alive for just one short minute, maybe two while about it, and you could bet your last sock-toe dollar that pesky fly wouldn't live to do his ticklish fiddling and stropping on any human's nose again.

"You, Woodrow, you!" Aunt Marty said. "Go look in that corncrib and take a look if any old flies worrying Dose."

"Uncle Dose don't care now," Woodrow said. "Uncle Dose don't care about nothing no more."

"Dead or alive, Dose cares about flies," Aunt Marty said.

There wasn't enough room in the house to stretch him out in. The house was full of people, and the people wanted plenty of room to stand around in. There was that banjo-playing fool in there, Hap Conson, and Hap had to have plenty of space when he was around. There was that jigging high-yellow gal everybody called Goodie, and Goodie took all the room there was when she histed up her dress and started shaking things.

Poor old Dose, dead a day and a night, couldn't say a word. That old fly was crawling all over Dose's nose, stopping every now and then to strop its wings and fiddle its legs. It had been only a day and a night since Dose had chased a fly right through the buzz saw at the lumber mill. That buzz saw cut Dose just about half in two, and he died mad as heck about the fly getting away all well and alive. It wouldn't make any difference to Dose, though, if he could wake up for a minute, maybe two while about it. If he could only do that, he would swat that pesky fly so hard there wouldn't be a flyspeck left.

"You, Woodrow, you!" Aunt Marty said. "Go like I told you do and see if any old flies worrying Dose."

"You wouldn't catch me swatting no flies on no dead man," Woodrow said.

"Don't swat them," Aunt Marty said. "Just shoo them."

Back the other side of the house they were trying to throw a makeshift coffin together for Dose. They were doing a lot of trying and only a little bit of building. Those lazybones out there just didn't have their minds on the work at all. The undertaker wouldn't come and bring one, because he wanted sixty dollars, twenty-five down. Nobody had no sixty dollars, twenty-five down.

Soon as they got the coffin thrown together, they'd go and bury poor old Dose, provided Dose's jumper was all starched and ironed by then. The jumper was out there swinging on the clothesline, waving in the balmy breeze, when the breeze came that way.

Old Dose Muffin, lying tickled-nosed in the corncrib, was dead and wanted burying as soon as those lazy, big-mouthed, good-for-nothing sawmill hands got the grave dug deep enough. He could have been put in the ground a lot sooner if that jabbering preacher and that mush-mouthed black boy would have laid aside their jawboning long enough to finish the coffin they were trying to throw together. Nobody was in a hurry like he was.

That time-wasting old Marty hadn't started washing out his jumper till noon, and if he had had his way, she would have got up and started at the break of day that morning. That banjo-playing fool in the house there, Hap Conson, had got everybody's mind off the burial, and nobody had time to come out to the corncrib and swat that pesky fly on Uncle Dose's nose and say howdy-do. That skirt-histing high-yellow in there, Goodie, was going to shake the house down, if she didn't shake off her behind first, and there wasn't a soul in the world cared enough to stop ogling Goodie long enough to come out to the crib to see if any pesky flies needed chasing away.

Poor old Dose died a ragged-pants sawmill hand, and he didn't have no social standing at all. He had given up the best job he had ever had in his life, when he was porter in the white-folks' hotel, because he went off chasing a fly to death just because the fly lit on his barbecue sandwich just when he was getting ready to bite into it. He chased that fly eight days all over the country, and the fly wouldn't have stopped long enough then to let Dose swat him if it hadn't been starved dizzy. Poor old Dose came back home, but he had to go to work in the sawmill and lost all his social standing.

"You, Woodrow, you!" Aunt Marty said. "How many times does it take to tell you go see if any old flies worrying Dose?"

"I'd be scared to death to go moseying around a dead man, Aunt Marty," Woodrow said. "Uncle Dose can't see no flies no way."

"Dose don't have to be up and alive like other folks to know about flies," she said. "Dose sees flies, he dead or alive."

The jumper was dry, the coffin was thrown together, and the grave was six feet deep. They put the jumper on Dose, stretched him out in the box, and dropped him into the hole in the ground.

That jabbering preacher started praying, picking out the pine splinters he had stuck into his fingers when he and that mush-mouthed black boy were throwing together the coffin. That banjo-playing Hap Conson squatted on the ground, picking at the thing like it was red-hot coals in a tin pan. Then along came that Goodie misbehaving, shaking everything that wouldn't be still every time she was around a banjo-plucking.

They slammed the lid on Dose, and drove it down to stay with a couple of rusty twenty-penny nails. They shoveled in a few spades of gravel and sand.

"Hold on there," Dose said.

Marty was scared enough to run, but she couldn't. She stayed right there, and before long she opened one eye and squinted over the edge into the hole.

"What's the matter?" Marty asked, craning her neck to see down into the ground. "What's the matter with you, Dose?"

The lid flew off, the sand and gravel pelting her in the face, and Dose jumped to his feet, madder than he had ever been when he was living his life.

145

"I could wring your neck, woman!" Dose shouted at her.

"What don't please you, Dose?" Marty asked him. "Did I get too much starch in the jumper?"

"Woman," Dose said, shaking his fist at her, "you've been neglecting your duty something bad. You're stowing me away in this here ground with a pesky fly inside this here coffin. Now, you get a hump on yourself and bring me a fly swatter. If you think you can nail me up in a box with a fly inside it, you've got another think coming."

"I always do like you say, Dose," Marty said. "You just wait till I run get the swatter."

There wasn't a sound made anywhere. The shovelers didn't shovel, Hap didn't pick a note, and Goodie didn't shake a thing.

Marty got the swatter fast as she could, because she knew better than to keep Dose waiting, and handed it down to him. Dose stretched out in the splintery pine box and pulled the lid shut.

Pretty soon they could hear a stirring around down in the box.

"Swish!" the fly swatter sounded.

"Just hold on and wait," Marty said, shaking her head at the shovelers.

"Swish!" the fly swatter sounded.

"Dose got him," Marty said, straightening up. "Now shovel boys, shovel!"

The dirt and sand and gravel flew in, and the grave filled up. The preacher got his praying done, and most of the splinters out of his fingers. That banjo-playing fool, Hap Conson, started acting like he was going to pick that thing to pieces. And that behind-shaking high-yellow, Goodie, histed her dress and went misbehaving all over the place. Maybe by morning Hap and Goodie would be in their stride. Wouldn't be too sure about it, though, because the longer it took to get the pitch up, the longer it would last.

William Faulkner

from The Hamlet

FRENCHMAN'S BEND WAS a section of rich river-bottom country lying twenty miles southeast of Jefferson. Hill-cradled and remote, definite yet without boundaries, straddling into two counties and owning allegiance to neither, it had been the original grant and site of a tremendous pre-Civil War plantation, the ruins of which — the gutted shell of an enormous house with its fallen stables and slave quarters and overgrown gardens and brick terraces and promenades — were still known as the Old Frenchman's place, although the original boundaries now existed only on old faded records in the Chancery Clerk's office in the county courthouse in Jefferson, and even some of the once-fertile fields had long since reverted to the cane-and-cypress jungle from which their first master had hewed them.

He had quite possibly been a foreigner, though not necessarily French, since to the people who had come after him and had almost obliterated all trace of his sojourn, anyone speaking the tongue with a foreign flavor or whose appearance or even occupation was strange, would have been a Frenchman regardless of what nationality he might affirm, just as to their more urban coevals (if he had elected to settle in Jefferson itself, say) he would have been called a Dutchman. But now nobody knew what he had actually been, not even Will Varner, who was sixty years old and now owned a good deal of his original grant, including the site of his ruined mansion. Because he was gone now, the foreigner, the Frenchman, with his family and his slaves and his magnificence. His dream, his broad acres were parcelled out now into small shiftless mortgaged farms for the directors of Jefferson banks to squabble over before selling finally to Will Varner, and all that remained of him was the river bed which his slaves had straightened for almost ten miles to keep his land from flooding and the skeleton of the tremendous house which his heirs-at-large had been pulling down and chopping up — walnut newel posts and stair spindles, oak floors which fifty years later would have been almost priceless, the very clapboards themselves — for thirty years now for firewood. Even his name was forgotten, his pride but a legend about the land he had wrested from the jungle and tamed as a monument to that appellation which those who came after him in battered wagons and on muleback and even on foot, with flintlock rifles and dogs and children and home-made whiskey stills and Protestant psalm-books, could not even read, let alone pronounce, and which now had nothing to do with any once-living man at all — his dream and his pride now dust with the lost dust of his anonymous bones, his legend but the stubborn tale of the money he buried somewhere about the place when Grant overran the country on his way to Vicksburg.

The people who inherited from him came from the northeast, through the Tennessee mountains by stages marked by the bearing and raising of a generation of children. They came from the Atlantic seaboard and before that, from England and the Scottish and Welsh Marches, as some of the names would indicate — Turpin and Haley and Whittington, McCallum and Murray and Leonard and Littlejohn, and other names like Riddup and Armstid and Doshey which could have come from nowhere since certainly no man would deliberately select one of them for his own. They brought no slaves and no Phyfe and Chippendale highboys; indeed, what they did bring most of them could (and did) carry in their hands. They took up land and built one- and two-room cabins and never painted them, and married one another and produced children and added other rooms one by one to the original cabins and did not paint them either, but that was all. Their descendants still planted cotton in the bottom land and corn along the edge of the hills and in the secret coves in the hills made whiskey of the corn and sold what they did not drink. Federal officers went into the country and vanished. Some garment which the missing man had worn might be seen — a felt hat, a broadcloth coat, a pair of city shoes or even his pistol — on a child or an old man or woman. County officers did not bother them at all save in the heel of election years. They supported their own churches and schools, they married and committed infrequent adulteries and more frequent homicides among themselves and were their own courts judges and executioners. They were Protestants and Democrats and prolific; there was not one Negro landowner in the entire section. Strange Negroes would absolutely refuse to pass through it after dark.

Will Varner, the present owner of the Old Frenchman place, was the chief man of the country. He was the largest landholder and beat supervisor in one county and Justice of the Peace in the next and election commissioner in both, and hence the fountainhead if not of law at least of advice and suggestion to a countryside which would have repudiated the term constituency if they had ever heard it, which came to him, not in the attitude of *What must I do* but *What do you think you think you would like for me to do if you was able to make me do it*. He was a farmer, a usurer, a veterinarian; Judge Benbow of Jefferson once said of him that a milder-mannered man never bled a mule or stuffed a ballot box. He owned most of the good land in the country and held mortgages on most of the rest. He owned the store and the cotton gin and the combined grist mill and blacksmith shop in the village proper and it was considered, to put it mildly, bad luck for a man of the neighborhood to do his trading or gin his cotton or grind his meal or shoe his stock anywhere else. He was thin as a fence rail and almost as long, with reddish-gray hair and moustaches and little hard bright innocently blue eyes; he looked like a Methodist Sunday School superintendent who on week days conducted a railroad passenger train or vice versa and who owned the church or perhaps the railroad or perhaps both. He was shrewd secret and merry, of a Rabelaisian turn of mind and very probably still sexually lusty (he had fathered sixteen chidren to his wife, though only two of them remained at home, the others scattered, married and buried, from El Paso to the Alabama line) as the spring of his hair which even at sixty was still more red than gray, would indicate. He was at once active and lazy; he did nothing at all (his son managed all the family business) and spent all his time at it,

149

out of the house and gone before the son had come down to breakfast even, nobody knew where save that he and the old fat white horse which he rode might be seen anywhere within the surrounding ten miles at any time, and at least once every month during the spring and summer and early fall, the old white horse tethered to an adjacent fence post, he would be seen by someone sitting in a home-made chair on the jungle-choked lawn of the Old Frenchman's homesite. His blacksmith had made the chair for him by sawing an empty flour barrel half through the middle and trimming out the sides and nailing a seat into it, and Varner would sit there chewing his tobacco or smoking his cob pipe, with a brusque word for passers cheerful enough but inviting no company, against his background of fallen baronial splendor. The people (those who saw him sitting there and those who were told about it) all believed that he sat there planning his next mortgage foreclosure in private, since it was only to an itinerant sewing-machine agent named Ratliff — a man less than half his age — that he ever gave a reason: "I like to sit here. I'm trying to find out what it must have felt like to be the fool that would need all this" — he did not move, he did not so much as indicate with his head the rise of old brick and tangled walks topped by the columned ruin behind him — "just to eat and sleep in." Then he said — and he gave Ratliff no further clue to which might have been the truth — "For a while it looked like I was going to get shut of it, get it cleared up. But by God folks have got so lazy they won't even climb a ladder to pull off the rest of the boards. It looks like they will go into the woods and even chop up a tree before they will reach above eyelevel for a scantling of pine kindling. But after all, I reckon I'll just keep what there is left of it, just to remind me of my one mistake. This is the only thing I ever bought in my life I couldn't sell to nobody."

The son, Jody, was about thirty, a prime bulging man, slightly thyroidic, who was not only unmarried but who emanated a quality of invincible and inviolable bachelordom as some people are said to breathe out the odor of sanctity or spirituality. He was a big man, already promising a considerable belly in ten or twelve years, though as yet he still managed to postulate something of the trig and unattached cavalier. He wore, winter and summer (save that in the warm season he dispensed with the coat) and Sundays and week days, a glazed collarless white shirt fastened at the neck with a heavy gold collar-button beneath a suit of good black broadcloth. He put on the suit the day it arrived from the Jefferson tailor and wore it every day and in all weathers thereafter until he sold it to one of the family's Negro retainers, so that on almost any Sunday night one whole one or some part of one of his old suits could be met — and promptly recognized — walking the summer roads, and replaced it with the new succeeding one. In contrast to the unvarying overalls of the men he lived among he had an air not funereal exactly but ceremonial — this because of that quality of invincible bachelorhood which he possessed: so that, looking at him you saw, beyond the flabbiness and the obscuring bulk, the perennial and immortal Best Man, the apotheosis of the masculine Singular, just as you discern beneath the dropsical tissue of the '09 halfback the lean hard ghost which once carried a ball. He was the ninth of his parents' sixteen children. He managed the store of which his father was still titular owner and in which they dealt mostly in foreclosed mortgages, and the gin, and oversaw the scattered farm holdings which his father at first and later the two of them together had been acquiring during the last forty years.

One afternoon he was in the store, cutting lengths of plowline from a spool of new cotton rope and looping them in neat seamanlike bights onto a row of nails in the wall, when at a sound behind him he turned and saw, silhouetted by the open door, a man smaller than common, in a wide hat and a frock coat too large for him, standing with a curious planted stiffness. "You Varner?" the man said, in a voice not harsh exactly, or not deliberately harsh so much as rusty from infrequent use.

"I'm one Varner," Jody said, in his bland hard quite pleasant voice. "What can I do for you?"

"My name is Snopes. I heard you got a farm to rent."

"That so?" Varner said, already moving so as to bring the other's face into the light. "Just where did you hear that?" Because the farm was a new one, which he and his father had acquired through a foreclosure sale not a week ago, and the man was a complete stranger.

He had never even heard the name before.

The other did not answer. Now Varner could see his face — a pair of eyes of a cold opaque gray between shaggy graying irascible brows and a short scrabble of iron-gray beard as tight and knotted as a sheep's coat. "Where you been farming?" Varner said.

"West." He did not speak shortly. He merely pronounced the one word with a complete inflectionless finality, as if he had closed a door behind himself.

"You mean Texas?"

"No."

"I see. Just west of here. How much family you got?"

"Six." Now there was no perceptible pause, nor was there any hurrying on into the next word. But there was something. Varner sensed it even before the lifeless voice seemed deliberately to compound the inconsistency: "Boy and two girls. Wife and her sister."

"That's just five."

"Myself," the dead voice said.

"A man don't usually count himself among his own field hands," Varner said. "Is it five or is it seven?"

"I can put six hands into the field."

Now Varner's voice did not change either, still pleasant, still hard: "I don't know as I will take on a tenant this year. It's already almost first of May. I figure I might work it myself, with day labor. If I work it at all this year."

"I'll work that way," the other said. Varner looked at him.

"Little anxious to get settled, ain't you?" The other said nothing. Varner could not tell whether the man was looking at him or not. "What rent were you aiming to pay?"

"What do you rent for?"

"Third and fourth," Varner said. "Furnish out of the store here. No cash."

"I see. Furnish in six-bit dollars."

"That's right," Varner said pleasantly. Now he could not tell if the man were looking at anything at all or not.

"I'll take it," he said.

Standing on the gallery of the store, above the half dozen overalled men sitting or squatting about it with pocket knives and slivers of wood, Varner watched his caller limp stiffly across the porch, looking neither right nor left, and descend and from among the tethered teams and saddled animals below the gallery choose a gaunt saddleless mule in a worn plow bridle with rope reins and lead it to the steps and mount awkwardly and stiffly and ride away, still without once looking to either side. "To hear that ere foot, you'd think he weighed two hundred pounds," one of them said. "Who's he, Jody?"

Varner sucked his teeth and spat into the road. "Name's Snopes," he said.

"Snopes?" a second man said. "Sho now. So that's him." Now not only Varner but all the others looked at the speaker — a gaunt man in absolutely clean though faded and patched overalls and even freshly shaven, with a gentle, almost sad face until you unravelled what were actually two separate expressions — a temporary one of static peace and quiet overlaying a constant one of definite even though faint harriedness, and a sensitive mouth which had a quality of adolescent freshness and bloom until you realized that this could just as well be the result of a lifelong abstinence from tobacco — the face of the breathing archetype and protagonist of all men who marry young and father only daughters and are themselves but the eldest daughter of their own wives. His name was Tull. "He's the fellow that wintered his family in a old cottonhouse on Ike McCaslin's place. The one that was mixed up in that burnt barn of a fellow named Harris over in Grenier County two years ago."

"Huh?" Varner said. "What's that? Burnt barn?"

"I never said he done it," Tull said. "I just said he was kind of involved in it after a fashion you might say."

"How much involved in it?"

"Harris had him arrested into court."

"I see," Varner said. "Just a pure case of mistaken identity. He just hired it done."

"It wasn't proved," Tull said. "Leastways, if Harris ever found any proof afterward, it was too late then. Because he had done left the

country. Then he turned up at McCaslin's last September. Him and his
family worked by the day, gathering for McCaslin, and McCaslin let
them winter in a old cottonhouse he wasn't using. That's all I know. I
ain't repeating nothing."

"I wouldn't," Varner said. "A man don't want to get the name of a
idle gossip." He stood above them with his broad bland face, in his
dingy formal black-and-white — the glazed soiled white shirt and the
bagging and uncared-for trousers — a costume at once ceremonial and
negligee. He sucked his teeth briefly and noisily. "Well well well," he
said. "A barn burner. Well well well."

That night he told his father about it at the supper table. With the
exception of the rambling half-log half-sawn plank edifice known as
Littlejohn's hotel, Will Varner's was the only house in the country with
more than one storey. They had a cook too, not only the only Negro
servant but the only servant of any sort in the whole district. They had
had her for years yet Mrs. Varner still said and apparently believed that
she could not be trusted even to boil water unsupervised. He told it that
evening while his mother, a plump cheery bustling woman who had
borne sixteen children and already outlived five of them and who still
won prizes for preserved fruits and vegetables at the annual County
Fair, bustled back and forth between dining room and kitchen, and his
sister, a soft ample girl with definite breasts even at thirteen and eyes
like cloudy hothouse grapes and a full damp mouth always slightly
open, sat at her place in a kind of sullen bemusement of rife young
female flesh, apparently not even having to make any effort not to
listen.

"You already contracted with him?" Will Varner said.

"I hadn't aimed to at all till Vernon Tull told me what he did. Now I
figure I'll take the paper up there tomorrow and let him sign."

"Then you can point out to him which house to burn too. Or are you
going to leave that to him?"

"Sho," Jody said. "We'll discuss that too." Then he said — and now
all levity was gone from his voice, all poste and riposte of humor's light
whimsy, tierce quarto and prime: "All I got to do is find out for sho
about that barn. But then it will be the same thing, whether he actually

did it or not. All he'll need will be to find out all of a sudden at
gathering time that I think he did it. Listen. Take a case like this." He
leaned forward now, over the table, bulging, protuberant, intense. The
mother had bustled out, to the kitchen, where her brisk voice could be
heard scolding cheerfully at the Negro cook. The daughter was not
listening at all. "Here's a piece of land that the folks that own it hadn't
actually figured on getting nothing out of this late in the season. And
here comes a man and rents it on shares that the last place he rented on
a barn got burnt up. It don't matter whether he actually burnt that barn
or not, though it will simplify matters if I can find out for sho he did.
The main thing is, it burnt while he was there and the evidence was
such that he felt called on to leave the country. So here he comes and
rents this land we hadn't figured on nothing out of this year nohow and
we furnish him outen the store all regular and proper. And he makes his
crop and the landlord sells it all regular and has the cash waiting and
the fellow comes in to get his share and the landlord says, 'What's this I
heard about you and that barn?' That's all. 'What's this I just heard
about you and that barn?' " They stared at one another — the slightly
protuberant opaque eyes and the little hard blue ones. "What will he
say? What can he say except 'All right. What do you aim to do?' "

"You'll lose his furnish bill at the store."

"Sho. There ain't no way of getting around that. But after all, a man
that's making you a crop free gratis for nothing, at least you can afford
to feed him while he's doing it. — Wait," he said. "Hell fire, we won't
even need to do that; I'll just let him find a couple of rotten shingles
with a match laid across them on his doorstep the morning after he
finishes laying-by and he'll know it's all up then and ain't nothing left
for him but to move on. That'll cut two months off the furnish bill and
all we'll be out is hiring his crop gathered." They stared at one another.
To one of them it was already done, accomplished: he could actually
see it; when he spoke it was out of a time still six months in the future
yet: "Hell fire, he'll have to! He can't fight it! He don't dare!"

"Hmph," Will said. From the pocket of his unbuttoned vest he took
a stained cob pipe and began to fill it. "You better stay clear of them
folks."

"Sho now," Jody said. He took a toothpick from the china receptacle on the table and sat back. "Burning barns ain't right. And a man that's got habits that way will just have to suffer the disadvantages of them."

He did not go the next day nor the one after that either. But early in the afternoon of the third day, his roan saddle horse hitched and waiting at one of the gallery posts, he sat at the roll-top desk in the rear of the store, hunched, the black hat on the back of his head and one broad black-haired hand motionless and heavy as a ham of meat on the paper and the pen in the other tracing the words of the contract in his heavy deliberate sprawling script. An hour after that and five miles from the village, the contract blotted and folded neatly into his hip pocket, he was sitting the horse beside a halted buckboard in the road. It was battered with rough usage and caked with last winter's dried mud, it was drawn by a pair of shaggy ponies as wild and active-looking as mountain goats and almost as small. To the rear of it was attached a sheet-iron box the size and shape of a dog kennel and painted to resemble a house, in each painted window of which a painted woman's face simpered above a painted sewing machine, and Varner sat his horse and glared in shocked and outraged consternation at its occupant, who had just said pleasantly, "Well, Jody, I hear you got a new tenant."

"Hell fire!" Varner cried. "Do you mean he set fire to another one? even after they caught him, he set fire to *another* one?"

"Well," the man in the buckboard said, "I don't know as I would go on record as saying he set ere a one of them afire. I would put it that they both taken fire while he was more or less associated with them. You might say that fire seems to follow him around, like dogs follows some folks." He spoke in a pleasant, lazy, equable voice which you did not discern at once to be even more shrewd than humorous. This was Ratliff, the sewing-machine agent. He lived in Jefferson and he travelled the better part of four counties with his sturdy team and the painted dog kennel into which an actual machine neatly fitted. On successive days and two counties apart the splashed and battered buckboard and the strong mismatched team might be seen tethered in the nearest shade and Ratliff's bland affable ready face and his neat tieless blue shirt one of the squatting group at a crossroads store, or — and still squatting and still doing the talking apparently though actually doing a good deal more listening than anybody believed until afterward — among the women surrounded by laden clotheslines and tubs and blackened wash pots beside springs and wells, or decorous in a splint chair on cabin galleries, pleasant, affable, courteous, anecdotal and impenetrable. He sold perhaps three machines a year, the rest of the time trading in land and livestock and second-hand farming tools and musical instruments or anything else which the owner did not want badly enough, retailing from house to house the news of his four counties with the ubiquity of a newspaper and carrying personal messages from mouth to mouth about weddings and funerals and the preserving of vegetables and fruit with the reliability of a postal service. He never forgot a name and he knew everyone, man, mule and dog, within fifty miles. "Just say it was following along behind the wagon when Snopes druv up to the house De Spain had given him, with the furniture piled into the wagon bed like he had druv up to the house they had been living in at Harris's or wherever it was and said 'Get in here' and the cookstove and beds and chairs come out and got in by their selves. Careless and yet good too, tight, like they was used to moving and not having no big help at it. And Ab and that big one, Flem they call him — there was another one too, a little one; I remember seeing him once somewhere. He wasn't with them. Leastways he ain't now. Maybe they forgot to tell him when to get outen the barn. — setting on the seat and them two hulking gals in the two chairs in the wagon bed and Miz Snopes and her sister, the widow, setting on the stuff in back like nobody cared much whether they come along or not either, including the furniture. And the wagon stops in front of the house and Ab looks at it and says, 'Likely it ain't fitten for hawgs.' "

Sitting the horse, Varner glared down at Ratliff in protuberant and speechless horror. "All right," Ratliff said. "Soon as the wagon stopped Miz Snopes and the widow got out and commenced to unload. Them two gals ain't moved yet, just setting there in them two chairs, in their Sunday clothes, chewing sweet gum, till Ab turned round and cussed them outen the wagon to where Miz Snopes and the widow was wrastling with the stove. He druv them out like a pair of heifers just a little too valuable to hit hard with a stick, and then him and Flem set there and watched them two strapping gals take a wore-out broom and a lantern outen the wagon and stand there again till Ab leant out and snicked the nigh one across the stern with the end of the reins. 'And then you come back and help your maw with that stove,' he hollers after them. Then him and Flem got outen the wagon and went up to call on De Spain.''

"To the barn?" Varner cried. "You mean they went right straight and —''

"No no. That was later. The barn come later. Likely they never knowed just where it was yet. The barn burnt all regular and in due course; you'll have to say that for him. This here was just a call, just pure friendship, because Snopes knowed where his fields was and all he had to do was to start scratching them, and it already the middle of May. Just like now," he added in a tone of absolutely creamlike innocence. "But then I hear tell he always makes his rent contracts later than most." But he was not laughing. The shrewd brown face was as bland and smooth as ever beneath the shrewd impenetrable eyes.

"Well?" Varner said violently. "If he sets his fires like you tell about it, I reckon I don't need to worry until Christmas. Get on with it. What do he have to do before he starts lighting matches? Maybe I can recognize at least some of the symptoms in time."

"All right," Ratliff said. "So they went up the road, leaving Miz Snopes and the widow wrastling at the cookstove and them two gals standing there now holding a wire rat-trap and a chamber pot, and went up to Major de Spain's and walked up the private road where that pile of fresh horse manure was and the nigger said Ab stepped in it on deliberate purpose. Maybe the nigger was watching them through the front window. Anyway Ab tracked it right across the front porch and knocked and when the nigger told him to wipe it offen his feet, Ab shoved right past the nigger and the nigger said he wiped the rest of it off right on that ere hundred-dollar rug and stood there hollering 'Hello. Hello, De Spain' until Miz de Spain come and looked at the

rug and at Ab and told him to please go away. And then De Spain come home at dinner time and I reckon maybe Miz de Spain got in behind him because about middle of the afternoon he rides up to Ab's house with a nigger holding the rolled-up rug on a mule behind him and Ab setting in a chair against the door jamb and De Spain hollers 'Why in hell ain't you in the field?' and Ab says, he don't get up or nothing, 'I figger I'll start tomorrow. I don't never move and start to work the same day,' only that ain't neither here nor there; I reckon Miz de Spain had done got in behind him good because he just set on the horse a while saying 'Confound you Snopes, confound you Snopes' and Ab setting there saying 'If I had thought that much of a rug I don't know as I would keep it where folks coming in would have to tromp on it.'"
Still he was not laughing. He just sat there in the buckboard, easy and relaxed, with his shrewd intelligent eyes in his smooth brown face, well-shaved and clean in his perfectly clean faded shirt, his voice pleasant and drawling and anecdotal, while Varner's suffused swollen face glared down at him.

"So after a while Ab hollers back into the house and one of them strapping gals comes out and Ab says, 'Take that ere rug and wash it.' And so next morning the nigger found the rolled-up rug throwed onto the front porch against the door and there was some more tracks across the porch too only it was just mud this time and it was said how when Miz de Spain unrolled the rug this time it must have been hotter for De Spain than before even — the nigger said it looked like they had used brickbats instead of soap on it — because he was at Ab's house before breakfast even, in the lot where Ab and Flem was hitching up to go to the field sho enough, setting on the mare mad as a hornet and cussing a blue streak, not at Ab exactly but just sort of at all rugs and all horse manure in general and Ab not saying nothing, just buckling hames and choke strops until at last De Spain says how the rug cost him a hundred dollars in France and he is going to charge Ab twenty bushels of corn for it against his crop that Ab ain't even planted yet. And so De Spain went back home. And maybe he felt it was all neither here nor there now. Maybe he felt that long as he had done something about it Miz de Spain would ease up on him and maybe come gathering time he would

a even forgot about that twenty bushels of corn. Only that never suited
Ab. So here, it's the next evening I reckon, and Major laying with his
shoes off in the barrel-stave hammock in his yard and here comes the
bailiff hemming and hawing and finally gets it out how Ab has done
sued him —"

"Hell fire," Varner murmured. "Hell fire."

"Sho," Ratliff said. "That's just about what De Spain hisself said
when he finally got it into his mind that it was so. So it come Sat-dy
and the wagon druv up to the store and Ab got out in that preacher's hat
and coat and tromps up to the table on that clubfoot where Uncle Buck
McCaslin said Colonel John Sartoris his-self shot Ab for trying to steal
his clay-bank riding stallion during the war, and the Judge said, 'I done
reviewed your suit, Mr Snopes, but I ain't been able to find nothing
nowhere in the law bearing on rugs, let alone horse manure. But I'm
going to accept it because twenty bushels is too much for you to have to
pay because a man as busy as you seem to stay ain't going to have time
to make twenty bushels of corn. So I am going to charge you ten
bushels of corn for ruining that rug.' "

"And so he burnt it," Varner said. "Well well well."

"I don't know as I would put it just that way," Ratliff said, repeated.
"I would just put it that that same night Major de Spain's barn taken
fire and was a total loss. Only somehow or other De Spain got there on
his mare about the same time, because somebody heard him passing in
the road. I don't mean he got there in time to put it out but he got there
in time to find something else already there that he felt entitled to
consider enough of a foreign element to justify shooting at it, setting
there on the mare and blasting away at it or them three or four times
until it run into a ditch on him where he couldn't follow on the mare.
And he couldn't say neither who it was because any animal can limp if
it wants to and any man is liable to have a white shirt, with the
exception that when he got to Ab's house (and that couldn't a been
long, according to the gait the fellow heard him passing in the road) Ab
and Flem wasn't there, wasn't nobody there but the four women and
De Spain never had time to look under no beds and such because there
was a cypress-roofed corn crib right next to that barn. So he rid back to

where his niggers had done fetched up the water barrels and was soaking towsacks to lay on the crib, and the first person he see was Flem standing there in a white-colored shirt, watching it with his hands in his pockets, chewing tobacco. 'Evening,' Flem says. 'That ere hay goes fast' and De Spain setting on the horse hollering 'Where's your paw? Where's that —' and Flem says, 'If he ain't here somewhere he's done went back home. Me and him left at the same time when we see the blaze.' And De Spain knowed where they had left from too and he knowed why too. Only that wasn't neither here nor there neither because, as it was just maintained, any two fellows anywhere might have a limp and a white shirt between them and it was likely the coal oil can he seen one of them fling into the fire when he shot the first time. And so here the next morning he's setting at breakfast with a right smart of his eyebrows and hair both swinged off when the nigger comes in and says it's a fellow to see him and he goes to the office and it's Ab, already in the preacher hat and coat and the wagon done already loaded again too, only Ab ain't brought that into the house where it could be seen. 'It looks like me and you ain't going to get along together,' Ab says, 'so I reckon we better quit trying before we have a misunderstanding over something. I'm moving this morning.' And De Spain says, 'What about your contract?' And Ab says, 'I done cancelled it.' and De Spain setting there saying 'Cancelled. Cancelled' and then he says, 'I would cancel it and a hundred more like it and throw in that barn too just to know for sho if it was you I was shooting at last night.' And Ab says, 'You might sue me and find out. Justices of the Peace in this country seems to be in the habit of finding for plaintiffs.' "

"Hell fire," Varner said quietly again. "Hell fire."

"So Ab turned and went stomping out on that stiff foot and went back —"

"And burnt the tenant house," Varner said.

"No no. I ain't saying he might not a looked back at it with a certain regret, as the fellow says, when he druv off. But never nothing else taken all of a sudden on fire. Not right then, that is. I don't —"

"That's so," Varner said. "I recollect you did say he had to throw the balance of the coal oil into the fire when De Spain started shooting at him. Well well well," he said, bulging, slightly apoplectic. "And now, out of all the men in this country, I got to pick him to make a rent contract with." He began to laugh. That is, he began to say "Ha. Ha. Ha." rapidly, but just from the teeth, the lungs: no higher, nothing of it in the eyes. Then he stopped. "Well, I can't be setting here, no matter how pleasant it is. Maybe I can get there in time to get him to cancel with me for just a old cottonhouse."

"Or at least maybe for a empty barn," Ratliff called after him.

An hour later Varner was sitting the halted horse again, this time before a gate, or a gap that is, in a fence of sagging and rusted wire. The gate itself or what remained of it lay unhinged to one side, the interstices of the rotted palings choked with grass and weed like the ribs of a forgotten skeleton. He was breathing hard but not because he had been galloping. On the contrary, since he had approached near enough to his destination to believe he could have seen smoke if there had been smoke, he had ridden slower and slower. Nevertheless he now sat the horse before the gap in the fence, breathing hard through his nose and even sweating a little, looking at the sagging broken-backed cabin set in its inevitable treeless and grassless plot and weathered to the color of an old beehive, with that expression of tense and rapid speculation of a man approaching a dud howitzer shell. "Hell fire," he said again quietly. "Hell fire. He's been here three days now and he ain't even set the gate up. And I don't even dare to mention it to him. I don't even dare to act like I knowed there was even a fence to hang it to." He twitched the reins savagely. "Come up!" he said to the horse. "You hang around here very long standing still and you'll be a-fire too."

The path (it was neither road nor lane: just two parallel barely discernible tracks where wagon wheels had run, almost obliterated by this year's grass and weeds) went up to the sagging and stepless porch of the perfectly blank house which he now watched with wire-taut wariness, as if he were approaching an ambush. He was watching it with such intensity as to be oblivious to detail. He saw suddenly in one of the sashless windows and without knowing when it had come there, a face beneath a gray cloth cap, the lower jaw moving steadily and rhythmically with a curious sidewise thrust, which even as he shouted "Hello!" vanished again. He was about to shout again when he saw beyond the house the stiff figure which he recognized even though the frock coat was missing now, doing something at the gate to the lot. He had already begun to hear the mournful measured plaint of a rusted well-pulley, and now he began to hear two flat meaningless loud female voices. When he passed beyond the house he saw it — the narrow high frame like an epicene gallows, two big absolutely static young women beside it, who even in that first glance postulated that immobile dreamy solidarity of statuary (this only emphasized by the fact that they both seemed to be talking at once and to some listener — or perhaps just circumambience — at a considerable distance and neither listening to the other at all) even though one of them had hold of the well-rope, her arms extended at full reach, her body bent for the down pull like a figure in a charade, a carved piece symbolizing some terrific physical effort which had died with its inception, though a moment later the pulley began again its rusty plaint but stopped again almost immediately, as did the voices also when the second one saw him, the first one paused now in the obverse of the first attitude, her arms stretched downward on the rope and the two broad expressionless faces turning slowly in unison as he rode past.

He crossed the barren yard littered with the rubbish — the ashes, the shards of pottery and tin cans — of its last tenants. There were two women working beside the fence too and they were all three aware of his presence now because he had seen one of the women look around. But the man himself (Durn little clubfooted murderer, Varner thought with that furious helpless outrage) had not looked up nor even paused in whatever it was he was doing until Varner rode directly up behind him. The two women were watching him now. One wore a faded sunbonnet, the other a shapeless hat which at one time must have belonged to the man and holding in her hand a rusted can half full of bent and rusted nails. "Evening," Varner said, realizing too late that he was almost shouting. "Evening, ladies." The man turned, deliberately, holding a hammer — a rusted head from which both claws had been broken, fitted onto an untrimmed stock of stove wood — and once more Varner looked down into the cold impenetrable agate eyes beneath the writhen overhang of brows.

"Howdy," Snopes said.

"Just thought I'd ride up and see what your plans were," Varner said, too loud still; he could not seem to help it. I got too much to think about to have time to watch it, he thought, beginning at once to think, Hell fire. Hell fire, again, as though proving to himself what even a second's laxity of attention might bring him to.

"I figure I'll stay," the other said. "The house ain't fitten for hogs. But I reckon I can make out with it."

"But look here!" Varner said. Now he was shouting; he didn't care. Then he stopped shouting. He stopped shouting because he stopped speaking because there was nothing else to say, though it was going through his mind fast enough: Hell fire. Hell fire. Hell fire. I don't dare say Leave here, and I ain't got anywhere to say Go there. I don't even dare to have him arrested for barn-burning for fear he'll set my barn a-fire. The other had begun to turn back to the fence when Varner spoke. Now he stood half-turned, looking up at Varner not courteously and not exactly patiently, but just waiting. "All right," Varner said. "We can discuss the house. Because we'll get along all right. We'll get along. Anything that comes up, all you got to do is come down to the store. No, you don't even need to do that: just send me word and I'll ride right up here as quick as I can get here. You understand? Anything, just anything you don't like—"

"I can get along with anybody," the other said. "I been getting along with fifteen or twenty different landlords since I started farming. When I can't get along with them, I leave. That all you wanted?"

All, Varner thought. All. He rode back across the yard, the littered grassless desolation scarred with the ashes and charred stick-ends and blackened bricks where pots for washing clothes and scalding hogs had sat. I just wish I never had to have but just the little I do want now, he thought. He had been hearing the well-pulley again. This time it did not cease when he passed, the two broad faces, the one motionless, the other pumping up and down with metronome-like regularity to the wheel's not-quite-musical complaint, turning slowly again as though riveted and synchronized to one another by a mechanical arm as he went on beyond the house and into the imperceptible lane which led to the broken gate which he knew would still be lying there in the weeds when he saw it next. He still had the contract in his pocket, which he had written out with that steady and deliberate satisfaction which, it now seemed to him, must have occurred in another time, or more likely, to another person altogether. It was still unsigned. *I could put a fire-clause in it,* he thought. But he did not even check the horse. *Sho,* he thought. *And then I could use it to start shingling the new barn.* So he went on. It was late, and he eased the horse into a rack which it would be able to hold nearly all the way home, with a little breathing on the hills, and he was travelling at a fair gait when he saw suddenly, leaning against a tree beside the road, the man whose face he had seen in the window of the house. One moment the road had been empty, the next moment the man stood there beside it, at the edge of a small copse — the same cloth cap, the same rhythmically chewing jaw materialized apparently out of nothing and almost abreast of the horse, with an air of the complete and purely accidental which Varner was to remember and speculate about only later. He had almost passed the other before he pulled the horse up. He did not shout now and now his big face was merely bland and extremely alert. "Howdy," he said. "You're Flem, ain't you? I'm Varner."

"That so?" the other said. He spat. He had a broad flat face. His eyes were the color of stagnant water. He was soft in appearance like Varner himself, though a head shorter, in a soiled white shirt and cheap gray trousers.

"I was hoping to see you," Varner said. "I hear your father has had a little trouble once or twice with landlords. Trouble that might have been serious." The other chewed. "Maybe they never treated him right; I don't know about that and I don't care. What I'm talking about is a mistake, any mistake, can be straightened out so that a man can still stay friends with the fellow he ain't satisfied with. Don't you agree to that?" The other chewed steadily. His face was as blank as a pan of uncooked dough. "So he won't have to feel that the only thing that can prove his rights is something won't that will make him have to pick up and leave the country next day," Varner said. "So that there won't come a time some day when he will look around and find out he has run out of new country to move to." Varner ceased. He waited so long this time that the other finally spoke, though Varner was never certain whether this was the reason or not:

"There's a right smart of country."

"Sho," Varner said pleasantly, bulging, bland. "But a man don't want to wear it out just moving through it. Especially because of a matter that if it had just been took in hand and straightened out to begin with, wouldn't have amounted to nothing. That could have been straightened out in five minutes if there had just been some other fellow handy to take a hold of a fellow that was maybe a little high-tempered to begin with say, and say to him, 'Hold up here, now; that fellow don't aim to put nothing on you. All you got to do is consult with him peaceable and it will be fixed up. I know that to be a fact because *I got his promise to that effect.*' " He paused again. "Especially if this here fellow we are speaking of, that could take a hold of him and tell him that, was going to get a benefit out of keeping him quiet and peaceable." Varner stopped again. After a while the other spoke again:

"What benefit?"

"Why, a good farm to work. Store credit. More land if he felt he could handle it."

"Ain't no benefit in farming. I figure on getting out of it soon as I can."

"All right," Varner said. "Say he wanted to take up some other line, this fellow we're speaking of. He will need the good will of the folks he aims to make his money off of to do it. And what better way —"

"You run a store, don't you?" the other said.

"— better way —" Varner said. Then he stopped. "What?" he said.

"I hear you run a store."

Varner stared at him. Now Varner's face was not bland. It was just completely still and completely intent. He reached to his shirt pocket and produced a cigar. He neither smoked nor drank himself, being by nature so happily metabolized that, as he might have put it himself, he could not possibly have felt better than he naturally did. But he always carried two or three. "Have a cigar," he said.

"I don't use them," the other said.

"Just chew, hah?" Varner said.

"I chew up a nickel now and then until the suption is out of it. But I ain't never lit a match to one yet."

"Sho now," Varner said. He looked at the cigar; he said quietly: "And I just hope to God you and nobody you know ever will." He put the cigar back into his pocket. He expelled a loud hiss of breath. "All right," he said. "Next fall. When he has made his crop." He had never been certain just when the other had been looking at him and when not, but now he watched the other raise his arm and with his other hand pick something infinitesimal from the sleeve with infinitesimal care. Once more Varner expelled his breath through his nose. This time it was a sigh. "All right," he said. "Next week then. You'll give me that long, won't you? But you got to guarantee it." The other spat.

"Guarantee what?" he said.

Two miles further on dusk overtook him, the shortening twilight of late April, in which the blanched dogwoods stood among the darker trees with spread raised palms like praying nuns; there was the evening star and already the whippoorwills. The horse, travelling supperward, was going well in the evening's cool, when Varner pulled it to a stop and held it for a full moment. "Hell fire," he said. "He was standing just exactly where couldn't nobody see him from the house."

Guy Owen

from The Ballad of the Flim-Flam Man

PRETTY SOON WE drove out of the swamps and into corn and cotton and tobacco country. The corn was all eared out and the tobacco was cropped way up the stalks, but the cotton hadn't busted out yet. Only a few bolls was leaking white. The August sun was clear as a bell in the blue sky.

Mr. Jones, he studied his map and we turned off on a bumpy clay road that won't even marked and headed back into the sticks, through scraggy pine thickets, back where the owls roost with the chickens. After a mile or so we passed some ramshackly tobacco barns with rusty tin roofs, then we come to a bunch of signs, tacky wooden signs, that was religious. There was one every mile or so, sort of new looking. "Prepare to Meet Thy God," "Are You Saved?", "Repent or Ye Shall Perrish." The one I remember best, it was this big red heart that said "Jesus Loves," a sort of six-foot valentine, which some rapscallion had shot twice with a shotgun.

Mr. Jones says, "I hope their religion is more orthodox than their spelling."

I never did take to such ignorant signs nohow. I could maybe stand cluttering up the roads with ads for falsies or toilet paper, even, but not religion, for God's sake. I'm not too religious, I reckon, but that kind of thing bothers me. These crazy bastards had so many signs saying "Prepare to Meet God" you expected to meet Him around the next curve, dressed up maybe in a tux or something. I swear.

Pa was the same way, so I guess I took it after him. He never could stand to see one of them religious signs. He'd cuss and carry on something awful every time he glimpsed one, working himself up into a lather, until he'd just have to haul out his old rusty pistol and shoot it as full of holes as rat cheese. It always seemed to rest him, getting it out of his system that way.

Anyhow, the only thing we met was the Reverend Doakus, not God at all, this poor excuse for a gospel slinger. We spied his little one-horse tent up the road with his gaudy billboard topped by two flags, and all right close to a big country store. A ladder was still leaning against a large sign that said DYNAMITE DOAKUS. It was getting on toward sundown, so we decided to stop there for the night.

We went in the store to get a bite to eat, and that's when we met up with old Dynamite, who turned out to be a right lively customer.

I recognized him right off, because his picture was plastered all over his signs and the storefront, only they didn't make him look as bald as he was. He was setting on a nail keg gnawing on a moonpie and drinking a bellywasher. There was a plumpish, sexy-looking brunette eating beside him, with this little lady, Miss Dobbins, that run the store, hovering around them and waiting on them like they was maybe God and the Virgin Mary.

I just bought a box of gingersnaps and a can of Vienna sausages and eased away from the counter. All the tacky signs had took my appetite and, besides, I didn't want to get too friendly with Doakus. I didn't like his looks much the first time I saw his picture tacked up back there at Lovick's store by the baboon in the circus poster, and seeing him in the flesh didn't improve matters a speck.

But not Mr. Jones. He didn't do nothing but waltz right over and shake old Dynamite's paw so hard he nearabout dropped his moonpie. I thought Mr. Jones would purely eat the both of them up, from all his sweet talk and glad hand. It would of made me sick, but of course I reasoned he had some cunning scheme behind it all.

Thinks I, You can include me out of this one, old hoss. Me and that kind of religion just don't mix.

But no, he introduced himself as Mr. Jonathan Edwards, shaking hands again, then waved over to me. Said I was Mr. Mather and was working my way through the seminary by helping him sell Bibles during the summer and was a crackerjack salesman and had wide experience playing the guitar and leading the choir at church singings and I don't know what all. I had to nod and grin like a possum, soaking in the prime malarkey. But I won't in the mood for it and I went on nibbling at my gingersnaps, setting on a twenty-pound saltlick and leaning against the far counter.

And old Doakus was so flattered and taken in he warmed up and got right sociable. He introduced his lady friend, Miss Letty Queen.

"She takes care of my organ for me," he says in a deep voice, laughing sort of and winking at the Flim-Flam Man. "She's Brother Dynamite's organist."

I'll be hanged if they ain't the exact words he used. And he kept on referring to himself as Brother Dynamite, a habit I've never been exactly mad about. Truth is, the old onionhead looked to me more like a wet firecracker than a stick of dynamite.

I commenced feeling right sorry for the organ lady, her having to listen to him all the time. But I reckon she deserved him and could put up with his rotten mouth. I watched her setting there close by him in this purple silk dress that she'd sweated through, her meaty legs crossed so you could see where her stockings was rolled. She kept a pukey little smile on her face, turning it on I and Mr. Jones. I hate to admit it but she looked sexy as all hell. But built for comfort instead of speed, as the old saying goes.

Mr. Jones, he got wound up then, and it was a pleasure just to hear him stretch his blanket and sling the bull. I can't recall it all, he spread it on so thick. He run on about what a joy it was for him to devote his autumn years to selling Bibles, spreading what little good he could in his humble manner, trying to be a little beacon of positive light in a world of chaos and darkness.

Mr. Jones didn't let old Bogus — that's what my pardner called him, not to his face naturally — he never let Bogus get a word in edgewise. He went on a mile a minute, every now and then slapping the Bible which anchored his coat pocket. He said he'd been a minister of the gospel once in his life and it was a great disappointment when he had to give it up, one he'd never really recover from until his dying day. Said he'd had a nice little Church of God congregation out in the Midwest.

Then he pointed to his throat and his voice sort of cracked. It was his voice, he said, that forced him into retirement. He had this operation at the Mayo Clinic for cancer of the throat, and after that his voice never could hold up under the strain of a good sermon. Said he wasn't bitter, because taking all things into consideration reviewing his life, he was fortunate to be free and alive, able to do what little service for the people he could.

Which, I had to agree, was true enough.

Well, the upshot of it was old Bogus and the organist expressed their sympathies and the store lady said she'd never been so touched in all her life and wouldn't take a penny for our eats.

Bogus says, "I'd be much obliged if you'd attend our little service tonight."

"We wouldn't miss it for the world, would we, Brother Mather?"

Then the preacher asked Mr. Jones to testify, if he was so moved, and lead in a prayer, and begged me to play.

I told him I had a blister on my thumb.

But Mr. Jones said he would consider it a rare privilege and honor to participate, though his voice would not allow him to testify. He could feel it weakening just from their pleasant conversation. "But you can rely on me, sir. We'll certainly take some part in your revival before it's over."

Thinks I, Amen to that. I knew my pardner hadn't stopped there just to buy a moonpie.

Bogus and Miss Queen stood up to leave and get ready for the tent meeting. He said he didn't think we'd be disappointed. So far he had accomplished a power of good. It was hard to be humble about all the good he had wrought, with the Lord's help, of course.

"I don't claim no special healing powers, Brother Edwards, but at our first meeting Monday an old lady that hadn't seen a speck in ten years, not since her husband died, got back her sight and walked out of my tent right by herself."

"You don't mean it."

"Oh, but he does," says Miss Queen. Kind of snotty.

After they'd left, Miss Dobbins took up and run on about what a ring-tailed miracle it was, the Widow Baldwin suddenly seeing after all them years. The poor soul had died of a heart attack the next night on the way to the tent, but that just went to prove it was even more of a miracle.

Mr. Jones asked if we could park behind the store too, close to Bogus's house trailer. She said we could, she'd be honored to have us. So I went out and drove our red truck around back, out of the common view. We still had a few cases of moonshine left and I judged Mr. Jones aimed to work the tent meeting and get shut of what we wouldn't keep for home consumption, as he called it. There's no place like a tent meeting for peddling panther juice.

Anyhow, about dark we moseyed on over towards the meeting place. Right in front of the tent, near the pasture gate where the cars and wagons drove in, was a big sign. It was topped by two flags and said in big letters: "For All People of All Belief," and under that: "Soul-Stirring Scriptural Gospel Preaching." In even bigger letters it said: "Blazing the Old-Timey Sawdust Trail with Dynamite Doakus."

Mr. Jones whispers, "Now, lad, you'll get an opportunity to observe a real flim-flammer operate. This you have to see to believe." Mr. Jones said he knew because his father had been an evangelist in his day — which was news to me. I never dreamed of the Flim-Flam Man having a bunkshooter for a father.

"I think I've been here before," I says. I remembered all the times I'd been drug to revivals by poor Aunt Doshie — though it never did a particle of good.

We walked under the tent and took a back seat and I gawked a bit. There was mostly old folks inside, men in overalls and women with their hair done up in buns. There was a scattering of young girls, mostly culls, fanning theirselves. It was hot, though both sides of the tent was rolled up as far as they'd go. I felt mighty sorry for all them folks because you could see they was actually looking forward to hearing the evening's message. A pity.

Directly, Old Bogus bounced up on his little platform in a loud checked coat and a blazing tie. He give himself a little time to warm up the crowd, starting out with a few jokes as old as the Bible, just to show he was a regular sort. The crowd didn't laugh much, though. I judged they hadn't *come* to laugh.

Next he had everybody on their feet singing "Amazing Grace" and "Old Time Religion." The sexy organist set down and played the organ, which was close by the pulpit. It looked like she had six or seven pillows on her bench. Why, I don't know, because she had plenty of padding built in of her own. One thing I'll say for Miss Queen though: she could play the hell out of the organ. She naturally made that "Old Time Religion" get up and *hump*.

When Bogus let her, she could play. But he kept hogging the show. He was always breaking in and lining out the verses, begging the folks to put their souls into the next verse, to make the old tent shimmy with some soul-shaking singing. Said it would wake up the Devil and make him mad as fire — and I reckon there was truth in that, too.

By now the crowd was a little more peart. I dare say he judged they was ripe for his message, because all of a sudden he shucked off his checked coat and loosened the knot in his yellow tie and started in. Sweat was already popping out on his face and onion head, and considerable lightning bugs was swirling around his jug ears.

Peering around, he said he saw some new faces under his blessed tent. Maybe some folks there had never heard Brother Dynamite before and he hoped and prayed it would be a real experience for them, one they'd not likely forget.

It was.

Course he hadn't come here to uphold Brother Dynamite. He'd come to divide the Good Book with these simple people and put shame on the horny head of Old Scratch. Amen.

"I don't rightly know what I'm gonna say to you tonight, but I got a notion I'm gonna make some of you stand up in your chairs and grovel on the mourners' bench before you quit this tent."

Then he naturally pitched in and flung himself all over the place. He waved his arms like a windmill gone crazy, and skipped off and on the platform like a goat jumping on and off a barrel. Said he was proud to be a simple instrument of the Lord's. He knew some high-toned folks that give themselves airs and thought he was ridiculous and dog-hauled him for believing in and preaching the old-fashioned gospel. But he wanted to do what he could to save good old-timey religion before it was too late. Before the communists and invisible demons took over and divided the world betwixt them. He was just a simple backwoods preacher, but wherever he pitched his tent, the devil had to pack up his satchel and go.

"Amen!" somebody shouts.

"Glory halleluyah!"

Things begun to get livelier. The preacher got louder and louder, cavorting and prancing about more. He tore into the modernists that was turning the church into a cocktail club and ripped into the evils of strong drink and communism and greed and any other sin he could lay his hands on handy. Oh, he was dead set against sin. Then he snatched up the Bible and divided out a passel of scripture, sweating more and more. Pretty soon things got as lively as a mess of frog legs in a skillet.

Directly, old Bogus called for tithes and offerings, though he said he hated to do it. It was the only part of the ministry that went against his grain. Said he was a humble and poor man and led a simple life, which he urged them all to embrace so they might be happy and simple like him. Then he held up a letter and said it contained about the worst news he'd ever had and called it catastrophic and a calamity. It turned out the rent was due on his home in Queen City and his wife and five little girls was about to be thrown out into the cold street — and he had no one to turn to for succor except them.

He never passed the plate. Old Bogus just held out his hand and asked anybody who was a true Christian to come up and manifest it. And Miss Queen, she struck up "Nearer My God To Thee," and almost all of them poor folks went up the aisle and shelled out. Mr. Jones went up, too, and handed him some folding money. Me, I wouldn't give him one buffalo, old Doakus, and I'm glad now I didn't.

But the way the others forked it over I judge he got a heap more by having them put it right in his paw than he would of by passing the hat. You just naturally couldn't walk up there, with the light shining right on you, and hand him a measly dime.

What happened after that, I can't even hope to tell, and I'm sorely tempted not to try. I'd heard Pa tell of such doings when he was a pup, but I always thought he was stretching it, like he generally did. He used to tell about them old-timey brush arbor meetings — just to aggravate Aunt Doshie. About how the folks all fell out and whooped it up and the young bucks went just to see the girls' tails when they was thrashing their frocks up.

Anyhow, the way the crowd there got religion was a sight to behold in this world. I thought they'd purely shake that little tent down over our ears and suffocate us all. And that's a cold fact. I just hunkered down in a back seat, out of sight sort of, taking it all in next to this whisky-slobbering brother in a blue denim jumper. I reckon my eyes was popping out of my head because Mr. Jones put a finger to his mouth to caution me — quiet. I didn't mean to make fun, mind you. I just set there hunched over, solemn as an owl.

To tell the truth though, they wouldn't of noticed if I'd jumped up and recited the Gettysburg Address. For crying out loud, I could of set the damn tent on *fire*, and they wouldn't of took note of it. A bunch of them was whooping it up over in the Amen Corner to theirselves, and a scattering up front had already sprawled out face down, trembling. They was working their legs and bowed up in knots, and popping their teeth, and quaking like a mule passing briars in a thunderstorm. One old buzzard was circling around on all fours, barking like a dog, uncommonly like a black and tan. A handful was setting bolt upright, their noses flared out like spooked mules and their eyes bulging, and jabbering in some kind of language I couldn't make heads nor tails of.

Mr. Jones said later it was the unknown tongue, and I reckon it was *unknown*, at that. And all of them was making their noises, if it won't nothing but to shout "Amen!" every now and then — just to prove they had religion, too, more than likely. I reckon the whippoorwills outside was scared spitless, for I never heard another peep out of them.

And old Dynamite, why, he knocked the socks off any gospel slinger I ever laid eyes on. He was spitting out words so fast you'd of thought he was an auctioneer asking for bids on Beulah Land. The words fairly flew out of his mouth — and considerable spit, too, if you want the whole truth. He spoke so familiar of hell you'd of thought he was born and raised there. I couldn't make much of the words generally — I never tried hard — but he had a right catchy rhythm, and he kept time by bouncing his old bald head up and down like a dang cork and rolling his eyes back till the whites all showed as clean as the girls' drawers — which interested me more.

All of a sudden, when a new candidate keeled off a bench and commenced chewing grass and sawdust, Bogus rushed down and doused the back of their necks with this what-you-may-call-it he had corked up in a glass bottle. Healing oil, he called it. Some sort of sauce. He'd souse them up good and rub it into their necks like it was vaseline, talking, spewing all the time, never so much as missing a beat.

And if it was a girl needing the oil, he'd lean close over her and maybe give her a goose or two. I didn't *see* him do it, but I wouldn't put it past him, the old ring-tailed rascal. One thing for sure, none of them girls would of cared, the shape they was in, carrying on so — not even if the Devil slipped them a good one, I bet. He never did souse that barking fool, though. He never could run him down and catch him. Come to think of it, I reckon old Bogus was scared the son of a bitch might bite him!

All of a sudden, when things got sort of calm and dull the old baldheaded knocker nearabout broke up the meeting. He was sweating now like a boar chinch in somebody's belly button, mopping his waddled jowls with a snot rag as big as a diaper. By jinks, he ups and cracks his heels together and shouts out, "I'm going to heaven, you all. Watch old Dynamite go through them pearly gates. Look out, Peter, here I come!"

And be swiggered if the old codger didn't climb the tent pole, with the whole crowd singing out "Halleluyah!" at his heels. He'd climb a little stretch, then clamp his knees in and stop and preach some more, with the folks all begging him to go on, shouting encouragement, some of them clapping their hands. And that crazy scudder that thought he was a dog treed him up the pole and barked considerable — though I admit it won't much like a hound that's treed. I wouldn't want to exaggerate.

Then Dynamite, he'd snake up the pole a little higher, yelling out at the top of his lungs, "Look out, Peter. Throw them gates open, 'cause Brother Dynamite's on the way!"

Every so often he'd stop and just pant awhile and bulge his eyes out and blow, kind of like a treed possum. Then he'd commence slipping a foot or so, like someone had greased the pole, holding on for dear life. Said it was old Satan dragging him down, and he popped his heels and joggled his feet, trying to fling Old Scratch off. But no, he couldn't shake him and he slid another yard or so. He allowed it was sin weighing him down, dragging like lead, his sins and the sins of all the congregation. And them poor souls groaned and pleaded and I don't know what all.

Directly, he sung out and commenced to climb some more. He mortally tore up the pole like a monkey, jerking his knees up to his chin and yanking up, the way you see a cat do that's chased hellbent for leather up a tree. Only this time he never stopped, just huffed and puffed right on up there. When he reached the top he slapped the canvas and let out a bellow that must of echoed a solid mile. And they pitched in below and capped it until my ears rung.

"It hain't easy," Bogus shouts, "it hain't easy gitting through the narrow gates. It's no soft job for the fainthearted. No, sir. I tell you it takes some get-up-and-go. It takes *humping* to git to Beulah Land." Then he croaks "Glory be, I'm a-coming, I'm a-coming."

I reckon he was, too, the way he was shagging the tent pole.

Then Brother Dynamite up and loosed his grip, sliding down the pole with his eyes shut and his big feet dancing on thin air. Oh, I tell you, it was lively, lively.

Time he struck the ground he bounced back on the platform and took up his sermon again, if you can name it that. He commenced to putting the stopper on it, kindly rounding it off. The shouting and the barking and such like swaged down a trifle, and the unknown tongues, too. Bogus allowed everybody could get to heaven, just like he'd showed them, if they'd follow his example. Then he ripped into Judas, who he didn't seem to admire much and next he climbed over on Peter and flogged him awhile. I saw he intended to wind up with Peter, if his breath didn't fail him.

At last, he mopped his red face again and struck a pose, one arm stretched out and his shadow froze behind him on the tent. He reared back and roars, "Let me leave you with this question. How many Peters are there here tonight?"

I declare, I just set still and waited for the tent to cave in. But no, it just showed what a double-distilled fool I was. Because you could of heard a gnat sneeze. There won't a solitary snort and nobody offered to snigger.

Then old Bogus called on Mr. Jones.

The Flim-Flam Man, he stood up and prayed over them a little, and I judged they needed it after all the commotion. There won't no flies on his prayer neither, it was short and sweet.

Which was the end of the meeting. Folks got up in a daze and staggered out of the tent, kind of like they was in a dream, or a nightmare. Some rose up from the ground with sawdust and grass stains on their clothes.

There was a dozen or so young bucks waiting at the tent flaps for the girls, and I saw the grins on their faces. They just took them stunned skirts by the arms as they crept out. And won't they all ripe for plucking, though?

It didn't seem fair to me somehow. It's like taking advantage of a woman that's stewed with booze, or shooting a dove that's lit on a post. But I wouldn't of been interested nohow. The frizzled-headed gals was pure rutabagas.

But there won't time to fret about the mud turtles that was about to be plucked. I gathered me a crowd of young bucks and old farmers and ambled in the dark over to the truck. They won't a bit laggard about it. In no time flat I sold about fifty dollars worth of bottled corn, more I'll bet than Bogus's collection come to. Which is no more than right, since Doodle's spirits was even more soul-stirring than old Dynamite's ranting.

When I went back to report to my pardner, he was standing tall and solemn under the tent, shaking hands up front with old Bogus and a white-haired deacon.

I thinks to myself, What's he leading up to now, Lord?

Jefferson Humphries

Quincy

MRS. ELBERT WAS driving the yardman home. It was midday and the sky was a pale blue so bright it stung her eyes and made her squint and blink. In the rearview mirror of the old white Chrysler she saw her brother Quincy, looking small and drawn and bright pink and as if lightning had struck him and left everything intact except his brain. The sight of him pulled her spirits down and seemed to drag them through the red clay ditches on the sides of the road. He was like a crime she suddenly remembered having committed, a black cancer on her soul which could never be lifted. The thought of him subtly and persistently tainted her every pleasure like a thimbleful of Ennis's acrid sweat baked into a cake. She could not let herself despise Quincy because after all it was not his fault he was eighty-eight years old and had lost his sense. She was a Presbyterian and he was a burden God had visited on her, not to test her strength and her virtue but to prove them. She sometimes told herself it would have been better to live in a shack like Ennis and have it fixed up nice and pleasant like some Negroes — Viney for instance who cooked for them and who was white in everything but her skin, who was clean and did not sweat — than to have been born a Clanton and grown up in a lovely house in a blue-blooded family with other blue-blooded people for friends and have been sent to college and elected to Phi Beta Kappa and married a blue-blooded man and had two blue-blooded daughters who had married rich if not blue-blooded doctors and lived in big houses, one in Savannah, Georgia, and the other in Alexandria, Virginia, and still have had to put up with Quincy. But she knew having had such privileges and having been blessed so meant that God favored her and had raised her up high so she could bear great burdens and suffer nobly and bring virtue to the community. God raised people to bear crosses and her cross was as heavy as several of anybody else's. God had raised her up so she could suffer greater burdens and reap a greater reward when the time came.

She reached one long thin arm and adjusted the rearview mirror so that she could see herself. She had been a beautiful baby and a beautiful child and a beautiful young woman and a beautiful middle-aged woman and now she looked in the mirror and remembered having thought in her youth that beauty and old age were incompatible. But she was sure she came nearer beauty than any other woman her age she knew of, though she had watched with alarm her slender figure grow brittle and bony and the curves in her body turn to sharp and abrupt angles. God had never seen fit to make her fat, and for this she was grateful. Most of her friends had let themselves go and had been punished for it by getting fat. Fat was repugnant to her in very much the same way Quincy was repugnant to her. She was grateful that God had not deemed it necessary to visit that on her among her other heavy burdens. Quincy was eighty-eight years old and didn't know his own name. He didn't know the difference between morning and afternoon, and he scarcely knew the difference between day and night. If there was anybody who *ought* to go on and die, it was Quincy. But Quincy seemed impervious to time. Even now he sat, small, plump, and rubicund on the back seat, as nimble as a frog and with about as much sense as one, she thought to herself. If there was anybody who *needed* to be dead, it was Quincy. He had been a successful lawyer in New York but he had never married, and when he retired he had had no one to take care of him but their mother, with whom he had moved in. For seven years Quincy's retirement had not been easy. He had done nothing but take care of their mother, who in her old age had lost her mind as well. She hadn't known where she was. In the summer she would take up the notion that they had sent her to "Hiwayer" to get rid of her, and it had been impossible to convince her of how absurd this was. None of them had ever been to Hawaii or ever had any desire to go there or to send her or anybody else there. The only reason she had known it existed was because of some program she looked at on television which she had called "Hiwayer Five." Mrs. Elbert thought the real name of the thing was "Hawaii Five-O." Quincy still looked at it. The old moron would sit in front of the television for hours at a time in one of the moth-eaten, narrow-lapelled, baggy suits and the inch-wide ties which he always wore. She had tried to tell him people didn't dress like that anymore when she had first come back and he had still had some sense, but now he was impervious to all suggestions. His hardheadedness was probably the reason God had punished him by making him into a moron. He would sit in front of the television and stare at it as if he had died there sometime before with his eyes open. She did not look at television, excepting the news and ballet and Shakespeare and other culturally enriching or current events programs. Mrs. Elbert was an intellectual. She was president of a study club and vice-president of the Presbyterian women's guild and had served two terms as president of the local historical society. She felt that if God had given you a good mind it was your Christian duty to cultivate it and do the best you could with it and not look at trash on the television. She had no doubt that among the first people God made to suffer for what they had done would be those responsible for the trash they showed on television. Immoral trash. And those responsible for the trash books they sold in the drugstore, which had pictures of practically naked men and women on them, and the films they showed, even on the television where little children could see, the ones she had happened to glimpse out of the corner of her eye at night when she was reading the Bible and happened to be passing by Quincy's television — it was impossible not to see it as the door to her room faced his and the television screen was situated squarely in the center of the door frame as one looked into Quincy's room from hers — why, they showed people stripped down to possible and doing things that made her blush and feel so weak she had to sit down on the end of her bed (from which the television screen remained visible, so that small figures moving in it reached out and jerked her gaze against its will in their direction, and even if they hadn't, Quincy turned the volume up so loud you could hear the thing anywhere in the house just like you were standing in front of it). They showed that *on television*, where children could see it all over the United States, and she knew it couldn't hold a candle to the things they showed in the movie houses and about which she had read in the paper. She had seen ads for movies with titles such as *Hot Nurses*, *Teen Lust*, *Hot Lip Hayride*, and there would be pictures of a man and a woman stripped down to possible locked in torrid embraces, or of a large-breasted, common-looking girl with her tongue sticking out. These ads made her blush and feel weak so that she had to sit down on the end of her bed. It was a shame, what passed for progress. The world had been a far better place when she was a girl.

She squinted out at the shacks they were passing. One yard was full of little nigger children of various sizes and shades and most of them were practically naked, playing in puddles of rainwater that had collected in the yard, bare earth save a few mangy patches of weeds and some chickens. There was a yellow girl standing in the doorway with her stomach swelled out, pregnant. Mrs. Elbert thought the girl was probably not even married. Viney, the cook, had told her that the colored mothers told their daughters not to use birth control, that the white people had devised birth control in order to gradually extinguish the Negro race. Why, you couldn't even try to help them but what they came up with some ignorant misunderstanding of it.

"Who was that colored girl, Ennis?" she asked.

"What you say, Miss Honey?" he replied.

The Negroes had called her Miss Honey since she had been a little girl. It was a link with her distant and televisionless childhood and made her feel young and pure and beautiful to hear herself so called by a Negro. It made her burden feel easier to bear.

"I said, do you know who that colored girl was we just passed, with all those children?"

The black idiot turned with an idiotic permanent half-grin on his face and looked out the back of the car. "Yebm," he said, "that's Tee Esther McAlpine."

"Who?" muttered Quincy absently. He didn't know where he was.

"He said it's a woman named Tee Esther McAlpine, honey," she shrieked at him. She always spoke in clearly enunciated tones and more loudly than most people; this, she had learned early in life, was the way to attract people's attention. You had only to say interesting, cheerful, pleasant things in a clearly enunciated, pleasant, cheerful tone and people would listen to you. She was an accomplished public speaker and had given more programs at historical society meetings and study club meetings than anyone else. When speaking to Quincy, however, she raised her voice to a *cheerful*, ear-splitting shriek, as if making him regain his sense was only a matter of sufficient decibels.

"A woman?" he muttered to himself. "I didn't see any woman."

"Yebm. She ain been live there but a mont. She been run off her old place."

"Run off? What for, Ennis?"

"Dey said the man she live with run her off. Said she were sleeping roun the neighborhood and he wadn't gon live wid no woman he didn't know whose her churren was."

"Well, he was just exactly right," she said. "I don't blame him a bit." There was nothing about anybody in town that Ennis didn't know. He asked so many questions of her that sometimes she wanted to lie down and cry. Sometimes she felt like picking up something heavy and hitting him with it if he asked another question. Colored people had been more intelligent and known how to behave themselves better when she had been a girl. Ennis was what came of giving them all that welfare and food stamps and what all. Why, they'd passed a law in Washington that she had to pay Ennis — idiot Ennis — the minimum wage! It was absurd. And that was not all. She had to pay Social Security to the government for him. So that Ennis could draw Social Security. And all he would do with it would be to go buy some cheap wine and get too drunk to do any work for her or any of the other white people who had given the government the money so it could give it to black idiots like Ennis. That was all the government did, take money away from the nice people who could have done something with it and give it to the idiotic ones who didn't know what to do with it and weren't willing to work for it. Every week she had to figure out how much Social Security tax to send the government. It was complicated arithmetic and gave her the headache. But she did not really mind this.

What she really minded was that Ennis would ask you anything and ask you *for* almost anything. Before Viney arrived in the morning, she had to fix Ennis's coffee. This morning while he drank his coffee she had showed him some photographs of her with her daughter and grand-children in Savannah and he had, to her great chagrin, insisted on taking each picture in his filthy hands and holding it three inches from his grimy face and breathing his whiskey breath on it — Ennis always smelled like whiskey and did not pay the slightest attention to the *people* in the pictures but asked every conceivable question about the clothes they had on and about the objects in the background. He wanted to know where everything had come from, how it had been made, and what they were going to do with it. There was no point in explaining the futility, much less the rudeness, of these questions to him. He did not think like white people and could not be made to. But Quincy was even worse than Ennis because he didn't know where he was. He would run away sometimes and walk through town in his baggy, moth-eaten suit introducing himself and telling people who had known him for forty years that he had just moved here from New York City and didn't know anybody. One morning he had come in her room and said he wanted to pay his bill, as if she ran a hotel. Another morning before she had even dressed or fixed her hair he came in and asked if they served breakfast in this place. Once when they were showing company to the door he had asked her where she was going and she had shrieked at him that she was not going anywhere, that she was his sister and lived there. He could be destructive. One day Ennis had not shown up for work and Quincy took it upon himself to trim the shrubs. He went directly to Mrs. Elbert's prize gardenia bush and amputated all its fine long branches at the very moment when they were heaviest with delicate flowers, so white and sweetly redolent of Mrs. Elbert's youth. Mrs. Elbert prized the bush because it reminded her of a much larger one which had grown in their parents' yard, not a gardenia but one with flowers of even finer hue and scent. When she had seen the strewn limp branches with their blooms already turning brown in the heat, Mrs. Elbert had cried bitter tears. She had looked heavenward through the water in her eyes and prayed for patience.

Another time Quincy had come in her room at night and said he thought it was only fair that she be told that he was an old man and had had several operations and could not be expected to be any sort of a husband to her. This made her blush and feel weak so that she had had to sit down on the end of her bed. He was even worse than their mother had been before she died, which was before Mrs. Elbert's husband had died and she had come back home to live with Quincy. She had not, thank God, had to live with her mother when she had lost her mind, but it could not have been any worse than living with Quincy now. He tainted even her smallest pleasures, such as having company. If anyone came to see them, Quincy would go up to them every few minutes and shake their hands and ask them if they knew who he was. It mortified her to have her friends see how she had to live, that her own brother had become a blithering idiot. Her friends all shook their heads and agreed that Mary Elbert bore a heavier burden than anyone else they knew of. Sometimes it just did not seem fair to have had a mother and a brother become morons *and* to have to live with the brother and put up with him twenty-four hours a day after she had lived a good life and raised two children in the Church and taken care of a husband with heart trouble until he died. At least he had died with his good sense intact.

The spring sun glanced fiercely off the white hood of the car into her eyes as they turned off onto the rutted dirt road which led to the clapboard shack, half of which was occupied by Ennis. It had no conveniences, not even hot water, and it just proved that he was common down to his soul that he was able to live that way. The other half was rented by a stringy colored woman named Florentine whom Ennis had shot with a slug bullet some years before when they were both drunk. When Florentine had been in the hospital she'd sworn to kill him when she got well. No doctor had given her any chance of survival — if she had been white she would have died as soon as the bullet hit her — but she had survived and moved right back in with Ennis and not killed him at all.

There was scarcely more than a blade or two of real grass in the front of the shack, the rest being weeds and hard-packed dirt. Rising from the starved, shocked-looking earth, however, was a low bushy tree in furious bloom — all over it were great stunningly white blossoms as if the roots had absorbed the glaring acid sun from the surface of the earth and forced it out of its own wood as buds and petals. It looked for all the world like the tree which had grown in her parents' yard. She was overcome with the sight. It made her feel weak and blush so that if she had been at home she would have sat down on the edge of the bed. She was so overwhelmed that she did not hear Ennis telling her to look out until she had driven into a thick post, all that remained of a gate that had once stood before the house.

Quincy fell off the back seat onto the floor. Ennis had seen what was coming and reached out to brace himself. Mrs. Elbert's small head, capped by two tightly wound buns of white hair, struck the windshield with such a terrific force that it looked as if a huge rock had flown up from the road and struck it from without. After the impact, she fell back into her seat as limp as a doll. The engine continued to roar. She did not move or speak. Ennis leaned over and looked at her. She had a pleased, almost beatific expression. A large, thin drop of blood trickled down to the end of her long nose and hung there. She seemed to smile.

Ennis reached over the seat and her, took the key in his palsied grip, and stopped the engine. A hissing steam rose from under the hood. All was quiet. A lark warbled gaily off in the crazily lush meadow of briars behind the house. Quincy stirred in the back.

"Oh my," he said, fumbling with the door handle. "Oh my gracious." He fumbled and fumbled without success. He furrowed his brow, grimaced.

"Wait jus a minute, Mist Quincy," said Ennis. "You stay yer a minute. I come roun and git you out in a minute." Ennis stepped gingerly from the car and closed the door, locking it from behind him. "You stay, Mist Quincy, don't you move, hear?" he bellowed hoarsely through the glass.

The old man blinked and took a deep breath. "Oh my," he moaned desperately.

Ennis opened the front door and with the most studied care lifted

Mrs. Elbert in his arms. He studied her face with controlled and piercing curiosity. She was breathing steadily. She appeared whole save for a tiny crimson stitch in the stippled membranous skin of her forehead.

Ennis climbed the two plank and brick steps to the porch and leaned gently against the parched grey door. He ducked his head and bore Mrs. Elbert into the cool darkness beyond.

It was cool and damp in the treehouse. The sunlight was stained soft green by the leaves and there was a smell of woodshavings, brightly spiced by the hundreds of frail white blooms, open and wilting, giving off a sweetness of gradual death. A squirrel chattered through the leaves at Mary Elbert. She drew further back from the ladder to avoid being seen. Her starched petticoats rustled loudly. She held her breath. The squirrel scolded. She looked down on her older brother Quincy. His belongings were being loaded into the buggy which would take him to the train, which would bear him far, far away, to school, away from her. She looked around her at the corncob doll and dollhouse he had made for her, at his slingshot and his marbles, which he had just that morning told her she could have. He had told her that the tree-house now was hers alone, and she must take care of it. That was when she had run from him. No one had been able to find her. No one knew where she was. Her mother called for her: "Mary! Mary! Come and tell Brother goodbye, dear!" Their father said, "There's no time. He spoke to her this morning. You'll write, won't you, Quincy?" She didn't hear his answer. Tears welled up in her eyes. She yanked one of the blue ribbons from her hair and flung it out at them. It caught briefly on a flower and descended but no one saw it. The buggy was leaving the yard. Mary wept. The squirrel scolded. The corncob doll watched her with its flat, expressionless gaze. She picked it up and threw it at the squirrel. It fell, striking the ground and breaking into several pieces. The squirrel ran to a neighboring tree. There was no sound but the breathing and weeping of Mary, high in the silent white flowers and the cool green leaves, no sound at all but the purest silence.

She awoke, head pounding, to the sight of Ennis's bloodshot eyes suspended inches above hers, the smell of his whiskey breath. "Ennis!" she barked, sitting bolt upright.

He recoiled and stepped backwards, removing his Western Auto cap and scratching his head nervously. "How you feel, Miss Mary? Is you feel anything broke?" he inquired.

"Fine. Fine," she said, feeling her head and neck carefully. She looked around the room. Two curtainless windows poured a styptic clarity into the dank closeness, framing motes of dust. There was a ragged hole in the wall opposite for a fireplace and above it a plank mantel. From a mason jar on the mantel erupted an incongruous riot of white blooms cut from the tree outside. The room was heavily redolent of old wood-ashes, bitter sweat, mildewed linen, burned cooking oil, and these nectarous floral avatars of her childhood. She spied a large hot plate on a table, and a toaster oven, gifts from her and other white benefactors. She realized she must be lying on his bed and abruptly stood up. A crunch of newspaper accompanied this motion: newspaper was neatly spread over the sheets on the sway-backed ancient mattress.

"Well, I . . ." she fumbled at her dress, smoothing it.

"Yebm, I speck you might be a lil so in the head. I takes me a bufferin when I has the so head."

Quincy's voice broke on them through the open door. "Sister! Oh Sister!" It sounded oddly distant, aerial.

Mrs. Elbert passed a small quantity of gas and cleared her throat as if observing some phonic symmetry. He had hardly ever called her "Sister" since he had left home for boarding school.

"Ennis. Catch him before he tries to run off."

They strode out onto the porch, Mrs. Elbert leading. Quincy was nowhere to be seen. He had left the car; the door hung open where he had gotten out.

The tinny theme music of a TV soap opera advertised the presence of Florentine behind them. "Laws, is dat Miss Mary?" she crooned, leaning against the screen door of her one room in a slip. She grinned. The few teeth remaining in her head were enormous. One was gold. A tiny blue television screen shone like a moon in the dark behind her.

She had curtains, all of which were pulled.

"How are you, Florentine?" asked Mrs. Elbert peremptorily, flashing an empty smile and returning her furrowed gaze to the lush horizon.

Florentine pushed open the door. Its spring whined and it slapped the wood frame behind her. "Y'all looking for Mister Quincy?"

Neither of the others replied.

Florentine shifted her weight languidly from one huge pancake foot to the other. "I been stanin yonder watchin him."

"Where he at, woman?" Ennis snapped.

"Clomb up thater tree, what he done." Florentine nodded at the tree festooned with the white blossoms.

Mrs. Elbert gasped and she and Ennis ran into the yard and looked up.

Florentine shuffled to the edge of the porch, folded her arms, and squinted up into the tree. "Mr. Quincy too *old* to be clombin tree. I don't reckon he gon clomb it. But he done clomb it. That old white man hop up yonder easas a skwull. What you speck make a old white gentermuns ack thataway?"

At the very top of the tree, in his black suit and hat, Quincy clung to a thin branch. He smiled and behind his thick spectacles his eyes sparkled. "Sister!" he cried, and with the recklessness of a small boy leaned outward, swaying precariously.

Ennis maneuvered to catch him. He was not so very high, perhaps fifteen feet. He must have weighed no more than a hundred and thirty pounds. It could be done. Mrs. Elbert raised her hand to her mouth in horror. She stood next to Ennis whose arms were outstretched and trembling.

"Quincy!" she cried, "come down from there this instant."

Quincy flung out one arm and leg and most of the branch broke off in his other hand. For a long instant, he appeared to fly. An extraordinary vision danced in the heads of Florentine, Ennis, and Mrs. Elbert: an old gnomish gentleman clad in suit, white shirt and tie, clasping in one hand a branch of white blossoms, floated in the blue spring firmament, spangled with afternoon sun, leaving his hat in midair as he

191

began to fall from under it. He gave a kick and twirled as he fell, fell, fell, seemed to take minutes falling. Florentine's eyes followed him downward like a cat's intent upon a pendulum as he kicked, twirled himself out of Ennis's reach and into his sister's.

It was too late to move. Mrs. Elbert began to shriek, "Murder alive!" but all that got out was "Murder a-." A loud thump followed as Quincy struck her in the chest. Their bodies on the ground made a popping, cracking thud, punctuated by the purest silence.

Truman Capote

Children on Their Birthdays
(This Story is for Andrew Lyndon)

YESTERDAY AFTERNOON THE six-o'clock bus ran over Miss Bobbit. I'm not sure what there is to be said about it; after all, she was only ten years old, still I know no one of us in this town will forget her. For one thing, nothing she ever did was ordinary, not from the first time that we saw her, and that was a year ago. Miss Bobbit and her mother, they arrived on that same six-o'clock bus, the one that comes through from Mobile. It happened to be my cousin Billy Bob's birthday, and so most of the children in town were here at our house. We were sprawled on the front porch having tutti-frutti and devil cake when the bus stormed around Deadman's Curve. It was the summer that never rained; rusted dryness coated everything; sometimes when a car passed on the road, raised dust would hang in the still air an hour or more. Aunt El said if they didn't pave the highway soon she was going to move down to the seacoast; but she'd said that for such a long time. Anyway, we were sitting on the porch, tutti-frutti melting on our plates, when suddenly, just as we were wishing that something would happen, something did; for out of the red road dust appeared Miss Bobbit. A wiry little girl in a starched, lemon-colored party dress, she sassed along with a grown-up mince, one hand on her hip, the other supporting a spinsterish umbrella. Her mother, lugging two cardboard valises and a wind-up victrola, trailed in the background. She was a gaunt shaggy woman with silent eyes and a hungry smile.

All the children on the porch had grown so still that when a cone of wasps started humming the girls did not set up their usual holler. Their attention was too fixed upon the approach of Miss Bobbit and her mother, who had by now reached the gate. "Begging your pardon," called Miss Bobbit in a voice that was at once silky and childlike, like a pretty piece of ribbon, and immaculately exact, like a movie-star or a schoolmarm, "but might we speak with the grown-up persons of the house?" This, of course, meant Aunt El; and, at least to some degree, myself. But Billy Bob and all the other boys, no one of whom was over thirteen, followed down to the gate after us. From their faces you would have thought they'd never seen a girl before. Certainly not like Miss Bobbit. As Aunt El said, whoever heard tell of a child wearing makeup? Tangee gave her lips an orange glow, her hair, rather like a costume wig, was a mass of rosy curls, and her eyes had a knowing, penciled tilt; even so, she had a skinny dignity, she was a lady, and what is more, she looked you in the eye with manlike directness. "I'm Miss Lily Jane Bobbit, Miss Bobbit from Memphis, Tennessee," she said solemnly. The boys looked down at their toes, and, on the porch, Cora McCall, who Billy Bob was courting at the time, led the girls into a fanfare of giggles. "*Country* children," said Miss Bobbit with an understanding smile, and gave her parasol a saucy whirl. "My mother," and this homely woman allowed an abrupt nod to acknowledge herself, "my mother and I have taken rooms here. Would you be so kind as to point out the house? It belongs to Mrs. Sawyer." Why, sure, said Aunt El, that's Mrs. Sawyer's, right there across the street. The only boarding house around here, it is an old tall dark place with about two dozen lightning rods scattered on the roof: Mrs. Sawyer is scared to death in a thunderstorm.

Coloring like an apple, Billy Bob said, please ma'am, it being such a hot day and all, wouldn't they rest a spell and have some tutti-frutti? and Aunt El said yes, by all means, but Miss Bobbit shook her head. "Very fattening, tutti-frutti; but *merci* you kindly," and they started across the road, the mother half-dragging her parcels in the dust. Then, and with an earnest expression, Miss Bobbit turned back; the sunflower yellow of her eyes darkened, and she rolled them slightly sideways, as if trying to remember a poem. "My mother has a disorder of the tongue, so it is necessary that I speak for her," she announced rapidly and heaved a sigh. "My mother is a very fine seamstress; she has made dresses for the society of many cities and towns, including Memphis and Tallahassee. No doubt you have noticed and admired the dress I am wearing. Every stitch of it was handsewn by my mother. My mother can copy any pattern, and just recently she won a twenty-five dollar prize from the *Ladies Home Journal*. My mother can also crochet, knit and embroider. If you want any kind of sewing done, please come to my mother. Please advise your friends and family. Thank you." And then, with a rustle and a swish, she was gone.

Cora McCall and the girls pulled their hair-ribbons nervously, suspiciously, and looked very put out and prune-faced. I'm *Miss* Bobbit, said Cora, twisting her face into an evil imitation, and I'm Princess Elizabeth, that's who I am, ha, ha, ha. Furthermore, said Cora, that dress was just as tacky as could be; personally, Cora said, all my clothes come from Atlanta; plus a pair of shoes from New York, which is not even to mention my silver turquoise ring all the way from Mexico City, Mexico. Aunt El said they ought not to behave that way about a fellow child, a stranger in the town, but the girls went on like a huddle of witches, and certain boys, the sillier ones that liked to be with the girls, joined in and said things that made Aunt El go red and declare she was going to send them all home and tell their daddies, to boot. But before she could carry forward this threat Miss Bobbit herself intervened by traipsing across the Sawyer porch, costumed in a new and startling manner.

The older boys, like Billy Bob and Preacher Star, who had sat quiet while the girls razzed Miss Bobbit, and who had watched the house into which she'd disappeared with misty, ambitious faces, they now straightened up and ambled down to the gate. Cora McCall sniffed and poked out her lower lip, but the rest of us went and sat on the steps. Miss Bobbit paid us no mind whatever. The Sawyer yard is dark with mulberry trees and it is planted with grass and sweet shrub. Sometimes after a rain you can smell the sweet shrub all the way into our house; and in the center of this yard there is a sundial which Mrs. Sawyer installed in 1912 as a memorial to her Boston bull, Sunny, who died after having lapped up a bucket of paint. Miss Bobbit pranced into the yard toting the victrola, which she put on the sundial; she wound it up, and started a record playing, and it played the Court of Luxemborg. By now it was almost nightfall, a firefly hour, blue as milkglass; and birds like arrows swooped together and swept into the folds of trees. Before storms, leaves and flowers appear to burn with a private light, color, and Miss Bobbit, got up in a little white skirt like a powderpuff and with strips of gold-glittering tinsel ribboning her hair, seemed, set against the darkening all around, to contain this illuminated quality. She held her arms arched over her head, her hands lily-limp, and stood straight up on the tips of her toes. She stood that way for a good long while, and Aunt El said it was right smart of her. Then she began to waltz around and around, and around and around she went until Aunt El said, why, she was plain dizzy from the sight. She stopped only when it was time to rewind the victrola; and when the moon came rolling down the ridge, and the last supper bell had sounded, and all the children had gone home, and the night iris was beginning to bloom, Miss Bobbit was still there in the dark turning like a top.

We did not see her again for some time. Preacher Star came every morning to our house and stayed straight through to supper. Preacher is a rail-thin boy with a butchy shock of red hair; he has eleven brothers and sisters, and even they are afraid of him, for he has a terrible temper, and is famous in these parts for his green-eyed meanness: last fourth of July he whipped Ollie Overton so bad that Ollie's family had to send him to the hospital in Pensacola; and there was another time he bit off half a mule's ear, chewed it and spit it on the ground. Before Billy Bob got his growth, Preacher played the devil with him, too. He used to drop cockleburrs down his collar, and rub pepper in his eyes, and tear up his homework. But now they are the biggest friends in town: talk alike, walk alike; and occasionally they disappear together for whole days, Lord knows where to. But during these days when Miss Bobbit did not appear they stayed close to the house. They would stand around in the yard trying to slingshot sparrows off telephone poles; or sometimes Billy Bob would play his ukulele, and they would sing so loud Uncle Billy Bob, who is Judge for this county, claimed he could hear them all the way to the courthouse: *send me a letter, send it by mail, send it in care of the Birming-ham jail.* Miss Bobbit did not hear them; at least she never poked her head out the door. Then one day

Mrs. Sawyer, coming over to borrow a cup of sugar, rattled on a good deal about her new boarders. You know, she said, squinting her chicken-bright eyes, the husband was a crook, uh huh, the child told me herself. Hasn't an ounce of shame, not a mite. Said her daddy was the dearest daddy and the sweetest singing man in the whole of Tennessee. . . . And I said, honey, where is he? and just as off-hand as you please she says, Oh, he's in the penitentiary and we don't hear from him no more. Say, now, does that make your blood run cold? Uh huh, and I been thinking, her mama, I been thinking she's some kinda foreigner: never says a word, and sometimes it looks like she don't understand what nobody says to her. And you know, they eat everything *raw. Raw* eggs, *raw* turnips, carrots — no meat whatsoever. For reasons of health, the child says, but ho! she's been straight out on the bed running a fever since last Tuesday.

That same afternoon Aunt El went out to water her roses, only to discover them gone. These were special roses, ones she'd planned to send to the flower show in Mobile, and so naturally she got a little hysterical. She rang up the Sheriff, and said, listen here, Sheriff, you come over here right fast. I mean somebody's got off with all my Lady Anne's that I've devoted myself to heart and soul since early spring. When the Sheriff's car pulled up outside our house, all the neighbors along the street came out on their porches, and Mrs. Sawyer, layers of cold cream whitening her face, trotted across the road. Oh shoot, she said, very disappointed to find no one had been murdered, oh shoot, she said, nobody's stole them roses. Your Billy Bob brought them roses over and left them for little Bobbit. Aunt El did not say one word. She just marched over to the peach tree, and cut herself a switch. Ohhh, Billy Bob, she stalked along the street calling his name, and then she found him down at Speedy's garage where he and Preacher were watching Speedy take a motor apart. She simply lifted him by the hair and, switching blueblazes, towed him home. But she couldn't make him say he was sorry and she couldn't make him cry. And when she was finished with him he ran into the backyard and climbed high into the tower of a pecan tree and swore he wasn't ever going to come down. Then his daddy stood at the window and called to him: Son, we aren't mad with you, so come down and eat your supper. But Billy Bob wouldn't budge. Aunt El went and leaned against the tree. She spoke in a voice soft as the gathering light. I'm sorry, son, she said, I didn't mean whipping you so hard like that. I've fixed a nice supper, son, potato salad and boiled ham and deviled eggs. Go away, said Billy Bob, I don't want no supper, and I hate you like all-fire. His daddy said he ought not to talk like that to his mother, and she began to cry. She stood there under the tree and cried, raising the hem of her skirt to dab at her eyes. I don't hate you, son. . . . If I didn't love you I wouldn't whip you. The pecan leaves began to rattle; Billy Bob slid slowly to the ground, and Aunt El, rushing her fingers through his hair, pulled him against her. Aw, Ma, he said, Aw, Ma.

After supper Billy Bob came and flung himself on the foot of my bed. He smelled all sour and sweet, the way boys do, and I felt very sorry for him, especially because he looked so worried. His eyes were almost shut with worry. You're s'posed to send sick folks flowers, he said righteously. About this time we heard the victrola, a lilting faraway sound, and a night moth flew through the window, drifting in the air delicate as the music. But it was dark now, and we couldn't tell if Miss Bobbit was dancing. Billy Bob, as though he were in pain, doubled up on the bed like a jackknife; but his face was suddenly clear, his grubby boy-eyes twitching like candles. She's so cute, he whispered, she's the cutest dickens I ever saw, gee, to hell with it, I don't care, I'd pick all the roses in China.

Preacher would have picked all the roses in China, too. He was as crazy about her as Billy Bob. But Miss Bobbit did not notice them. The sole communication we had with her was a note to Aunt El thanking her for the flowers. Day after day she sat on her porch, always dressed to beat the band, and doing a piece of embroidery, or combing curls in her hair, or reading a Webster's dictionary — formal, but friendly enough; if you said good-day to her she said good-day to you. Even so, the boys never could seem to get up the nerve to go over and talk with her, and most of the time she simply looked through them, even when they tomcatted up and down the street trying to get her eye. They wrestled, played Tarzan, did foolheaded bicycle tricks. It was a sorry business. A great many girls in town strolled by the Sawyer house two and three times within an hour just on the chance of getting a look. Some of the girls who did this were: Cora McCall, Mary Murphy Jones, Janice Ackerman. Miss Bobbit did not show any interest in them either. Cora would not speak to Billy Bob any more. The same was true with Janice and Preacher. As a matter of fact, Janice wrote Preacher a letter in red ink on lace-trimmed paper in which she told him he was vile beyond all human beings and words, that she considered their engagement broken, that he could have back the stuffed squirrel he'd given her. Preacher, saying he wanted to act nice, stopped her the next time she passed our house, and said, well, hell, she could keep that old squirrel if she wanted to. Afterwards, he couldn't understand why Janice ran away bawling the way she did.

Then one day the boys were being crazier than usual; Billy Bob was sagging around in his daddy's World War khakis, and Preacher, stripped to the waist, had a naked woman drawn on his chest with one of Aunt El's old lipsticks. They looked like perfect fools, but Miss Bobbit, reclining in a swing, merely yawned. It was noon, and there was no one passing in the street, except a colored girl, baby-fat and sugar-plum shaped, who hummed along carrying a pail of blackberries. But the boys, teasing at her like gnats, joined hands and wouldn't let her go by, not until she paid a tariff. I ain't studyin' no tariff, she said, what kinda tariff you talkin' about, mister? A party in the barn, said Preacher, between clenched teeth, mighty nice party in the barn. And she, with a sulky shrug, said, huh, she intended studyin' no barn parties. Whereupon Billy Bob capsized her berry pail, and when she, with despairing, piglike shrieks, bent down in futile gestures of rescue, Preacher, who can be mean as the devil, gave her behind a kick which sent her sprawling jellylike among the blackberries and the dust. Miss Bobbit came tearing across the road, her finger wagging like a metronome; like a schoolteacher she clapped her hands, stamped her foot, said: "It is a well-known fact that gentlemen are put on the face of this earth for the protection of ladies. Do you suppose boys behave this way in towns like Memphis, New York, London, Hollywood or Paris?" The boys hung back, and shoved their hands in their pockets. Miss Bobbit helped the colored girl to her feet; she dusted her off, dried her eyes, held out a handkerchief and told her to blow. "A pretty pass," she said, "a fine situation when a lady can't walk safely in the public daylight."

Then the two of them went back and sat on Mrs. Sawyer's porch; and for the next year they were never far apart, Miss Bobbit and this baby elephant, whose name was Rosalba Cat. At first, Mrs. Sawyer raised a fuss about Rosalba being so much at her house. She told Aunt El that it went against the grain to have a nigger lolling smack there in plain sight on her front porch. But Miss Bobbit had a certain magic, whatever she did she did it with completeness, and so directly, so solemnly, that there was nothing to do but accept it. For instance, the tradespeople in town used to snicker when they called her *Miss* Bobbit; but by and by she was Miss Bobbit, and they gave her stiff little bows as she whirled by spinning her parasol. Miss Bobbit told everyone that Rosalba was her sister, which caused a good many jokes; but like most of her ideas, it gradually seemed natural, and when we would overhear them calling each other Sister Rosalba and Sister Bobbit none of us cracked a smile. But Sister Rosalba and Sister Bobbit did some queer things. There was the business about the dogs. Now there are a great many dogs in this town, rat terriers, bird dogs, bloodhounds; they trail along the forlorn noon-hot streets in sleepy herds of six to a dozen, all waiting only for dark and the moon, when straight through the lonesome hours you can hear them howling: someone is dying, someone is dead. Miss Bobbit complained to the Sheriff; she said that certain of the dogs always planted themselves under her window, and that she was a light sleeper to begin with; what is more, and as Sister Rosalba said, she did not believe they were dogs at all, but some kind of devil. Naturally the Sheriff did nothing; and so she took the matter into her own hands. One morning, after an especially loud night, she was seen stalking through the town with Rosalba at her side, Rosalba carrying a flower basket filled with rocks; whenever they saw a dog they paused while Miss Bobbit scrutinized him. Sometimes she would shake her head, but more often she said, "Yes, that's one of them, Sister Rosalba," and Sister Rosalba, with ferocious aim, would take a rock from her basket and crack the dog between the eyes.

Another thing that happened concerns Mr. Henderson. Mr. Henderson has a back room in the Sawyer house; a tough runt of a man who formerly was a wildcat oil prospector in Oklahoma, he is about seventy years old and, like a lot of old men, obsessed by functions of the body. Also, he is a terrible drunk. One time he had been drunk for two weeks; whenever he heard Miss Bobbit and Sister Rosalba moving around the house, he would charge to the top of the stairs and bellow down to Mrs. Sawyer that there were midgets in the walls trying to get at his supply of toilet paper. They've already stolen fifteen cents' worth, he said. One evening, when the two girls were sitting under a tree in the yard, Mr. Henderson, sporting nothing more than a nightshirt, stamped out after them. Steal all my toilet paper, will you? he hollered, I'll show you midgets. . . . Somebody come help me, else these midget bitches are liable to make off with every sheet in town. It was Billy Bob and Preacher who caught Mr. Henderson and held him until some grown men arrived and began to tie him up. Miss Bobbit, who had behaved with admirable calm, told the men they did not know how to tie a proper knot, and undertook to do so herself. She did such a good job that all the circulation stopped in Mr. Henderson's hands and feet and it was a month before he could walk again.

It was shortly afterwards that Miss Bobbit paid us a call. She came on Sunday and I was there alone, the family having gone to church. "The odors of a church are so offensive," she said, leaning forward and with her hands folded primly before her. "I don't want you to think I'm a heathen, Mr. C.; I've had enough experience to know that there is a God and that there is a Devil. But the way to tame the Devil is not to go down there to church and listen to what a sinful mean fool he is. No, love the Devil like you love Jesus: because he is a powerful man, and will do you a good turn if he knows you trust him. He has frequently done me good turns, like at dancing school in Memphis. . . . I always called in the Devil to help me get the biggest part in our annual show. That is common sense; you see, I knew Jesus wouldn't have any truck with dancing. Now, as a matter of fact, I have called in the Devil just recently. He is the only one who can help me get out of this town. Not that I live here, not exactly. I think always about somewhere else,

201

somewhere else where everything is dancing, like people dancing in the streets, and everything is pretty, like children on their birthdays. My precious papa said I live in the sky, but if he'd lived more in the sky he'd be rich like he wanted to be. The trouble with my papa was he did not love the Devil, he let the Devil love him. But I am very smart in that respect; I know the next best thing is very often the best. It was the next best thing for us to move to this town; and since I can't pursue my career here, the next best thing for me is to start a little business on the side. Which is what I have done. I am sole subscription agent in this county for an impressive list of magazines, including *Reader's Digest*, *Popular Mechanics*, *Dime Detective* and *Child's Life*. To be sure, Mr. C., I'm not here to sell you anything. But I have a thought in mind. I was thinking those two boys that are always hanging around here, it occurred to me that they are men, after all. Do you suppose they would make a pair of likely assistants?"

Billy Bob and Preacher worked hard for Miss Bobbit, and for Sister Rosalba, too. Sister Rosalba carried a line of cosmetics called Dewdrop, and it was part of the boys' job to deliver purchases to her customers. Billy Bob used to be so tired in the evening he could hardly chew his supper. Aunt El said it was a shame and a pity, and finally one day when Billy Bob came down with a touch of sunstroke she said, all right, that settled it, Billy Bob would just have to quit Miss Bobbit. But Billy Bob cussed her out until his daddy had to lock him in his room; whereupon he said he was going to kill himself. Some cook we'd had told him once that if you ate a mess of collards all slopped over with molasses it would kill you sure as shooting; and so that is what he did. I'm dying, he said, rolling back and forth on his bed, I'm dying and nobody cares.

Miss Bobbit came over and told him to hush up. "There's nothing wrong with you, boy," she said. "All you've got is a stomach ache." Then she did something that shocked Aunt El very much: she stripped the covers off Billy Bob and rubbed him down with alcohol from head to toe. When Aunt El told her she did not think that was a nice thing for a little girl to do, Miss Bobbit replied: "I don't know whether it's nice or not, but it's certainly very refreshing." After which Aunt El did all she could to keep Billy Bob from going back to work for her, but his daddy said to leave him alone, they would have to let the boy lead his own life.

Miss Bobbit was very honest about money. She paid Billy Bob and Preacher their exact commission, and she would never let them treat her, as they often tried to do, at the drugstore or to the picture show. "You'd better save your money," she told them. "That is, if you want to go to college. Because neither one of you has got the brains to win a scholarship, not even a football scholarship." But it was over money that Billy Bob and Preacher had a big falling out; that was not the real reason, of course: the real reason was that they had grown cross-eyed jealous over Miss Bobbit. So one day, and he had the gall to do this right in front of Billy Bob, Preacher said to Miss Bobbit that she'd better check her accounts carefully because he had more than a suspicion that Billy Bob wasn't turning over to her *all* the money he collected. That's a damned lie, said Billy Bob, and with a clean left hook he knocked Preacher off the Sawyer porch and jumped after him into a bed of nasturtiums. But once Preacher got a hold on him, Billy Bob didn't stand a chance. Preacher even rubbed dirt in his eyes. During all this, Mrs. Sawyer, leaning out an upper-story window, screamed like an eagle, and Sister Rosalba, fatly cheerful, ambiguously shouted, Kill him! Kill him! Kill him! Only Miss Bobbit seemed to know what she was doing. She plugged in the lawn hose, and gave the boys a close-up, blinding bath. Gasping, Preacher staggered to his feet. Oh, honey, he said, shaking himself like a wet dog, honey, you've got to decide. "Decide *what?*" said Miss Bobbit, right away in a huff. Oh, honey, wheezed Preacher, you don't want us boys killing each other. You got to decide who is your real true sweetheart. "Sweetheart, my eye," said Miss Bobbit. "I should've known better than to get myself involved with a lot of country children. What sort of businessman are you going to make? Now, you listen here, Preacher Star: I don't want a sweetheart, and if I did, it wouldn't be you. As a matter of fact, you don't even get up when a lady enters the room."

Preacher spit on the ground and swaggered over to Billy Bob. Come on, he said, just as though nothing had happened, she's a hard one, she is, she don't want nothing but to make trouble between two good friends. For a moment it looked as if Billy Bob was going to join him in a peaceful togetherness; but suddenly, coming to his senses, he drew back and made a gesture. The boys regarded each other a full minute, all the closeness between them turning an ugly color: you can't hate so much unless you love, too. And Preacher's face showed all of this. But there was nothing for him to do except go away. Oh, yes, Preacher, you looked so lost that day that for the first time I really liked you, so skinny and mean and lost going down the road all by yourself.

They did not make it up, Preacher and Billy Bob; and it was not because they didn't want to, it was only that there did not seem to be any straight way for their friendship to happen again. But they couldn't get rid of this friendship: each was always aware of what the other was up to; and when Preacher found himself a new buddy, Billy Bob moped around for days, picking things up, dropping them again, or doing sudden wild things, like purposely poking his finger in the electric fan. Sometimes in the evenings Preacher would pause by the gate and talk with Aunt El. It was only to torment Billy Bob, I suppose, but he stayed friendly with all of us, and at Christmas time he gave us a huge box of shelled peanuts. He left a present for Billy Bob, too. It turned out to be a book of Sherlock Holmes; and on the flyleaf there was scribbled, "Friends Like Ivy On the Wall Must Fall." That's the corniest thing I ever saw, Billy Bob said. Jesus, what a dope he is! But then, and though it was a cold winter day, he went in the backyard and climbed up into the pecan tree, crouching there all afternoon in the blue December branches.

But most of the time he was happy, because Miss Bobbit was there, and she was always sweet to him now. She and Sister Rosalba treated him like a man; that is to say, they allowed him to do everything for them. On the other hand, they let him win at three-handed bridge, they never questioned his lies, nor discouraged his ambitions. It was a happy while. However, trouble started again when school began. Miss Bobbit refused to go. "It's ridiculous," she said, when one day the principal, Mr. Copland, came around to investigate, "really ridiculous; I can read and write and there are *some* people in this town who have every reason to know that I can count money. No, Mr. Copland, consider for a moment and you will see neither of us has the time nor energy. After all, it would only be a matter of whose spirit broke first, yours or mine. And besides, what is there for you to teach me? Now, if you knew anything about dancing, that would be another matter; but under the circumstances, yes, Mr. Copland, under the circumstances, I suggest we forget the whole thing." Mr. Copland was perfectly willing to. But the rest of the town thought she ought to be whipped. Horace Deasley wrote a piece in the paper which was titled "A Tragic Situation." It was, in his opinion, a tragic situation when a small girl could defy what he, for some reason, termed the Constitution of the United States. The article ended with a question: *Can she get away with it?* She did; and so did Sister Rosalba. Only she was colored, so no one cared. Billy Bob was not as lucky. It was school for him, all right; but he might as well have stayed home for the good it did him. On his first report card he got three F's, a record of some sort. But he is a smart boy. I guess he just couldn't live through those hours without Miss Bobbit; away from her he always seemed half-asleep. He was always in a fight, too; either his eye was black, or his lip was split, or his walk had a limp. He never talked about these fights, but Miss Bobbit was shrewd enough to guess the reason why. "You are a dear, I know, I know. And I appreciate you, Billy Bob. Only don't fight with people because of me. Of course they say mean things about me. But do you know why that is, Billy Bob? It's a compliment, kind of. Because deep down they think I'm absolutely wonderful."

And she was right: if you are not admired no one will take the trouble to disapprove. But actually we had no idea of how wonderful she was until there appeared the man known as Manny Fox. This happened late in February. The first news we had of Manny Fox was a series of jovial placards posted up in the stores around town: Manny Fox Presents the Fan Dancer Without the Fan; then, in smaller print: Also, Sensational Amateur Program Featuring Your Own Neighbors — First Prize, A Genuine Hollywood Screen Test. All this was to take place the following Thursday. The tickets were priced at one dollar each, which around here is a lot of money; but it is not often that we get any kind of flesh entertainment, so everybody shelled out their money and made a great todo over the whole thing. The drugstore cowboys talked dirty all week, mostly about the fan dancer without the fan, who turned out to be Mrs. Manny Fox. They stayed down the highway at the Chucklewood Tourist Camp; but they were in town all day, driving around in an old Packard which had Manny Fox's full name stenciled on all four doors. His wife was a deadpan pimento-tongued redhead with wet lips and moist eyelids; she was quite large actually, but compared to Manny Fox she seemed rather frail, for he was a fat cigar of a man.

They made the pool hall their headquarters, and every afternoon you could find them there, drinking beer and joking with the town loafs. As it developed, Manny Fox's business affairs were not restricted to theatrics. He also ran a kind of employment bureau: slowly he let it be known that for a fee of $150 he could get for any adventurous boys in the county high-class jobs working on fruit ships sailing from New Orleans to South America. The chance of a lifetime, he called it. There are not two boys around here who readily lay their hands on so much as five dollars; nevertheless, a good dozen managed to raise the money. Ada Willingham took all she'd saved to buy an angel tombstone for her husband and gave it to her son, and Acey Trump's papa sold an option on his cotton crop.

But the night of the show! That was a night when all was forgotten: mortgages, and the dishes in the kitchen sink. Aunt El said you'd think we were going to the opera, everybody so dressed up, so pink and sweet-smelling. The Odeon had not been so full since the night they gave away the matched set of sterling silver. Practically everybody had a relative in the show, so there was a lot of nervousness to contend with. Miss Bobbit was the only contestant we knew real well. Billy Bob couldn't sit still; he kept telling us over and over that we mustn't applaud for anybody but Miss Bobbit; Aunt El said that would be very rude, which sent Billy Bob off into a state again; and when his father bought us all bags of popcorn he wouldn't touch his because it would make his hands greasy, and please, another thing, we mustn't be noisy and eat ours while Miss Bobbit was performing. That she was to be a contestant had come as a last-minute surprise. It was logical enough, and there were signs that should've told us; the fact, for instance, that she had not set foot outside the Sawyer house in how many days? And the victrola going half the night, her shadow whirling on the window shade, and the secret, stuffed look on Sister Rosalba's face whenever asked after Sister Bobbit's health. So there was her name on the program, listed second, in fact, though she did not appear for a long while. First came Manny Fox, greased and leering, who told a lot of peculiar jokes, clapping his hands, ha, ha. Aunt El said if he told another joke like that she was going to walk straight out: he did, and she didn't. Before Miss Bobbit came on there were eleven contestants, including Eustacia Bernstein, who imitated movie stars so that they all sounded like Eustacia, and there was an extraordinary Mr. Buster Riley, a jug-eared old wool-hat from way in the back country who played "Waltzing Matilda" on a saw. Up to that point, he was the hit of the show; not that there was any marked difference in the various receptions, for everybody applauded generously, everybody, that is, except Preacher Star. He was sitting two rows ahead of us, greeting each act with a donkey-loud boo. Aunt El said she was never going to speak to him again. The only person he ever applauded was Miss Bobbit. No doubt the Devil was on her side, but she deserved it. Out she came, tossing her hips, her curls, rolling her eyes. You could tell right away it wasn't going to be one of her classical numbers. She tapped across the stage, daintily holding up the sides of a cloud-blue skirt. That's the cutest thing I ever saw, said Billy Bob, smacking his thigh, and Aunt El had to agree that Miss Bobbit looked real sweet. When she started to twirl the whole audience broke into spontaneous applause; so she did it all over again, hissing, "Faster, faster," at poor Miss Adelaide, who was at the piano doing her Sunday-school best. "I was born in China, and raised in Jay-pan . . ." We had never heard her sing before, and she had a rowdy sandpaper voice. ". . . if you don't like my peaches, stay away from my can, o-ho o-ho!" Aunt El gasped; she gasped again when Miss Bobbit, with a bump, up-ended her skirt to display blue-lace underwear, thereby collecting most of the whistles the boys had been saving for the fan dancer without the fan, which was just as well, as it later turned out, for that lady, to the tune of "An Apple for the Teacher" and cries of gyp gyp, did her routine attired in a bathing suit. But showing off her bottom was not Miss Bobbit's final triumph. Miss Adelaide commenced an ominous thundering in the darker keys, at which point Sister Rosalba, carrying a lighted Roman candle, rushed onstage and handed it to Miss Bobbit, who was in the midst of a full split; she made it, too, and just as she did the Roman candle burst into fiery balls of red, white and blue, and we all had to stand up because she was singing "The Star Spangled Banner" at the top of her lungs. Aunt El said afterwards that it was one of the most gorgeous things she'd ever seen on the American stage.

Well, she surely did deserve a Hollywood screen test and, inasmuch as she won the contest, it looked as though she were going to get it. Manny Fox said she was: honey, he said, you're real star stuff. Only he skipped town the next day, leaving nothing but hearty promises. Watch the mails, my friends, you'll all be hearing from me. That is what he said to the boys whose money he'd taken, and that is what he said to Miss Bobbit. There are three deliveries daily, and this sizable group gathered at the post office for all of them, a jolly crowd growing gradually joyless. How their hands trembled when a letter slid into their mailbox. A terrible hush came over them as the days passed. They all knew what the other was thinking, but no one could bring himself to say it, not even Miss Bobbit. Postmistress Patterson said it plainly, however: the man's a crook, she said, I knew he was a crook to begin with, and if I have to look at your faces one more day I'll shoot myself.

Finally, at the end of two weeks, it was Miss Bobbit who broke the spell. Her eyes had grown more vacant than anyone had ever supposed they might, but one day, after the last mail was up, all her old sizzle came back. "O.K., boys, it's lynch law now," she said, and proceeded to herd the whole troupe home with her. This was the first meeting of the Manny Fox Hangman's Club, an organization which, in a more social form, endures to this day, though Manny Fox has long since been caught and, so to say, hung. Credit for this went quite properly to Miss Bobbit. Within a week she'd written over three hundred descriptions of Manny Fox and dispatched them to Sheriffs throughout the

South; she also wrote letters to papers in the larger cities, and these attracted wide attention. As a result, four of the robbed boys were offered good-paying jobs by the United Fruit Company, and late this spring, when Manny Fox was arrested in Uphigh, Arkansas, where he was pulling the same old dodge, Miss Bobbit was presented with a Good Deed Merit award from the Sunbeam Girls of America. For some reason, she made a point of letting the world know that this did not exactly thrill her. "I do not approve of the organization," she said. "All that rowdy bugle blowing. It's neither good-hearted nor truly feminine. And anyway, what is a good deed? Don't let anybody fool you, a good deed is something you do because you want something in return." It would be reassuring to report she was wrong, and that her just reward, when at last it came, was given out of kindness and love. However, this is not the case. About a week ago the boys involved in the swindle all received from Manny Fox checks covering their losses, and Miss Bobbit, with clodhopping determination, stalked into a meeting of the Hangman's Club, which is now an excuse for drinking beer and playing poker every Thursday night. "Look boys," she said, laying it on the line, "none of you ever thought to see that money again, but now that you have, you ought to invest it in something practical — like me." The proposition was that they should pool their money and finance her trip to Hollywood; in return, they would get ten percent of her life's earnings which, after she was a star, and that would not be very long, would make them all rich men. "At least," as she said, "in this part of the country." Not one of the boys wanted to do it: but when Miss Bobbit looked at you, what was there to say?

Since Monday, it has been raining buoyant summer rain shot through with sun, but dark at night and full of sound, full of dripping leaves, watery chimings, sleepless scuttlings. Billy Bob is wide-awake, dry-eyed, though everything he does is a little frozen and his tongue is as stiff as a bell tongue. It has not been easy for him, Miss Bobbit's going. Because she'd meant more than that. Than what? Than being thirteen years old and crazy in love. She was the queer things in him, like the pecan tree and liking books and caring enough about people to let them hurt him. She was the things he was afraid to show anyone else. And in the dark the music trickled through the rain: won't there be nights when we will hear it just as though it were really there? And afternoons when the shadows will be all at once confused, and she will pass before us, unfurling across the lawn like a pretty piece of ribbon? She laughed to Billy Bob; she held his hand, she even kissed him. "I'm not going to die," she said. "You'll come out there, and we'll climb a mountain, and we'll all live there together, you and me and Sister Rosalba." But Billy Bob knew it would never happen that way, and so when the music came through the dark he would stuff the pillow over his head.

Only there was a strange smile about yesterday, and that was the day she was leaving. Around noon the sun came out, bringing with it into the air all the sweetness of wisteria. Aunt El's yellow Lady Anne's were blooming again, and she did something wonderful, she told Billy Bob he could pick them and give them to Miss Bobbit for good-bye. All afternoon Miss Bobbit sat on the porch surrounded by people who stopped by to wish her well. She looked as though she were going to Communion, dressed in white and with a white parasol. Sister Rosalba had given her a handkerchief, but she had to borrow it back because she couldn't stop blubbering. Another little girl brought a baked chicken, presumably to be eaten on the bus; the only trouble was she'd forgotten to take out the insides before cooking it. Miss Bobbit's mother said that was all right by her, chicken was chicken; which is memorable because it is the single opinion she ever voiced. There was only one sour note. For hours Preacher Star had been hanging around down at the corner, sometimes standing at the curb tossing a coin, and sometimes hiding behind a tree, as if he didn't want anyone to see him. It made everybody nervous. About twenty minutes before bus time he sauntered up and leaned against our gate. Billy Bob was still in the garden picking roses; by now he had enough for a bonfire, and their smell was as heavy as wind. Preacher stared at him until he lifted his head. As they looked at each other the rain began again, falling fine as sea spray and colored by a rainbow. Without a word, Preacher went over and started helping Billy Bob separate the roses into two giant bouquets: together they carried them to the curb. Across the street there were bumblebees of talk, but when Miss Bobbit saw them, two boys whose flower-masked faces were like yellow moons, she rushed down the steps, her arms outstretched. You could see what was going to happen; and we called out, our voices like lightning in the rain, but Miss Bobbit, running toward those moons of roses, did not seem to hear. That is when the six-o'clock bus ran over her.

Credits

Contributors

ERSKINE CALDWELL, born in 1903 in Moreland, Georgia, is the author of over fifty volumes. Books such as *Tobacco Road* (1932), *God's Little Acre* (1933), and *Southways* (1938) identify him as one of the main spokesmen in what is sometimes known as the gothic school of Southern writing. His dark humor and his social realism mark his large influence on American literature.

TRUMAN CAPOTE was born Truman Streckfus Persons in New Orleans in 1924. His first novel, *Other Voices, Other Rooms*, published when the author was only twenty-four, established him as an important figure in American letters. Capote sustained that reputation with such titles as *A Tree of Night and Other Stories* (1949), *The Grass Harp* (1951), *Breakfast at Tiffany's* (1958), *In Cold Blood* (1965), and *A Christmas Memory* (1966). He died in New York in 1984.

CLYDE EDGERTON is a native of Bethesda, North Carolina. A graduate of UNC Chapel Hill, he teaches at St. Andrews College in Laurinburg, N.C. *Raney* is his first novel.

WILLIAM FAULKNER, the South's best known writer, was born in 1897 in New Albany, Mississippi. His awards include the Nobel Prize for literature (1949), National Book Awards for *Collected Stories* (1951) and for *A Fable* (1951), and Pulitzer Prizes for *A Fable* and for *The Reivers* (1963). He died in Byhalia, Mississippi, on July 6, 1962.

JESSE HILL FORD was born in Troy, Alabama, in 1928. A graduate of Vanderbilt and the University of Florida, he has worked as a reporter for the Nashville *Tennessean* and as writer-in-residence at Memphis State University. His books include *Mountains of Gilead* (1961), *The Conversion of Buster Drumwright* (1964), *The Libera-*

tion of Lord Byron Jones (1965), *Fishes, Birds and Sons of Men: Stories* (1967), *The Feast of Saint Barnabas* (1969), and *The Raider* (1975).

MARTHA LACY HALL, a native of Magnolia, Mississippi, lives in Baton Rouge where, until recently, she was managing editor of the Louisiana State University Press. She is a regular contributor to such magazines as the *Southern Review*, the *Sewanee Review*, and the *New Orleans Review*.

JEFFERSON HUMPHRIES was born in 1955 in Greene County, Alabama. He was educated at Duke and Yale Universities and has received an Academy of American Poets Prize. His essays, short fiction, and poems have appeared in *Massachusetts Review*, *Michigan Quarterly Review*, the *Southern Review*, *Oxford Literary Review*, and elsewhere. His most recent books are *Losing the Text* (University of Georgia) and *The Puritan and the Cynic* (Oxford University Press). He is an associate professor of French and comparative literature at LSU.

GEORGE WILLIAM KOON, a native of Columbia, South Carolina, writes for a variety of magazines and is head of the English department at Clemson University. His biography of Hank Williams came out in 1983. The first volume of his *A Collection of Classic Southern Humor* appeared in 1984.

AUGUSTUS BALDWIN LONGSTREET (1790-1870) was born in Augusta, Georgia, and educated at Yale and at the Litchfield, Connecticut, Law School. He was a member of the Georgia legislature and a judge of that state's superior court. His sketches of Georgia life appeared in the Milledgeville and Augusta papers before being collected into *Georgia Scenes* (1835). He became a Methodist minister in 1838 and served successively as president of Emory College, Centenary College, the University of Mississippi, and the University of South Carolina.

GUY OWEN was born in 1925 in Clarkton, North Carolina, an area
that became the "Cape Fear County" of his novels. He received a
Ph.D. from UNC Chapel Hill and taught at Stetson University
before settling in 1962 at N.C. State University. He is well known
as a fiction writer, as editor of the *Southern Poetry Review*, and as a
teacher of creative writing. He died in Raleigh in 1981.

WALKER PERCY's first novel, *The Moviegoer*, won the National
Book Award for 1962. His other novels are *The Last Gentleman*
(1967), *Love in the Ruins* (1971), *Lancelot* (1977), and *The Second
Coming* (1980). His essays, collected in *The Message in the Bottle*,
appeared in 1975. *Lost in the Cosmos: The Last Self-Help Book*
was published in 1983. Percy lives in Covington, Louisiana.

MARK TWAIN (1835-1910), in the flesh of Samuel L. Clemens, was a
river steamboat pilot, Confederate volunteer, journalist, inventor,
and lecturer. He gave up most of his many professions to answer
what he terms "a 'call' to literature, of a low order — i.e.,
humorous." His *Huckleberry Finn* has sold over thirteen million
copies, making it one of the most popular books of all times.

EUDORA WELTY was born in Jackson, Mississippi, where she has
lived most of her life. One of the South's finest writers, she has
won the National Medal for literature, the American Academy of
Arts and Letters Howells Medal, the National Institute of Arts and
Letters Gold Medal for the Novel, the Pulitzer Prize, and the
Presidential Medal of Freedom. Her novels are *The Robber Bride-
groom* (1942), *Delta Wedding* (1946), *The Ponder Heart* (1954),
Losing Battles (1970), and *The Optimist's Daughter* (1972). Har-
court Brace Jovanovich published her collected stories in 1980.

TENNESSEE WILLIAMS (1911-1983) was born Thomas Lanier
Williams in Columbus, Mississippi, and grew up in St. Louis. His
first major success was *The Glass Menagerie*, which won the New
York Drama Critics' Circle Prize for the best play of 1945. *A*

Streetcar Named Desire (1947) and *Cat on a Hot Tin Roof* (1955) each won a Pulitzer Prize. His best known fiction is probably the 1950 novel, *The Roman Spring of Mrs. Stone*. Williams died in New York City.

TOM WOLFE grew up in Richmond, Virginia, and lives now in New York City. *The Kandy-Kolored Tangerine-Flake Streamline Baby* (1965), *The Pump House Gang* (1968), *The Electric Kool-Aid Acid Test* (1968), and *The Right Stuff* (1979) may be the best known of his many books.

Also Available From Peachtree Publishers

CLASSIC SOUTHERN HUMOR

Fiction and Occasional Fact
By Some of the South's Best Storytellers

Eudora Welty
Why I Live at the P.O.

Lee Smith
Cakewalk

Flannery O'Connor
Revelation

Barry Hannah
Horning In—A.

John Kennedy Toole
from A Confederacy of Dunces

Lee K. Abbott, Jr.
*A Modern Story of Woe and
Lovecraft*

Mark Steadman
John Fletcher's Night of Love

Lewis Grizzard
Good Men of God

William Price Fox
*Doug Broome, Hamburger
King*

Harry Crews
*Tuesday Night with Cody,
Jimbo, and a Fish of Some
Proportion*

Marion Montgomery
I Got a Gal

Ferrol Sams
from Run with the Horsemen

Roy Blount, Jr.
Heterosexism and Dancing

Florence King
*Would Youall Be Good Enough
to Excuse Me While I Have an
Identity Crisis?*

Lisa Alther
The Art of Dying Well

Franklin Ashley
*Listen, Buddy, We Don't
Throw Gutter Balls Here*

Larry King
*The Best Little Whorehouse
in Texas*